DK small business guides

managing
your
finances

DK small business *guides*

managing your finances

COLIN BARROW

A Dorling Kindersley Book

Dorling **DK** Kindersley

LONDON, NEW YORK, SYDNEY, DELHI, PARIS,
MUNICH, and JOHANNESBURG

Senior Art Editor Jamie Hanson
US Editors Gary Werner, Margaret Parrish
US Consultant Stuart Gittleman
DTP Designer Julian Dams
Production Controller Michelle Thomas

Managing Editor Adèle Hayward
Senior Managing Editor Stephanie Jackson
Senior Managing Art Editor Nigel Duffield

Produced for Dorling Kindersley by
Grant Laing Partnership
48 Brockwell Park Gardens,
London SE24 9BJ

Managing Editor Jane Laing
Project Editor Alison Bolus
Project Art Editor Christine Lacey
Picture Researcher Jo Walton

First American Edition, 2001

00 01 02 03 04 05 10 9 8 7 6 5 4 3 2 1

Published in the United States by
Dorling Kindersley Publishing, Inc.
95 Madison Avenue
New York, New York 10016

Library of Congress Cataloging-in-Publication Data
Barrow, Colin.
  Managing your finances / Colin Barrow.
    p.cm. – (Small business guides)
  Includes bibliographical references and index.
  ISBN 0-7894-7198-1 (alk paper)
  1. Business enterprises--Finance. 2. Corporations--Finance. I. Title. II. Series.

HG4026.B314 2001
658.15--dc21
                                        00-065659

Colour reproduction in Italy by GRB Editrice
Printed and bound by Mondadori in Verona, Italy

see our complete catalogue at
www.dk.com

CONTENTS

INTRODUCTION

When starting out in business, people rank independence as their primary motivation. Fewer than one in six have making money as their foremost reason, although few would list losing money as their key goal. Whatever your motives, successfully launching a small business or expanding an existing one is not a simple task. Good ideas, hard work, enthusiasm, skills, knowing your product or service, and how to make or deliver it, although essential, are not enough. Barely 40 percent of small firms survive intact to celebrate their fifth birthday.

Most of these failures occur within the first few years, and poor or non-existent financial management is the most cited reason for a small firm getting into difficulties. Owners and managers often need help in acquiring business skills in such areas as bookkeeping and accounting. Most failing businesses simply do not know their financial position. The order book can be full when the cash runs out.

Owners and managers also need to know what sorts of financing are available and how to put themselves in the best possible position to raise the funds. Surprisingly, there is no shortage of funds. Problems lie, rather, in the business proposition itself, or, more often, in the way the proposition is made to the financier. This calls for a business plan, a statement of business purpose, with the consequences spelled out in financial terms. For most people this calls for new knowledge.

Managing Your Finances provides you with this knowledge. Aimed at those who want to either start up a business or review their prospects, it shows you how to keep accurate financial records and how to translate plans and projections into cash. It outlines how to estimate how much cash your business needs and how much you can expect "outsiders" to put in. It also explains the use of ratios in analyzing the profitability of your business and the effect on it of various factors.

By following the wide range of advice and techniques offered in this book, you will ensure that your business is properly financed and controlled from the outset.

ESTIMATING finances

A well-prepared business plan is the foundation upon which the financial success of your business will depend. In preparing the business plan, you will have to forecast the amount of cash you are likely to need, when you will need it, and for how long. In making projections, you have to be ready for likely pitfalls and prepared for the unexpected events that may create problems with your cash flow.

PREPARING YOUR BUSINESS PLAN

A well-prepared business plan is the foundation upon which the financial success of your business depends. It will also help you to decide how much money is needed, by when, and for what purposes. A business plan is a selling document that conveys the excitement and promise of your business to a potential backer or shareholder. That audience can include outsiders, such as the bank, venture capitalists, or even current and prospective employees who need to be confident that there is a future in the business for them.

Perhaps the most important step in managing the finances of any new venture or expanding an existing one is the construction of a business plan. The plan should be prepared and written by you with the help of other people who are vital to its implementation. Such a plan must include your goals for the enterprise, both short and long term, as well as a description of the products or services you will offer, and the market opportunities you have anticipated for them. Finally, it should include an explanation of the resources, financial and other, that you are able to employ to achieve your goals in the face of competition.

No start-up or growing business should be without a current business plan that has been reviewed within the past six months. The planning horizon should be at least three years, because it takes this long to implement anything of strategic merit. The first year of the plan will form the framework for the operating budget. This is the profit and loss style description of how you will execute your business strategy. (For more information on profit and loss, see pp. 84–89.)

Why Have a Business Plan?

A business plan will be a useful tool both for you, as the owner of the business, and for any outsiders who are interested in your business, such as prospective employees and potential financial backers. Its benefits justify the work

CASE STUDY: The Benefits of Thorough Planning

MARTIN JENKINS planned to start a restaurant in downtown Atlanta. He had worked as a chef in a small hotel for five years and from this experience he had gained a sound knowledge of most aspects of the business. One area in which he was less experienced was financial planning. Acknowledging his ignorance, he read up on the subject and taught himself how to prepare a business plan. While gathering data for the cash flow forecast in his business plan, this potential entrepreneur made the discovery that if he delayed purchasing some of the necessary equipment, and leased others, he could halve his initial funding requirements. This had a profound effect on his overall financial strategy and meant that far less of his capital was tied up at the outset.

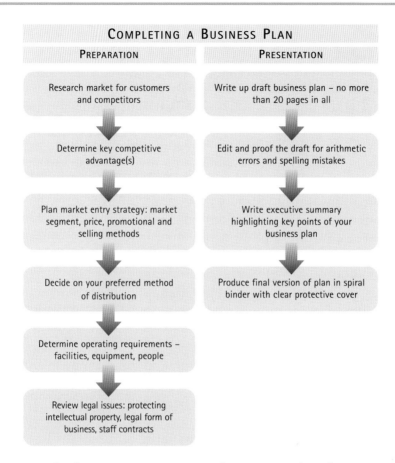

COMPLETING A BUSINESS PLAN

PREPARATION

Research market for customers and competitors

↓

Determine key competitive advantage(s)

↓

Plan market entry strategy: market segment, price, promotional and selling methods

↓

Decide on your preferred method of distribution

↓

Determine operating requirements – facilities, equipment, people

↓

Review legal issues: protecting intellectual property, legal form of business, staff contracts

PRESENTATION

Write up draft business plan – no more than 20 pages in all

↓

Edit and proof the draft for arithmetic errors and spelling mistakes

↓

Write executive summary highlighting key points of your business plan

↓

Produce final version of plan in spiral binder with clear protective cover

---

needed to prepare the plan. Constructing a business plan has four immediate benefits:

■ It tests the validity of your ideas.
■ It gives you the confidence to proceed.
■ It provides an overview of your financial requirements.
■ It gives you valuable planning experience.

TESTING YOUR IDEAS

The systematic approach required in creating a business plan means you make your mistakes on paper, rather than in the marketplace.

INCREASING YOUR CONFIDENCE

Once completed, a business plan will make you feel more confident in your ability to set up

and operate your planned venture. It may even compensate for any lack of capital and experience, provided of course that you have other factors in your favor, such as a sound idea and a sizable market opportunity for your proposed product or service.

GIVING AN OVERVIEW OF YOUR FINANCIAL REQUIREMENTS

Your business plan will show how much money is needed, what it is needed for, and when and for how long it is required.

Undercapitalization and early cash flow problems are two important reasons why new business activities fail, so if you have a soundly prepared business plan you can reduce these

TIME SAVER

Prepare a list of all essential expenses needed for your business. Tell your accountant about them while putting your business plan together. If you discuss these only after you have prepared your plan, you may end up having to substantially revise all your figures.

risks of failure. You can also safely experiment, on paper, with a range of viable strategies, and so concentrate on options that make the most efficient use of scarce financial resources.

It would be an overstatement to say that your business plan is the passport to sources of finance. It will, however, help you to display your grasp of the financial dynamics of your business to the full, and to communicate your ideas to others in a way that will be easier for them to understand and to appreciate the reasoning behind your ideas. These outside parties could be bankers, potential investors, partners, or advisory agencies. Once they know what you are trying to do, they will be better able to help and advise you.

Use your business plan to prepare yourself for the rigors and dangers of the marketplace

PROVIDING PLANNING EXPERIENCE

Preparing a business plan will give you an insight into the financial planning process. It is this process itself that is important to the long-term financial health of a business, and not simply the plan that comes out of it. Businesses are dynamic, as are the commercial and competitive environments in which they operate, and no one expects every event as recorded on a business plan to occur exactly as predicted. But the understanding and knowledge you will gain as you go through the process of constructing your plan will prepare your business for any changes that it may face, and so enable it to adjust quickly.

AVOIDING A HIGH-RISK START-UP

Despite these many valuable benefits, thousands of would-be entrepreneurs still attempt to start without a business plan. The most common such offenders are businesses that appear to need little or no capital at the outset, or whose founders have funds of their own; in both cases it is believed unnecessary to expose the project to harsh financial appraisal.

The former hypothesis is usually based on the easily exploded myth that customers will all pay cash on the spot and that suppliers will wait for months to be paid. In the meantime, the proprietor has the use of these funds to finance the business. Such model customers and suppliers are, unfortunately, thinner on the ground than optimistic entrepreneurs think. In any event, two important market rules still apply: either the product or service being offered fails to sell like hot cakes, and mountains of unpaid inventory builds up in the warehouse, all of which eventually have to be financed, or it does sell like hot cakes, as a result of which more financially robust entrepreneurs are attracted into the market. Without the staying power that adequate financing provides, these new competitors will rapidly kill off the business.

In the second scenario, those would-be entrepreneurs with funds of their own or, worse still, borrowed from friends and relatives, tend to think that the time spent in preparing a business plan could be more usefully spent looking for premises, buying a new car, or installing a computer. In short, anything that inhibits them from immediate action is viewed as a waste of time.

Most people's initial perception of their business venture is flawed in some major respect, so jumping in at the deep end is risky, and unnecessarily so. Flaws can often be discovered cheaply during the preparation of a business plan; they are always discovered in the marketplace, invariably at a much higher and often fatal cost.

Aiming Your Plan at Potential Financiers

All successful businesses need external financing at some stage in their development, and if you are to succeed in raising those funds it is important to examine what financiers expect from you.

It is often said that there is no shortage of money for new and growing businesses, the only scarce commodities being good ideas and people with the ability to exploit them. From the potential entrepreneur's position, this is often hard to believe. Out of every 1,000 business plans received by venture capital providers, only 100 or so are examined in any detail, less than 10 are pursued to the negotiating stage, and only one of those is finally invested in.

To a great extent, the decision whether to proceed beyond an initial reading of the plan will depend on the quality of the financial arguments and the revenue, or sales, model used to support the investment proposal. The business plan is the ticket of admission, giving the entrepreneur their first and often only chance to impress any prospective sources of financing with the quality of their proposal.

It follows that to have any chance at all of getting financial support, your business plan should pay high regard to the likely requirements of potential financiers. The two main potential sources of financing, banks and venture capitalists, each have different requirements.

WHAT THE BANKS LOOK FOR

Bankers and other sources of debt capital are looking for asset security to back their loan, and the near certainty of getting their money back. Essentially, banks are in the business of converting illiquid assets, such as property or stock, into liquid assets, such as cash or overdraft facilities. They will also charge an interest rate that reflects current market conditions and their view of the level of risk of the proposal. Depending on the nature of the business in question and the purpose for which the money is being used, bankers will take a two- to five-year view.

Bankers will usually expect a business to start repaying both the loan and the interest on a monthly or quarterly basis as soon as the loan has been granted, although in some cases a capital holiday of up to two years can be negotiated, during which time no repayments are made. In the early stages of any loan, the interest charges make up the lion's share of payments, in the same way as mortgage repayments, and you must allow for this in your cash flow projections.

Bankers hope that a business will succeed in order that they can lend more money in the future and provide more banking services, such as insurance or tax advice, to a loyal customer. It follows from this appreciation of lenders' needs that banks are much less interested in rapid growth and the consequent capital gain than they are in being assured of a steady stream of earnings almost from the outset of the business trading.

DOS AND DON'TS OF BORROWING MONEY

✓ Do borrow as much as your plan says you need.

✓ Do talk to several lenders before deciding from whom to borrow.

✓ Do explain the risks of your business as well as the rewards.

✓ Do make sure the loan term is long enough for you to reach breakeven.

✗ Don't borrow from anyone who can't afford it.

✗ Don't raise money until you need it and so incur unnecessary charges.

✗ Don't conceal information about your credit or business record from a prospective lender.

✗ Don't ignore government guaranteed programs; they can be better lending value.

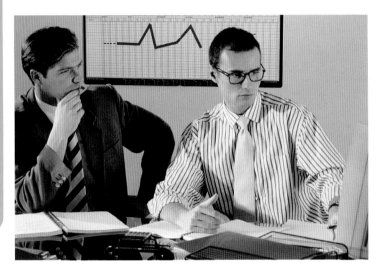

WHAT THE VENTURE CAPITALISTS LOOK FOR

Most new or fast-growing businesses generally do not make immediate profits, so money for such enterprises must come from elsewhere. Risk or equity capital – the capital of a business that comes from the issue of shares – as other types of funds are called, comes from venture capital firms, as well as being put in by founders, their families, and friends.

Because the inherent risks of investing in new and young ventures are greater than those of investing in established companies, venture capital fund managers have to offer their investors the chance of larger overall returns. To do that, fund managers not only have to keep failures to a minimum, they also have to pick some big winners – ventures with annual compound growth rates above 35 percent – to offset the inevitable mediocre performers. (Bearing in mind the massive growth in internet access, it is hardly surprising that the dot.com sector has sucked up so much equity financing.) Typically, a fund manager would expect any 10 investments to comprise one star, seven also-rans, and two flops. However, despite this outcome, venture capital fund managers are looking only for winners, so, unless you are projecting high growth in the short to medium term, the chances of getting venture capital are slim.

■ VENTURE CAPITALISTS AS SHAREHOLDERS

Not only are venture capitalists looking for winners, they are also looking for a shareholding in your business. The size of the shareholding will vary with each business.

If the venture capital firm sees that you have a great business idea, a first-class team, and a product/service that is ready to roll, they would be looking for a third or more of the shares in your business as their reward for putting up the money. That portion could be further reduced if the management is putting (or have put) in some of their own money, or if a bank is lending. If the idea is

TIME SAVER

Prepare your business plan before approaching venture capitalists. Send them your two-page executive summary, then phone them to find out if they want to see the full plan. This will save wasted meetings with venture capitalists who turn out to be unprepared to back you.

not fully developed, or your team is weak – in which case they may want to put in a director and a managing executive and work with you to strengthen the team – they may aim for more than a third of your business to compensate for the increased risk.

It all comes down to how much you need the money, how risky the venture is, how much money could be made from your business, and your skills as a negotiator.

Fast-growing companies typically have no cash available to pay dividends and, in the case of many dot.coms, may not have made any profits in any case, so investors can profit only by selling their holdings. With this in mind, the venture capitalists need to have an exit strategy in view at the outset, such as an initial public offering or a potential corporate buyer.

■ **SHORT-TERM INVESTMENT**
Unlike many entrepreneurs (and some lending bankers), who see their ventures as lifelong commitments to success and growth, venture capitalists have a relatively short-term horizon. Typically, they are looking to liquidate small company investments within two to six years, allowing them to pay out individual investors and to have funds available for tomorrow's winners. So your financial plan needs to accommodate this timescale.

BALANCING THE SOURCES

To be successful, your business must be targeted at the needs of these two sources of financing, and in particular at the balance between the two. Lending bankers ideally look for a ratio of 1:1, which means that half the business's finances are borrowed and half comes from risk capital. Banks have been known to go to a ratio of 4:1, but rarely willingly or at the outset of their involvement. Venture capital providers will almost always encourage entrepreneurs to take on new debt capital to match the level of equity, or share, funding.

If you are planning to raise money from friends and relatives either as debt or equity, then their needs must also be taken into account in your business plan.

BELIEVABLE GROWTH FORECASTS

Right at the heart of every investment or lending proposition is the need to demonstrate that the business will deliver a satisfactory financial result. The business plan needs to show, in summary form, the key results to be achieved. This should cover sales, cash flow, profits, margins, and investment returns for a sufficient period to give confidence.

Entrepreneurs are naturally ebullient when explaining the future prospects of their businesses. They frequently believe that the sky is the limit when it comes to growth and that the lack of money is the only thing that stands between them and their almost certain success.

It is true that if you are looking for venture capital, then the providers are also looking for rapid growth. However, it is also good to remember that financiers are dealing with thousands of investment proposals each year, and already have money tied up in hundreds of business sectors. It follows that they already have a perception of what the accepted financial results and marketing approaches currently are for any sector. Any new company's business plan showing projections that are outside the ranges perceived as acceptable within an industry will raise questions in the investor's mind.

Make your growth forecasts believable, supporting them with hard facts where possible. If your forecasts are on the low side, then approach the more cautious lending bankers, rather than venture capitalists. The former often see a modest forecast as a virtue, lending credibility to the business proposal as a whole, rather than being impressed by ambitious goals.

Take into account the interests of all potential readers when writing your financial plan

Presenting a Business Plan

Having decided on the contents of your business plan, you now need to consider how to present the material in order to make it into a professional and impressive document that will convince backers to support your idea.

Deciding on the Packaging

Every product is enhanced by appropriate packaging, and a business plan is no exception. Most experts prefer a simple spiral binding with a clear plastic cover front and back. This makes it easy for the reader to move from section to section, and it ensures that the document will survive the frequent handling that every successful business plan is likely to get. A letter-quality printer, using a 12-point typeface, double spacing, and wide margins, will result in a pleasing and easy-to-read plan.

There is no such thing as a universal business-plan format. That being said, experience has taught us that certain styles have been more successful than others. Following these guidelines will result in an effective business plan that covers most requirements. Not every subheading will be relevant, but the general format is robust and is equally suitable for new businesses of any size.

Cover and Title Page

First, the cover should show the name of your business, its address, phone and fax numbers, email address, and website (if you have one), and the date on which this version of the plan was prepared. It should confirm that this is the business's current view on its position and financing needs.

Second, the title page, immediately behind the front cover, should repeat the above information and also give the founder's name, address, and phone number. A home phone number can be helpful, particularly for investors, who often work irregular hours.

The Executive Summary

Ideally one page, but certainly no longer than two, the executive summary follows the title page. Writing this is the most difficult task, but it is the single most important part of the business plan. Done well, it can favorably dispose the reader from the outset. Done badly, or not at all, the plan may not get beyond the mail room. The executive summary can be written only after the business plan has been completed, because it summarizes all the contents of the plan.

The Table of Contents

This page follows the executive summary and is the "map" that will guide readers through the business proposal. If that map is obscure, muddled, or even missing, then you are likely to end up with lost or irritated readers who are in no mind to back your proposal.

Each main section should be listed, numbered, and given a page number. Elements within each section should also be numbered; for example, Section 1 would contain elements 1.1, 1.2, and so forth.

The Body of the Plan

The contents of the business plan should include the following main sections, each with its own heading:

- **The Business and its Management** Outline a brief history of the business and its performance to date and give details on key staff, current mission, capital structure, legal entity, and professional advisers.
- **Products and Services** Give a description of products and services, their applications, competitive advantage, and proprietary position. Include details on the state of readiness of new products and services, and development cost estimates.
- **Marketing** Provide a brief overview of the market by major segment, showing size and growth. Explain the current and proposed marketing strategy for each major segment, covering price, promotion, distribution

SUMMARY

BUSINESS DESCRIPTION:	New retail shop (women's fashions for the over 50s).
LOCATION:	Small suburban town.
PROPRIETOR:	Joan Smith (operating as a sole proprietor).
STAFF:	The proprietor only.
MARKET:	The main market is women, over 50, living in the town (population 66,500). The nearest stores catering for this market are in the city, 28 miles away.
PREMISES:	About 500 sq. ft. in a good location.
PROPOSED SHOP NAME:	"Simply Perfect"
ANNUAL SALES:	First-year estimate: approximately $48,500. Second-year estimate: approximately $60,000.
FINANCING:	Depending upon which shop is rented, capital of some $17,000 is required, of which the proprietor can raise $10,000, leaving a balance of $7,000 to be found. A three-year bank loan of $4,000 would be sufficient, together with an overdraft facility of $3,000 to allow for initial inventory purchases.
TIMESCALE:	The plan is to open the business by May 1, in time for the summer season, though inventory will be ordered earlier.

3

EXECUTIVE SUMMARY
This gives the essential details of your proposed business operations and forms a vital part of your business plan.

A description of the products or services, together with details on any rights or patents and details on competitive advantage

The reasons why customers need this product or service, together with some indication of market size and growth

The current position of the business, including a summary of past business results (for existing businesses)

How much money is needed to fund the growth and how and when the provider will benefit

A summary of forecasts of sales and profits, together with short- and longer-term aims and the strategies to be employed

---

channels, selling methods, location requirements, and the need for acquisitions, mergers, or joint ventures, if any.
■ **MANAGEMENT AND STAFFING** Give details on current key staff and on any recruitment needs to achieve the planned goals. Include information on staff retention strategies, reward systems, and training plans.
■ **OPERATIONS** Describe how your products are made, how your services are provided, how quality standards are assured, and how your output can be stepped up or down to meet the varying levels of demand implied in the business plan. It is important to demonstrate a degree of flexibility.
■ **FINANCIAL FORECAST AND CONTROLS** Provide a projected profit and loss statement (see pp. 84–89), together with a description of the key controls used to monitor and review your performance.
■ **FINANCING REQUIREMENTS** Show the finances needed to achieve the planned goals, together with timings. You should also demonstrate how the business would

Assessing the Contents of Your Business Plan

By answering the questions below you will get some idea of how well your business plan is progressing. Score 1, 2, or 3, following the key below, for each of the questions. Mark the options closest to your instincts, and be honest. Then add up your scores and refer to the results at the end of the questionnaire to see how you scored and to check the potential of your plan.

Whatever your score, remember that this type of self-assessment test is broad-brush. It is designed only to give an indication of whether you have the basic attitude, instincts, and capabilities to make a success of launching your own business. If your score is low, the chances are that you do not. If it is high, the opposite is true.

1 = Made a start   2 = Some data only   3 = Comprehensive

Title page ☐1 ☐2 ☐3
Name of business, contact details, date of business plan, contents

Executive summary ☐1 ☐2 ☐3
Your details; summary of key strategies; why you are better or different; summary of profit projections; summary of financial needs

The business and its management ☐1 ☐2 ☐3
You and your team's relevant experience; business goals and objectives; legal structure of the business

The marketing strategy ☐1 ☐2 ☐3
Market segment analysis; pricing strategy; promotion plans; product mix and range; e-commerce strategy; location; selling strategy

Management and staffing ☐1 ☐2 ☐3
Staff numbers; roles and responsibilities; recruitment needs

Operations ☐1 ☐2 ☐3
What facilities and equipment are needed; what services will be bought in?

Legal issues ☐1 ☐2 ☐3
What intellectual protection do you have as a barrier to entry; what other legal issues affect your business?

Financial forecasts ☐1 ☐2 ☐3
Summary of financial projections; monthly cash flows; profit-and-loss statements; balance sheets; break-even analysis

Financing requirements ☐1 ☐2 ☐3
How much money do you need; what is it needed for; how much money can you provide; how much do you need to raise from outside; what security is available?

Results

9 points or less
You still have a lot more information to gather or decisions to make. No serious plan could be drawn up at this stage.

Between 10 and 20 points
You have made progress, but still have a few gaps to fill. Concentrate your efforts on completing your plan.

More than 20 points
Your plan is now complete and ready for final editing.

proceed using only internal funding. The gap between the two levels of production is what the extra money will help to deliver.

■ **APPENDICES** could include a resumé for each of the key team members, technical data, patents, copyrights and designs, details on professional advisers, audited financial statements, consultants' reports, abstracts of market surveys, details of orders in hand, and so on.

ADDRESSING THE READER

Clearly a business plan will be more effective if it is written with the reader in mind. This will involve some research into the particular interests, foibles, and idiosyncrasies of those readers. Of the four likely types of readers, bankers are more interested in hearing about certainties and steady growth, venture capitalists are also interested in dreams of great things to come, potential partners are concerned with whether or not this is a venture they want to share in, and potential employees will want to be convinced that you can offer them interesting and secure employment.

It is a good idea to carry out your research before the final editing of your business plan, so that you can incorporate something of this knowledge into the way it is presented. You may find that slightly different versions of the plan have to be made for different audiences. This makes the reader feel that the proposal has been addressed to them rather than just being a "Dear Sir or Madam" type of missive. The fundamentals of the plan will, however, remain constant whatever the readership.

EDITING YOUR PLAN

The first draft of the business plan may have several authors and it can be written ignoring the niceties of grammar and style. Now would be a good time to talk over the proposal with your legal adviser, to keep you on the straight and narrow, and with a friendly banker or venture capitalist. Their opinions can give you an insider's view as to the strengths and weaknesses of your proposal at a stage when you still have time to alter it.

When the first draft has been revised, then comes the task of editing. Here grammar, spelling, and a consistent style do matter. The end result must be a crisp, correct, clear, and complete plan, no more than 20 pages long. If you are not a confident writer, you may need help with the editing. Your local librarian or college may be able to help by providing you with suitable contacts.

Making an Oral Presentation

I f any of your chosen financiers find your plan of interest, they will want to meet you to discuss particular aspects, to iron out any elements that are unclear, and to evaluate your skills and character. Anyone backing a business does so primarily because they believe in the management. They know from experience that

---

TIPS FOR PREPARING A SUCCESSFUL ORAL PRESENTATION

1 Rehearse beforehand, having found out how much time you have.

2 Allow at least as much time for questions as you take in your talk.

3 Use visual aids, and if possible bring and demonstrate your product or service.

4 Explain your strategy in a businesslike manner, demonstrating your grasp of the competitive market forces at work.

5 Listen to comments and criticisms carefully, avoiding a defensive attitude when you respond.

6 Make your replies to questions brief and to the point to allow for as many different questions to be put as possible.

7 Use eye contact, tone of voice, body language, and enthusiasm to create empathy between yourself and listeners.

things rarely go to plan, so your presentation must convince them that the team involved can respond effectively to changing conditions.

Any financier that you are presenting to will have read dozens of similar plans to your own and will be well rehearsed in the art of finding the ones worth backing. They may even have researched something of your business and financial history already. Your oral presentation must convince them that your business is a sound investment.

Maintaining Confidentiality

Finding an investor or a bank to lend to your business may take weeks or months. During that time, potential backers will diligently gather information about the business so that they will not have unpleasant surprises later. The business plan will be only the starting point for their investigations.

OBTAINING LEGAL PROTECTION

If you and the prospective financiers are strangers to one another, you may be reluctant to turn over business information to them until you know that they are serious. To allay these fears, ask for a confidentiality agreement.

The simple agreement to the right will suffice in most circumstances, but if substantial amounts of intellectual property are involved you may prefer a more formal agreement drafted by a lawyer. Do make sure that the document contains no binding commitment on you. The agreement should be limited to the potential investor's agreement to treat the information you give them as confidential, and to use it only to investigate lending to, or investing in, your proposed business.

THE SUBJECT OF RESEARCH

Investors may want to learn about your own financial status, job, or business history. They are interested in your financial stability, business know-how, and reputation for integrity because they will, in effect, be extending credit to you.

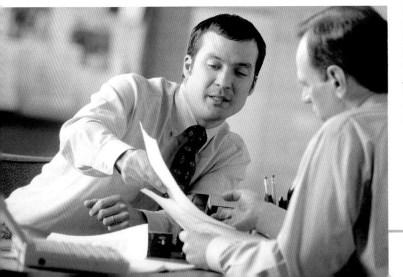

DISCUSSING YOUR PLAN
When presenting your business plan to a potential backer, your goal is to convince the listener that you are worth backing. A well-prepared plan and a confident manner will help to achieve this goal.

CONFIDENTIALITY AGREEMENT

This agreement provides you with safeguards against an interested party stealing your idea and either developing the concept or selling it to a third party.

This protects the contents of your business plan

WHEREAS

1. The purpose of communication between the Parties to this Agreement is for the Investor/Lender to evaluate the suitability as an investment or lending proposition, the business proposition as set out in the business plan.

2. The information to be communicated in strict confidence between the Parties to this Agreement includes the business plan, demonstrations, commercial and technical information, all forms of intellectual property, and includes material for which patent or similar registration may have been filed.

THEREFORE THE PARTIES HEREBY UNDERTAKE AS FOLLOWS:

FIRST: Each Party hereto agrees to maintain as confidential and not to use any of the information directly or indirectly disclosed by the other Party until or unless such information becomes public knowledge through no fault of the recipient Party, or unless the Parties to the Agreement complete a further Agreement making provision for utilization of information disclosed. Each Party undertakes to prevent the information disclosed from passing to other than those representatives who must be involved for the purpose of this Agreement.

You can discuss details only with those who have signed the agreement

SECOND: In the event that no further Agreement on utilization or publication of information is concluded each Party hereto undertakes to return to the other all confidential items submitted and to furnish certification that no copies or other records of those items have been retained.

THIRD: In the event that either Party requires the assistance of a further party in pursuing the purposes of the Agreement the approval of the other Party to this Agreement shall be secured.

You should confirm the state whose law the agreement comes under

FOURTH: Any information which either Party can prove was in his possession prior to disclosure hereunder and was not acquired from the other Party or his representatives is excepted from this Agreement.

FIFTH: The construction, validity, and performance of this Agreement shall be governed in all respects by the law of the state of -- and the Parties hereto submit to the jurisdiction of the courts of such state.

Principals concerned must sign here for agreement to be valid

SIGNED for

First Party ....

Position ....

For and on behalf of: ....

In the presence of: ....

SIGNED for

First Party ....

Position ....

For and on behalf of: ....

In the presence of: ....

FORECASTING CASH FLOW

The most reliable way to estimate the amount of money a business will require to meet its future needs is to make a cash-flow forecast; that is, determine the pattern and extent of cash payments and receipts by a business over a particular period. The different aspects of a business that need to be taken into account when drawing up an accurate cash-flow forecast are examined and explained here, in order to help you to feel as confident as possible that you have considered every necessary factor.

A profit is made if a business has any money left over after paying all the costs associated with making goods, or supplying a service. Typically such costs will fall under two headings: cost of sales and overhead. Cost of sales, or direct costs, includes raw materials if you are making products or the costs of providing a service. For example, a travel company might have to buy airline tickets and rent hotel rooms to "produce" a package holiday. Overhead, or indirect costs, are the cost of premises, telephone, insurance, and so forth.

ADDITIONAL COSTS TO CONSIDER

Even after these costs have been allowed for, however, a business may have other major expenses. For example, if fixed assets such as a computer or a van are required, these have to be allocated for in your cash calculations. As your business grows, it may need more inventory and it may attract more customers, who in turn take time to pay their bills. This gap between cash outflow and cash inflow will, in part, be offset by the increasing credit you will be able to take from your suppliers, but inevitably some financing will be required.

SETTING COSTS AGAINST INCOME

For the purpose of deciding how much money you need to start up or expand your business, you have to prepare a cash-flow forecast. This means estimating your likely future costs and your likely income from sales.

TAKE ACCOUNT OF ALL YOUR COSTS TO DETERMINE YOUR NET PROFIT

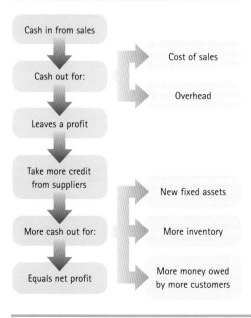

Cash in from sales

Cash out for:

Cost of sales

Leaves a profit

Overhead

Take more credit from suppliers

New fixed assets

More cash out for:

More inventory

Equals net profit

More money owed by more customers

Estimating Fixed Costs

Many costs have to be incurred before sales income can be generated, such as buying a car, office furniture, or a computer, or renting premises. You need to anticipate both the likely

		MINIMIZING FIXED COSTS			
ASSET	DO WE REALLY NEED IT?	DO WE NEED IT NOW?	DO WE REALLY NEED TO BUY IT?	COULD WE FINANCE IT SEPARATELY?	CAPITAL COST ($)
BOARDROOM TABLE	Nice, but not essential	No	No, could use hotel as needed	Yes	800
COLOR COPIER	Yes	Yes	No, could use copy center	Yes	1,400
DELIVERY VAN	Yes	No, not for eight weeks	Yes	Yes	21,000

amount and the timing of the purchase of these. Minimize your fixed costs by asking yourself the following questions about them.

DO WE REALLY NEED IT?

Business assets often have an element of vanity attached to them. For example, one company founder felt that a boardroom table and eight chairs were essential to his business from the outset. However, this meant paying the rent on a room that could now not be used for any productive purpose, incurring the cost of purchasing the furniture, and wasting a day on choosing and selecting the table and chairs. It was over two years before the company actually employed eight people, so this was really an unnecessary start-up cost.

DO WE NEED TO BUY IT?

Even if an asset is essential, it may not be necessary to buy it. For example, the founder of the business mentioned above could have held his board meetings at a local hotel for a fraction of the cost, or he could have searched out another entrepreneur, with an underutilized boardroom that he was eager to see being used.

A color photocopier may be nice to have, but for the relatively few occasions it is needed, using a copy center would suffice. This may still make sense even if there is a big difference between the cost per copy of using your own machine and the cost per copy at the copy

AN UNNECESSARY ASSET
Buying a color copier – which will tie up large amounts of cash – may well be a waste of money if you could manage with visits to a local copy center instead.

center, because it frees up scarce capital for other vital costs. If you need to produce color work often, then consider leasing a copier. Less capital is tied up, and you should benefit from terms such as free maintenance and possibly the option to buy the machine at a reduced price at the end of the lease period.

Do We Need to Buy It Now?

Timing is a vital element in determining the financing needs of a business. If a particular asset is not needed for several months, then do not buy it now. One owner-manager bought a refrigerated van for his food deliveries while still getting his production facility up and running. The van sat, unused, for three weeks before being misused to pick up and drop off garbage. It was not used to deliver fresh food to customers until eight weeks after its purchase.

Are These the Right Things to Buy?

Even when you know that an asset is essential to your business, it is not always easy to predict the right one to buy. In the example above, the van was discovered to be the wrong size for the job almost the first time it was used, and it had to be exchanged for a larger van. The business founder's predictions of sales demand were made with prudence and caution, but actual sales per customer turned out to be much better than expected. Unfortunately, much of the gain from extra sales was wasted on the loss in value of the original van.

Fact File

Cash is the money assets of a business, both in hand and at the bank. Profit is the excess of sales over costs and expenses during an accounting period. It follows, therefore, that many businesses that run an overdraft, and so technically have no cash, can nevertheless still be profitable.

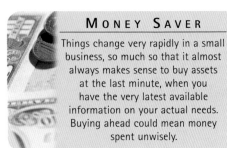

Money Saver

Things change very rapidly in a small business, so much so that it almost always makes sense to buy assets at the last minute, when you have the very latest available information on your actual needs. Buying ahead could mean money spent unwisely.

What Is the Best Way to Buy?

Rather than buy an essential asset outright, using cash or traditional financing such as an overdraft or loan, it may make sense to finance a particular asset directly. A car, for example, could be financed or leased, freeing up money for less tangible costs such as advertising, which a bank may not be so eager to support. (See pp. 59–60 for more details.)

Estimating Sales Revenue

The sales forecast is perhaps the most important set of numbers to come out of the business planning process. How much inventory to hold, how many staff to employ, and how much material to buy are all decisions that hinge on the sales forecast. These sales figures are also used to predict the cash-flow forecast and hence the funding requirements of the business.

These projections are also the key to valuing the business, and so they will determine whether or not bankers will lend and investors invest. Furthermore, they will give some guidance as to how much of an enterprise investors expect in exchange for funding. Naturally enough, potential backers do not accept a new business's sales forecast unchallenged, because in their experience new ventures nearly always miss the target by a wide margin.

While all forecasts may turn out to be wrong, it is important to demonstrate in your business plan that you have thought through all the different factors that could impact on your performance. You should also show how you can deliver satisfactory results even when many of these factors work against you. Backers want security, so they will inevitably be measuring the downside risk, to evaluate the worst case scenario and its likely effects, as well as looking toward an ultimate exit strategy.

RESEARCH SIMILAR BUSINESSES

Your overall projections will have to be believable. Most lenders and investors will have an extensive experience of similar business proposals. Unlike you, they will have the benefit of hindsight, being able to look back several years at other ventures they have backed, and see how they fared in practice as

---

CASE STUDY: Predicting Zero Sales Revenue

MEDSOFT WAS SET UP to sell dedicated computer systems to hospital consultants. The concept grew out of a chance meeting between Richard Kensall, a successful department store owner and disillusioned computer dealer, and an eager young doctor with a love of computers.

The doctor's problem was that he had too large a volume of patient data to classify and analyze. Some 16,000 specialists had a need to

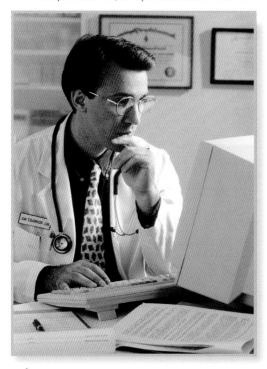

record details on 35 million patient consultations and 5 million admissions per year. A record had to be generated containing all details of each patient. At that time, almost all such records were generated and maintained manually. So, for Medsoft, the market opportunity was substantial and, with some further development, their product line was proven. The only problem was the time needed to get a decision made as to whether to buy or not, and then to get the cash.

Capital investment decisions such as this follow a long and complex procedure through the hospital administration. From finding a specialist who wanted to buy, to finally obtaining approval by the administration, could take up to nine months. Even after clearing all these hurdles, a project could fail if a regional hospital system had insufficient funds to pay for all the properly approved proposals. Consequently, Medsoft's business plan had to anticipate zero sales revenue for the first nine months at least, and only modest sums until well into the second year. Their resultant cash-flow forecast looked very sick indeed over this period, but in their business plan they were able to argue for this situation occurring. Fortunately, while investigating the decision-making process, they uncovered four types of potential customer who could "buy" within six months. These people were to be the focus of all sales effort for the first six months of Medsoft's life.

COMPREHENSIVE ACCESS
Once installed, Medsoft's dedicated computer system enabled hospital specialists to generate and update both the record details and the consultations with any of their patients at any time.

compared with the initial forecasts of their enthusiastic owners.

You could gather some useful knowledge on similar businesses yourself by researching filed company reports, trade magazines or by talking with the founders of similar ventures who will not be your direct competitors.

EVALUATE MARKET SHARE

How big is the market for your product or service? Is it growing or contracting? At what rate per year? What is the economic and competitive position? The answers to these questions can all provide a market share basis for your forecasts. An entry market share of more than a few percent would be most unusual. For all the hype, after a decade of hard work, the internet booksellers still account for less than 2 percent of all books sold, and Amazon is just one of a score of major players.

Beware, however, of turning this argument regarding small percentages on its head. Many sales forecasts are made on the premise that "if we capture only 1 percent of the potential market, we'll be a great success," with the belief that just 1 percent must be achievable. This argument is then advanced as part of the business plan, so that no time is "wasted" in doing basic market research. After all, the business has to sell to only this tiny percentage of possible buyers! In fact, this is ambitious and unrealistic thinking, which leads to more new business failures than any other single factor.

If the market is so huge that achieving sales to only 1 percent of it is very profitable, then inevitably there are large and established competitors. For a small firm to try to compete head on in this situation is little short of suicidal. It can be done, but only if sound research has clearly identified a market niche.

No investor will be impressed by clearly unsubstantiated statements, such as "in a market of $1 billion per annum we can easily capture 1 percent, which is $10 million a year," because they know that achieving this 1 percent of the market will not be nearly as easy as it sounds.

USE RULES OF THUMB

For some businesses there are useful generalizations, called rules of thumb, that can be used to estimate sales. This is particularly

ONLINE RESEARCH
Market research takes commitment and a methodical approach. Libraries are a good starting point that provide access to magazines, reports, and annual reports. You can also do research using the internet. You can then choose to view data on an international, national, or individual basis.

CASE STUDY: Steady Build-up of Sales

FOR THE PAST TWO YEARS Anthea Cody has been running a very successful outdoor clothing store called Exploration Works. Last year she took over an agency from Asian Adventure Vacations, one of the largest and most respected travel agents in the market. With virtually no marketing effort, 200 adventure vacations have been sold in the past six months, netting $40,000 in commissions. Sales of insurance policies and other services have added to this total, and could potentially add more.

When making her sales forecast, Anthea estimated that her inquiry-to-sales conversion rate on the adventure travel vacations sold to date had been 33 percent, while operating within the outdoor clothing store. For the purposes of her sales forecast, she made a conservative estimate that only 20 percent of inquiries would actually result in an adventure vacation being booked.

She expects a steady buildup of clients coming from the clothing store to talk about vacations. The number of new inquiries generated by promotional activity should also build up during the year, gradually overtaking inquiries from the clothes store. She expects this trend to continue. Based on the projection below, she is forecasting sales of 660 adventure travel vacations next year at an average price of $2,157. Once insurance and other service sales are added in, she expects to generate $160,948 over the year.

SALES FORECAST PROJECTION

	QUARTER 1	QUARTER 2	QUARTER 3	QUARTER 4	YEAR TOTAL
INQUIRIES GENERATED THROUGH PROMOTION	200	425	425	750	1,800
ADVENTURE STORE INQUIRIES	300	300	450	450	1,500
TOTAL INQUIRIES	500	725	875	1,200	3,300
VACATIONS SOLD	100	145	175	240	660
AVERAGE VACATION'S COST	$2,000	$2,000	$2,250	$2,250	$2,157
COMMISSION RECEIVED (10-11%)	$20,000	$29,000	$43,312	$59,136	$151,448
COMMISSION ON INSURANCE AND OTHER SERVICES RECEIVED (0.5-0.75%)	$1,000	$2,000	$3,000	$3,500	$9,500
TOTAL COMMISSION AND FEES EARNED	$21,000	$31,000	$46,312	$62,636	$160,948

true in retailing, where location studies, traffic counts, and population density are known factors that affect the volume of sales.

OBTAIN DATA FROM CUSTOMERS

How many customers and potential customers do you know who are likely to buy from you, and how much might they buy? Here you can use many types of data on which to base reasonable sales projections.

You can interview a sample of prospective customers, issue a press release or advertisement to gauge response, and exhibit at trade shows to get customer reactions.

TAKE SEASONALITY INTO ACCOUNT

When working out your sales forecast you should also look at seasonal factors that might cause sales to be high or low at certain periods in the year. For example, 80 percent of toys are sold in just three months of the year, leaving nine very flat sales months. Such seasonality would have a significant effect on your cash-flow projections.

INCORPORATE DESIRED INCOME

Forecasts will also accommodate the realistic goals of the proprietor. Indeed, you could go further and state that the whole purpose of the strategy is to ensure that certain forecasts are achieved. In a mature company with proven products and markets, this is more likely to be the case than with a new business. Nevertheless, an element of "How much do we need to earn?" must play a part in forecasting your sales, if only to signal when a strategy is simply not worth pursuing.

RELATE SALES FORECAST TO ACTIVITY

However they are arrived at, sales figures will convince no one unless they relate to the specific activities that will generate the necessary business.

If, for example, in your business salespeople have to make visits to generate orders, then knowing how many calls need to be made to get one order, and what the average order size could be, are essential pieces of information to include in your sales forecast.

GAIN APPROVAL

If your product or service needs to be on an association's or federation's approved list before it can be bought, then your cash-flow forecast should confirm that you have obtained the relevant approval to operate.

Calculating Working Capital

Once you have completed your sales forecast, you can use it to calculate the amount of raw material and inventory you will have to hold (if you are a manufacturing business or in subcontracting, for example) and how much money you will have tied up in customers, if you decide to sell on credit. This

CASE STUDY: Using Restaurant Rule of Thumb

TIM BROWN, who founded his second restaurant, called Alamo, in Los Angeles, with substantial backing from private investors, used a rule of thumb accepted by many restaurateurs to estimate his likely sales revenue. From the experience gained from setting up and running his first restaurant, he concurred with the accepted rule that once a restaurant has served 25,000 clients it can expect sufficient repeat business to break even.

In the event, during his first eight months of operation Brown served 20,000 customers at Alamo, and so was well on his way to the 25,000 break-even point he required to match his projected sales revenue forecast.

EXHIBITING AT TRADE SHOWS

Exhibiting at trade shows is an excellent way of viewing and assessing your competitors' merchandise. Trade shows also provide you with the opportunity to meet potential customers (and competitors) and to get personal reactions to your goods or services.

may be offset, in part at least, by the amount of credit you take from your suppliers. But the balance, which is known as the working capital, has to be funded by you.

The chart below shows the complete cash-flow cycle, tracing all the movements that occur within working capital. It should provide you with enough information to forecast the cash (and hence the financing) requirements of your business.

Forecasting Cash Requirements

Although a sales forecast can be drawn up on a quarterly basis, your cash-flow forecast should be broken down into months to give more detail. A cash-flow forecast, or pro forma cash-flow statement, for a travel agent on the next two pages shows how this is arrived at.

THE CASH-FLOW CYCLE

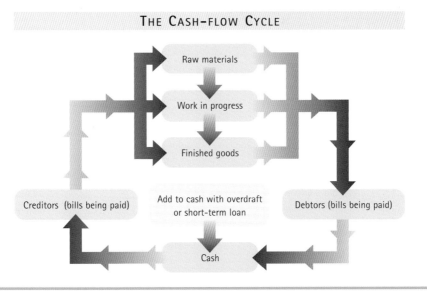

Raw materials

Work in progress

Finished goods

Creditors (bills being paid)

Add to cash with overdraft or short-term loan

Debtors (bills being paid)

Cash

Cash-flow Analysis

The business will need additional cash for most of the year, and anything less than $46,000 will be insufficient. In this example, this is the amount of the financing requirement called for in the business plan.

The owner is putting $10,000 of his own money into the business

Although sales are expected in month 1, the owner does not expect to get paid until month 2, or 3 for insurance commissions

The sales income figures come from the sales forecast

Ongoing expenses such as wages and leasing costs are charged monthly

Payments for major fixed assets such as fixtures, fittings, furniture, and website development come out in month 1

Pro Forma Cash-flow			
Month	**1**	**2**	**3**
Receipts			
Commission on Travel Sales		6,000	6,500
Commission on Insurance and Other Services			150
Owner's Cash Invested	10,000		
Total Receipts	10,000	6,000	6,650
Payments			
Rent	1,500	1,500	1,500
Heat, Light, and Power			875
Telephone System Leasing	166	166	166
Computer Systems and Software Leasing	416	416	416
Marketing and Promotion	1,041	1,041	1,041
Postage and Stationery	270	270	270
Telephone			893
Insurance and Legal	3,500		
Employee's Wages	3,000	3,000	3,000
Consultancy Services (Database and Website)	10,000	10,000	
Memberships and Subscriptions	1,500		
Travel and Entertainment	1,250		
Training and Staff Development		2,000	
Fixtures, Fittings, and Furniture	15,000		2,500
Bank Interest and Charges			1,250
Total Payments	37,643	18,393	11,911
Cash flow Surplus/Deficit (−)	(27,643)	(12,393)	(5,261)
Opening Bank Balance	0	(27,643)	(40,036)
Closing Bank Balance	(27,643)	(40,036)	(45,297)

Subscriptions are charged once a year

Utilities are paid quarterly

STATEMENT: YEAR ONE

4	5	6	7	8	9	10	11	12	TOTALS
7,500	8,500	9,500	11,000	13,000	14,500	15,812	17,250	19,800	129,362
250	300	300	350	450	450	600	600	700	4,150
5,000			5,000			5,000			25,000
12,750	8,800	9,800	16,350	13,450	14,950	21,412	17,850	20,500	158,512
1,500	1,500	1,500	1,500	1,500	1,500	1,500	1,500	1,500	18,000
		875			875			875	3,500
166	166	166	166	166	166	166	166	174	2,000
416	416	416	416	416	416	416	416	424	5,000
1,041	1,041	1,041	1,041	1,041	1,041	1,041	1,041	1,049	12,500
270	270	270	270	270	270	270	270	280	3,250
		893			893			896	3,575
									3,500
3,000	3,000	3,000	3,000	3,000	3,000	3,000	3,000	3,000	36,000
	5,000								25,000
									1,500
1,000			2,000						4,250
	2,000			2,000					6,000
									17,500
		1,250			1,250			1,250	5,000
7,393	13,393	9,411	8,393	8,393	9,411	6,393	6,393	9,448	146,575
5,357	(4,593)	389	7,957	5,057	5,539	15,019	11,457	11,052	11,937
(45,297)	(39,940)	(44,533)	(44,144)	(36,187)	(31,130)	(25,591)	(10,572)	885	
(39,940)	(44,533)	(44,144)	(36,187)	(31,130)	(25,591)	(10,572)	885	11,937	

Summarizing Financing Needs

You probably have a very good idea of why you need the funds that you are asking for, but unless the reader of your business plan has plenty of time to spare (which is unlikely) and can be bothered to figure it out without further explanation, you must clearly state to what use you will put the funds received.

A statement such as the one shown on the right clearly tells the reader of the plan how the funds will be spent.

The $100,000 required for plant and equipment will be needed several weeks or months before the business can open, while the $5,000 for the vehicle can, in all probability, be left closer to the time at which you will need it. The working capital requirement of $75,000 is needed in varying amounts over the first six months or so of business. Your funding request should clearly show this "timetable of anticipated funding." An example of this timetable of funding might be as shown in the table opposite.

FINANCING REQUIRED ($)	
TO PURCHASE:	
VEHICLE	5,000
PLANT AND EQUIPMENT	100,000
TO PROVIDE:	
WORKING CAPITAL FOR SIX MONTHS	75,000
TOTAL REQUIREMENT	180,000
MINUS INVESTMENT MADE (BY YOU)	30,000
NET FUNDING REQUIREMENT	150,000

MAKING YOUR REQUIREMENTS CLEAR

The bottom line of this summary clearly states that a net investment of $150,000 is required, and the uses to which this money will be put have been outlined above.

The timetable should be carried on for as long as external funding is required, and shows that:
- **AN EQUITY INVESTMENT** of $100,000 is made three months prior to start-up of business and remains in the business for the medium- to long-term future.
- **A BANK OVERDRAFT** facility of $75,000 is required, which is first used during month 3, reaches a peak of $70,000 during month 5,

---

CASE STUDY: Starting from Desired Income

JANE JENKINS set up her business 18 months after finishing a college degree. At first she was not sure what business to start, but she decided to see if she could turn her love of pottery into a money-making business. She began by visiting a number of potteries. "Their vase shapes were revolting, so I drew my own. I found that all my frustration evaporated just like that, and I knew what I wanted to do."

She persuaded some factories to make vases based on her own designs, then spent the next few months driving around the country, staying in cheap hotels *en route*. She equipped herself with sponges and colors so that she could apply her designs to her vases in the factories.

"At first people thought I was crazy and were skeptical but helpful." However, she soon won her first order, worth $600, from a fashionable store, and within two months she decided to meet her potential customers by exhibiting at a trade show.

Jane decided that unless she could earn at least $40,000 per annum in the second year of her new business, she would not want to start up. Her predicted profit margin was 40 percent, so this "objective" called for a sales forecast of $100,000. She used her market research and the resultant strategies to satisfy herself (and her backers) that this was a realistic goal.

	TIMETABLE OF ANTICIPATED FUNDING FOR FIRST YEAR				
DATE	REQUIREMENT PER CASH-FLOW FORECAST ($000)	SHARE ISSUE ($000)	YOUR CASH INTRODUCED ($000)	BANK LOAN ($000)	LEASE DEPOSIT ($000)
PRECOMMENCEMENT OF TRADING					
MONTH 1	100	100	30	–	–
MONTH 2	5	–	–	–	–
MONTH 3	70	–	–	45	5.00
COMMENCEMENT OF TRADING					
MONTH 4	20	–		60	4.85
MONTH 5	10	–		70	4.70
MONTH 6	-5	–		65	4.55
MONTH 7	-20	–		45	4.40
MONTH 8	-21	–		24	4.25
MONTH 9	-25	–		–	4.10
MONTH 10	-20	–		–	3.95
MONTH 11	-10	–		–	3.80
MONTH 12	-10	–		–	3.65

and is cleared by month 9 (i.e. the sixth month in business). Note that the full $75,000 facility appears not to be needed, but it is always advisable to obtain more than is required to cover any unforeseen circumstances. It is better to borrow too much than to have to go back and ask for more.

▦ A LEASE DEPOSIT of $5,000 is required in month 3, and this will be repaid over three years.

Expecting the Unexpected

There is little that disturbs a financier more than a firm that has to go back for more financing too soon after raising money, especially if the reason should have been seen and allocated for at the outset. So, in making projections, you have to be ready for likely pitfalls and be prepared for the unexpected events that will knock your cash flow off target. Forecasts and projections rarely go as planned, but the most common pitfalls can be anticipated.

You cannot really protect yourself against freak disasters or unforeseen delays, which hit large and small businesses alike. But some events are more likely than others to affect your cash flow, and it is against these that you can guard by careful planning. Not all of the events listed here may be relevant to your business, but some, if not many, will be.

BASED ON A FLAWED PREMISE

There is no doubt that forecasting sales is difficult. The number of things that can and will go awry are many and varied. In the first place, the entire premise on which the forecast is based may be flawed. Estimating the number of people who may come into a restaurant as "passing trade," the number of people who will order from a mail-order catalog, or the proportion of internet site hits that will turn into paying customers depends on performance ratios. For example, a direct mailing to a well-targeted list could produce anything from a 0.5 to a 3 percent response. If you build your sales forecast using the higher figure but actually achieve only the lower figure, then your sales income could be barely a sixth of the figure in your cash-flow projection.

Allow for late payers in your cash-flow projections, to avoid unpleasant surprises

SALES BUILDUP IS SLOWER THAN EXPECTED

Even if your forecasting premise is right, or nearly so, customers may take longer to make up their minds than you expect. Your forecast may include an assumption that people will order within two weeks of receiving your mail-order catalog. But until you start trading you will not know how accurate that assumption is likely to be. Even if you have been in business for years, buying patterns may change.

CUSTOMERS TAKE LONGER TO PAY THAN EXPECTED

While you set the terms and conditions under which you plan to do business, customers are a law unto themselves. If they can take extra credit, they will. Unless you are in a cash business, you can expect a proportion of your customers to be late payers. If you have good accounting systems, you will keep this to an acceptable figure, but you will never get every bill paid on time. You need to allow for this lag in your cash-flow projections.

BAD DEBTS

Unfortunately, late payers are not the only problem. Some customers will never pay. Thousands of businesses fail each year and individuals go bankrupt, each leaving behind a trail of unpaid bills. Some steps can be taken to minimize this risk, and we will discuss those later, but the risk cannot be eliminated altogether. You can try to research the rate of nonpayment in your sector and allow for it in your plans. As a general rule, the construction and restaurant industries have a relatively high incidence of bad debts, while business services have a lower rate.

REPEAT ORDERS TAKE LONGER TO COME IN THAN EXPECTED

It is often hard to know exactly what a customer's demand for your product or service is. Their initial order from you may last them months, weeks, or just days. For strategic reasons, they may want to divide up their business between a number of suppliers. If, for example, they have three suppliers and they order a month's worth at a time, it may be some time before it is your turn for an order. If your customer sales are sluggish or seasonal, then that time frame could extend further still. So even delighted customers may not come back for more for some time.

PRICES TOO LOW

The selling price is an important factor in estimating the amount of cash coming into a business and hence the amount of financing needed to operate that business.

Often the only way a new or small business can win certain customers is by matching a competitor's price. This may not be the price in your list, but it is the one at which you have to sell. Also, the mix of products or services you actually sell may be very different from your projection, and this can affect average prices. For example, a restaurant owner will have to forecast what wines his customers will buy. If the house wine is too good, then more customers might go for that rather than the more expensive and profitable wines on the list.

TOO MUCH INVENTORY

If your sales projections are too high, you will experience the double whammy of having less cash coming in and more going out than shown in your forecast. That is because in all probability you will have purchased supplies to meet demand. Your suppliers offering discounts for bulk purchases may have exacerbated the situation if you took up their offers.

LATE DELIVERIES

If your suppliers deliver late, you may in turn find you have nothing to sell. Such a delay will cause ill will with your customers, and you may have to wait weeks or months for another opportunity to supply them. This problem can be minimized using online order tracking

systems, but some late deliveries will still occur. Increasing stocks is one way to ensure against deficiencies in the supply chain, but that strategy too has an adverse impact on cash flow.

SUPPLIERS WILL NOT GIVE CREDIT

Few suppliers are eager to give small and particularly new businesses any credit. So, before you build in 30, 60, or even 90 days' credit into your financial projections, you need to confirm that normal terms of business will apply to what a supplier may view as an abnormal customer.

You need to remember that, while taking extended credit may help your cash flow in the short term, it could sour relationships in the long term. So, in circumstances where a product is in short supply, poor payers will be last on the list to get deliveries, and the problems identified above may be further exacerbated.

MISSED OR WRONG COST

If you are starting up, or expanding into new areas of business, it is possible that certain areas of cost are missing from your business plan. Business insurance and legal expenses are two often-overlooked items. Even where a cost is not left out altogether, it may be understated. So, for example, if you are including the cost of taking out a patent in your financing plan, it is safer to base the price on those quoted by the US Patent and Trademark Office, rather than just to assume that it will cost the same as it did a friend of yours a few years ago.

FRAUD AND THEFT

Retailers claim that they could knock 5 percent off everything they sell if they could only eliminate theft, which is an ever-increasing problem. Even more disturbing is theft within the business, as in the case study below, where the thief was the company's accountant.

Anticipating Worst-case Scenarios

Even events that have not been anticipated can be allowed for when estimating financing needs. An analysis using a cash-flow spreadsheet will allow you to identify worst-case scenarios that could knock you off course. From this, you will end up with a realistic estimate of the financing requirements of the business or project. The chart on the right illustrates the effects of some of the possible ways in which financing projections can go awry.

TESTING TO DESTRUCTION

Even events that have not been anticipated can be allowed for when estimating financing needs. A "what if" analysis using a cash-flow spreadsheet will allow you to identify worst-case scenarios that could knock you off course.

Some examples of incidents that could happen are: the expenses that you considered unlikely to happen actually occur; the sales buildup is slower than forecasted; the total sales in the period are lower than expected; suppliers demand payment on delivery; your credit customers take longer to pay up than expected; and operating costs are higher than anticipated. The chart opposite shows the effects of some of the possible ways in which a business' financing projections could go awry.

In the original forecast, this business looks like it may need only $6,300 of capital. But, once "tested to destruction" by having some realism built into the projections, the forecast shows that the business may actually need $31,800 if it is to survive its first few months. This "what if" forecast is usually repeated across a range of possible scenarios to see which set of circumstances could imperil the business. Working with the financial requirement of $6,300 rather than $31,800 would undoubtedly have caused major, if not terminal, problems for this business had the scenario explored actually come to pass.

CASE STUDY: The Effects of Fraud

JANE EDGE DISCOVERED that her founding partner, who was also the company's accountant, was defrauding her only when she decided to offer shares as incentives to the company's employees. Valuing the company required audited financial statements, which were not ready. Her partner claimed that the auditors were holding up clearing the statements on a few technicalities. When Jane contacted them, the auditors said that the company was late in producing the statements and that they had not even seen them! Eventually it was discovered that the partner had siphoned off a quarter of the business's assets for his own purposes.

Needless to say, the partner was fired and sued successfully, though no money was recovered. Unfortunately, the loss of money meant that the employee incentive plan had to be postponed, causing two key employees to leave and set up in business for themselves. The company never fully recovered from this setback.

Expect no credit

Missed cost item

Slower buildup and later payment

CASH IN	ORIGINAL FORECAST			REVISED FORECAST		
THE "WHAT IF" FORECAST						
	MONTH 1 ($)	MONTH 2 ($)	MONTH 3 ($)	MONTH 1 ($)	MONTH 2 ($)	MONTH 3 ($)
SALES		10,000	15,000			10,000
OWNER'S CAPITAL	4,000			4,000		
TOTAL	4,000	10,000	15,000	4,000		10,000
CASH OUT						
INVENTORY/RAW MATERIALS		5,000	7,500	5,000	7,500	10,000
ADVERTISING AND PROMOTION	200	300	500	200	300	500
INSURANCE				500		
HEAT, LIGHT, AND POWER			300			300
TELEPHONE			1,000			1,000
PROFESSIONAL SERVICES	500			500		
AUTO	200	200	200	200	200	200
TRAVEL AND ENTERTAINMENT	500	500	500	500	500	500
RENT	1,200	1,200	1,200	1,200	1,200	1,200
WAGES	1,100	1,100	1,100	1,100	1,100	1,100
CAPITAL EXPENDITURE	0	8,000	3,000	8,000	3,000	
TOTAL	3,700	16,300	15,300	17,200	13,800	14,800
NET CASH FLOW	300	-6,300	-300	-13,200	-13,800	-4,800
CUMULATIVE NET CASH FLOW	300	-6,000	-6,300	-13,200	-27,000	-31,800

The difference between "Cash in" and "Cash out"

The total cash needed by the business

RAISING the money

*T*here are many sources of funds available to small firms. However, not all are equally appropriate to all businesses, nor are they available to every type of business. So the legal structure under which you operate can affect the choice of funding sources open to you. Different sources carry with them very different obligations, responsibilities, and opportunities for a profitable business. The differences have to be understood to allow for an informed choice.

WAYS TO ORGANIZE YOUR BUSINESS

There are different legal frameworks for the ownership of a business – sole proprietorship, partnership, close corporation, public corporation, cooperative, or franchise chain – and not all sources of financing are open to every type of business. Once you know how much money is needed either to start up or to grow, and what that money is needed for, you will be in a better position to make an informed choice from the options.

Each business structure has a range of advantages and disadvantages, and each confers different responsibilities, liabilities, and opportunities for creating personal wealth. In general, the more money that is required and the more risky the venture, the more likely it is that incorporation will be the most suitable structure for your new business. However, most successful businesses are very likely to change their ownership structure as they grow and develop.

Only the issues that relate to financial management are considered here, although other factors are affected by legal structure. For example, some people think that operating as a public corporation is more prestigious than, say, a partnership.

Choose sole proprietorship if you want independence and responsibility for your business,

Operating as Sole Proprietor

The vast majority of new businesses are essentially one-man bands. As such, they are free to choose the simplest legal structure. They are known as "sole proprietorships." This structure has the merit of being relatively formality-free, and there are few rules about the records you have to keep. Your financial statements do not have to be audited, and financial information on your business need not be filed.

As a sole propritor there is no legal distinction between you and your business. Your business is one of your assets, in the same way as your house or car is. If your business should fail, your creditors have

CASE STUDY: Personal Liability – Debt

JAMES IS THE SOLE PROPRIETOR of a small manufacturing business. When business prospects look good, he orders supplies and uses them up. Unfortunately, there is then a sudden drop in demand for his products, so he cannot sell the items he has produced and the supplies continue to pile up in his warehouse.

When the company that sold James the supplies demands payment, he cannot pay the bill.

As sole proprietor, James is personally liable for this business obligation. This means that the creditor can sue him and go after not only his business assets but his other property as well. This can include his house, his car, and his personal bank account.

ADVANTAGES AND DISADVANTAGES OF BUSINESS TYPES

BUSINESS TYPE	ADVANTAGES	DISADVANTAGES
SOLE PROPRIETORSHIP	■ Simple and inexpensive to create and operate ■ Owner reports profit or loss on his or her personal tax return	■ Owner personally liable for business debts ■ No access to external capital ■ Life of business restricted to life of owner ■ Limited potential for value creation
GENERAL PARTNERSHIP	■ Simple and inexpensive to create and operate ■ Owners (partners) report their share of profit or loss on their personal tax returns ■ Some potential for value creation	■ Owners (partners) personally liable for business debts ■ Life of business restricted to life of first partner to die ■ Access to outside capital restricted to partners
LIMITED PARTNERSHIP	■ Limited partners have limited personal liability for business debts as long as they do not participate in management ■ General partners can raise cash without involving outside investors in management of business ■ Wider access to outside capital ■ Some potential for value creation	■ General partners personally liable for business debts ■ More expensive to create than general partnership ■ Life of business restricted to life of first partner to die
CORPORATION	■ Owners have limited personal liability for business debts ■ Some benefits (pensions, etc.) can be deducted as a business expense ■ Owners can split corporate profit among owners and corporation, paying lower overall tax rate ■ Access to full range of external capital ■ Business can live on after founder's death ■ Potential for value creation	■ More expensive to create and run than partnership or sole proprietorship ■ Owners must meet legal requirements for stock registration, account filing and paperwork ■ Separate taxable entity
COOPERATIVE	■ Owners have limited personal liability for business debts ■ Owners report their share of corporate profit or loss on their personal tax returns ■ Owners can use corporate loss to offset income from other sources	■ More expensive to create than a sole proprietorship ■ Owners must meet legal requirements for account filing, registration and paperwork ■ Restricted access to outside capital
FRANCHISE CHAIN	■ Access to a stream of capital and income from new franchisees, to fund expansion	■ Limited potential for value creation

a right not only to the assets of the business but also to your personal assets, subject only to the provisions of federal bankruptcy and state "homestead" exemptions. These rules often allow you to keep only a few absolutely basic essentials for yourself and your family. You may, however, be able to avoid the worst consequences of bankruptcy by distancing your assets (see p. 152).

Seek professional advice regarding your legal obligations before setting up as a sole proprietor

The capital to start and run the business must come from you or from loans. As a sole proprietor you have no access to equity capital, which has the attraction of being risk-free. In return for these drawbacks you can have the pleasure of being your own boss immediately, subject only to declaring your profits on your tax return and, if necessary, applying for a business permit.

Going into Partnership

A partnership is effectively a collection of sole proprietors. It is a common structure used by people who started out on their own but who want to expand.

There are very few restrictions on setting up in business with another person (or persons) in partnership, and several definite advantages. By pooling resources, you and your partner(s) may have more capital, you will be bringing (hopefully) several sets of skills to the business, and if you are ill the business can still carry on.

The legal regulations governing partnerships assume that competent business people should know what they are doing. The law merely provides a framework of agreement that applies "in the absence of an agreement to the contrary." It follows that many partnerships are entered into without legal formalities and sometimes without the parties themselves being aware that they have entered a partnership. Just giving other people the impression that you are partners may be enough to create an "implied partnership." In the absence of an agreement to the contrary, these rules apply to partnerships:

- All partners will contribute capital equally.
- All partners will share profits and losses equally.
- No partner will have interest paid on their capital.
- No partner will be paid a salary.
- All partners will have an equal say in the management of the business.

It is unlikely that all these provisions will suit you, so you would be well advised to get a partnership agreement drawn up in writing.

FINANCIAL DRAWBACKS

Partnerships have three serious financial drawbacks that merit particular attention.

CASE STUDY: Personal Liability – Personal Injury

ANN IS THE SOLE PROPRIETOR of a flower shop. One day Andrew, one of Ann's employees, is delivering flowers using a truck owned by the business. Andrew strikes and seriously injures a pedestrian. The injured pedestrian sues Andrew, claiming that he drove carelessly and caused the accident. The lawsuit names Ann as a codefendant. After a trial, the jury returns a verdict against Andrew, and therefore against Ann as owner of the business. Ann is personally liable to the injured pedestrian. This means that the pedestrian can go after all of Ann's assets, business and personal, unless she has sufficient insurance coverage to meet the claim.

CASE STUDY: Starting with a Partnership

JANE, STEPHANIE, AND TERRY-ANN, all librarians, planned to open an electronic information searching business with an emphasis on information of special interest to women. They would hold on to their daytime jobs until they could determine if their new business would be successful enough to support all three of them.

At a planning meeting to discuss buying personal computers, Jane said that she wanted the business to be run as professionally as possible, which to her meant promptly incorporating. The discussion about equipment was put off, and the three women tried to decide how to organize the legal structure of their business. After several frustrating hours, they agreed to continue the discussion later after doing some research into the organizational options.

Before the next meeting, Jane conferred with a small business adviser, who suggested that the women refocus their energy on the computers and getting their business operating, keeping its legal structure as simple as possible. One good way to do this, she suggested, was to form a partnership, using a written partnership agreement. Each partner would contribute equally to buying equipment and would share the workload fairly. Profits would be divided equally between the three.

Later, she advised, if the business succeeded and grew, it might make sense to incorporate and consider other issues, such as a health plan, retirement plan, and other benefits. But, for now, real professionalism meant getting on with the job, not consuming time and money forming an unneeded corporate entity.

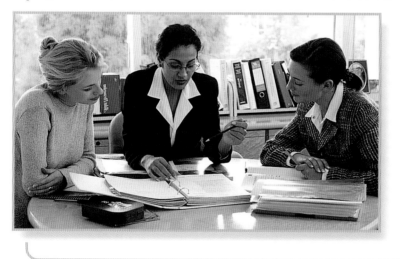

PART OF A TEAM
From the outset, the three partners met regularly and frequently to discuss any issues affecting their business.

First, if your partner makes a business mistake, perhaps by signing a disastrous contract, without your knowledge or consent, every member of the partnership must shoulder the consequences. Under these circumstances, as a partner your personal assets could be taken to pay the creditors, even though the mistake was no fault of your own.

Second, if your partner goes bankrupt in their personal capacity, for whatever reason, their share of the partnership can be seized by their creditors. As a private individual, you are not liable for your partner's private debts, but having to buy them out of the partnership at short notice could put both you and the business in financial jeopardy.

Third, if your partnership breaks up for any reason, those continuing with it will want to recover control of the business, those who remain partners will want to buy the departing partner out cheaply, while they want a higher price. The agreement you have on setting up the business should specify the procedure and how to value the leaver's stake; otherwise, resolving the situation will be costly.

Calculating the Buyout

The traditional route to value the departing partner's stake is to ask an independent accountant. This is rarely cost-effective. The valuation costs money and, worst of all, is not definite; consequently there is room for argument.

Another way of valuing the stake is to establish a formula, for example an agreed eight times the last audited pretax profits. This approach is simple but difficult to get right. A fast-growing business will be undervalued by a formula using historic data, unless the multiple is high; by the same token, a high multiple may overvalue the level of goodwill generated by the business, and thus unreasonably profit the departing partner.

Under a third option, one partner offers to buy out the others at a price he specifies. If they do not accept his offer, the continuing partners must buy the leaver out at that price. In theory, such a price should be acceptable to all.

Even death may not release you from partnership obligations, and in some circumstances your estate can remain liable. Unless you take public leave of your partnership by notifying your business contacts, and legally bringing your partnership to an end, you will remain liable – with all that that implies – indefinitely.

Limited Partnerships

One possibility that can reduce the more painful consequences of entering a partnership is to have your involvement registered as a limited partnership. A "limited" partnership is a very different business to a "general" partnership. It is a legal animal that, in certain ircumstances, combines the best attributes of a partnership and a corporation.

A limited partnership works like this. There must be one or more general partners with the same basic rights and responsibilities (including unlimited liability) as in any general partnership, and one or more limited partners

---

CASE STUDY: Creating a Limited Partnership

Judith and Tony have been partners in a small picture-frame shop for two years. Building on their increasing success, they want to expand into a bigger store in a much better location, where they can stock a large selection of fine art prints as well as frames. To raise the extra money, they create a limited partnership, offering a $30,000 investor a 10 percent interest in the total net profits of the store for the next three years, as well as the return of the invested capital at the end of that period. They sell four limited partnership interests to this value and so raise $120,000, which they use to put their expansion plans into operation. Three years later they return the invested capital to all four investors.

who are usually passive investors. The big difference between a general partner and a limited partner is that the limited partner is not personally liable for the debts of the partnership. The most a limited partner can lose is the amount that he or she:

▪ paid or agreed to pay into the partnership as a capital contribution; or

▪ received from the partnership after it became insolvent.

To keep this limited liability, a limited partner may not participate in the management of the business, except in very few exceptional circumstances. A limited partner who does get actively involved in the management of the business risks losing immunity from personal liability and so having the same legal exposure as a general partner.

The advantage of a limited partnership as a business structure is that it provides a way for the business owners to raise money (from the limited partners) without either having to take in any new partners – who would be active in the business and therefore enlarge the number of people involved in decision making – or having to form a corporation. In addition, a general partnership that has been operating for years can create a limited partnership in order to finance expansion.

Choose limited partnership status if you want to avoid liability for the debts of your partnership

states followed suit, and Britain caught up in 1854. Today most countries have a legal structure that incorporates the concept of limited liability.

As the name suggests, in this form of business your liability is limited to the amount you contribute to the business by way of share capital.

A corporation has a legal identity of its own, separate from the people who own or run it. This means that, in the event of failure, creditors' claims are restricted to the assets of the business. The shareholders of the business are not liable as individuals for the business debts beyond the paid-up value of their shares. This applies even if the shareholders are working directors (unless of course the company has been operating fraudulently). In practice, the ability to limit liability is restricted these days because most lenders often insist on personal guarantees from the directors.

Other advantages include the freedom to raise capital by selling shares. Disadvantages of choosing this structure include the legal requirement for the company's books to be audited and filed for public inspection.

A corporation can be formed by one or more people, one of whom must be a director. A company secretary must also be appointed; he or she can be a shareholder, a director, or an

Forming a Corporation

The concept of limited liability – in which the owners of the business are not liable, in the last resort, for the debts of their business – can be traced back to the Romans. It was rarely used, however, because it was granted as a special favor by those in power only to their friends. Some 2,000 years later the idea was revived when, in 1811, New York State brought in a general limited liability law for manufacturing companies. Most American

FACT FILE

A corporation is a business that is owned by one or more people who may or may not be involved in the day-to-day running of the business. The owners, known as shareholders, have a limited personal liability for the debts incurred by the company, which is itself a separate legal entity. The day-to-day running of a corporation is entrusted to its directors, who may also be shareholders.

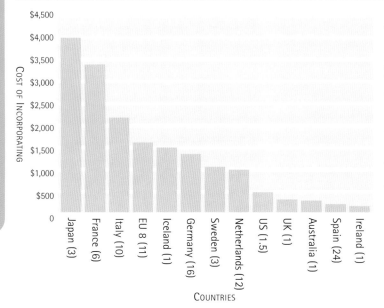

Countries: Japan (3), France (6), Italy (10), EU 8 (11), Iceland (1), Germany (16), Sweden (3), Netherlands (12), US (1.5), UK (1), Australia (1), Spain (24), Ireland (1)

COUNTRIES

ASSESSING THE COST
This shows the cost and time to incorporate a business. The time in weeks is shown in brackets. The massive variation in regulations worldwide means that setting up a corporation can cost anything from a few hundred dollars up to $4,000. The time to set up also varies, from one week to four months.

outside person unconnected with the business, such as an accountant or lawyer.

The simplest method of starting a corporation is to form your own from scratch with the name and other details that you have decided upon. You will need to register it with the appropriate agency of the state in which you register.

Alternatively, you can buy one "off the shelf" from a registration agent, who will then adapt it to suit your own purposes. This will involve changing the name, shareholders, and articles of association. It will take a couple of weeks for your agent to register these changes with the relevant authorities. There will, of course, be a fee to pay.

CASE STUDY: Forming a Cooperative

SEVERAL YEARS AGO RACHEL attended a local college to improve her skills in cake baking and decoration. Although her evening classes lasted only a few weeks, she soon found she had an

aptitude for the subject. Her skills were well above average, a fact that was acknowledged by friends and fellow students alike. She often received requests to produce birthday or wedding cakes, usually from friends and relatives.

Although she frequently found herself making one or two cakes a week, Rachel considered this as a hobby rather than a business.

The idea of starting a business came when Rachel met Jane, who had recently moved into the area and was eager to supplement her husband's income. She too was a good pastry cook, and together with her friend Mary was already taking occasional cake orders from friends. The three decided to start up in business together. None of them expected or even wanted to make a fortune from the business. They would be happy to stay small, and their satisfaction would come from being independent and doing something they really enjoyed.

All three had other friends who occasionally helped them out if they got too busy and who at

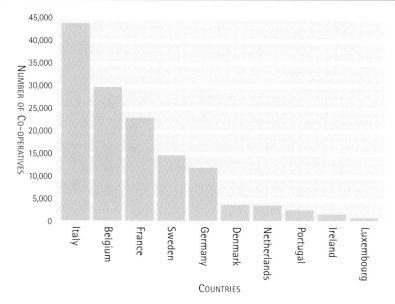

EUROPEAN COOPERATIVES
The revival of the cooperative in Europe reflects people's inherent desire to work together in a democratically owned and run business. The range in the number of cooperatives across Europe is extremely wide: from very few in Luxembourg to a massive 44,000 in Italy.

Cooperating with Others

A cooperative is an enterprise owned and controlled by the people working in it. Once in danger of becoming extinct, the

some stage might want to get involved on a more permanent basis. After considering other legal forms for their business, they decided that a cooperative was ideally suited to their purpose. Each member has equal control through the principle of "one person one vote," and membership must be open to any friends who satisfy the stipulated qualifications.

Within three months of setting up together as the Commemoration Cakes Cooperative, the business was receiving three or four inquiries a day, with most of those converting into firm orders. Their website was attracting some large enquiries from the corporate sector, one of which had already resulted in an order for 80 cakes for an annual sales conference.

workers' cooperative is now enjoying something of a revival. There are around 200,000 cooperatives operating in Europe, of which Italy undoubtedly has the lion's share (see graph above), and many states in the United States have laws to help those people who dream of forming a non-hierarchical business of true equals – an organization that is owned and controlled democratically by its members – to form a cooperative.

A cooperative is certainly not a legal structure designed to give entrepreneurs control of their own destiny and deliver maximum profits, but it does have other advantages, not the least being that you are all equal members with equal rights. You may be able to operate a cooperative as a closely held or regular corporation, or as a partnership. You can also organize under your state's cooperative corporation law, after consulting your attorney and accountant.

If a cooperative does not formally register itself with the necessary authorities, and this is not mandatory, it will be treated in law as a partnership with unlimited liability.

COMMON RULES GOVERNING COOPERATIVES

1. Each member of the cooperative has equal control through the principle of "one person one vote."

2. Membership must be open to anyone who satisfies the stipulated qualifications.

3. Profits can be retained in the business or distributed in proportion to members' involvement, for example hours worked.

4. Members must benefit primarily from their participation in the business.

5. Interest on loan or share capital is limited in some specific way, even if the profits are high enough to allow a greater payment.

Taking up Franchising

Another way either to start up or expand a business is via franchising. Buying a franchise falls somewhere in between working for somebody else as an employee and starting a business of your own as an independent entrepreneur. The main appeal is that you can sell a recognized product or service, but you are not in business all by yourself, with no backup resources to support you. In addition, good franchises offer three financial benefits:

1 **A PROVEN PLAN FOR RUNNING THE BUSINESS**
The franchisor (the company that sells a franchise) will have an operations manual that can serve as a roadmap to get you

started. This is particularly helpful if you do not have any business experience. They will also have systems in place for bookkeeping and financial control.

2 **HELP FROM THE FRANCHISOR** The better franchisors have people available who are experienced in marketing, personnel policies, accounting, and day-to-day operations to whom you can turn if you run into problems. With a well-run franchise organization, being able to call on these resources in effect provides you with expert advisers at an affordable cost.

3 **EXTERNAL FINANCING** A franchise is a proven business model, and so it is much more likely that banks would be prepared to put up funds to finance it.

EXPANDING A BUSINESS

Franchising is also a method of expanding a business using other people's energy and capital. Each new franchisee will pay a capital sum to buy into the network, a share of ongoing

SUCCESSFUL FRANCHISE
Fast-food chains lead the way in franchise operations, and McDonald's is probably the most widely recognized of all such establishments.

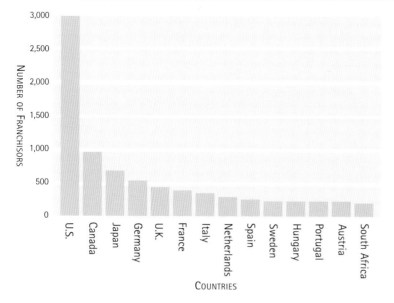

NUMBER OF FRANCHISORS

COUNTRIES

WORLD FRANCHISING
As this chart shows, the U.S. completely dominates the world with its number of franchisors, many of which are fast-food chains.

costs, and a fee based on sales. So, in effect, the franchisors gets a stream of new, risk-free money to finance their expansion. Most of the fast-food chains, such as McDonald's and Burger King, are all franchise operations, but the concept extends into many other areas too, including car rental, office and business services, clothing, health care, and real-estate services.

Franchisors should not see selling franchises as a quick route to expanding a business idea. It needs patient and skilled management, plus considerable experience, to iron out all the problems before you can start to persuade franchisees to part with their money. You should run several pilot operations for at least a year to prove the concept and to assess problem areas. A thorough operations manual and audited financial statements will be needed. It also helps to get the franchise department of your bank involved so that they can endorse the operation.

CHOOSING A SOURCE OF FINANCING

Different sources of money have different conditions attached. Some financiers require an involvement in the business, others may take take months or even years to arrange the funding. Some are costly but involve the recipient in little risk, while others are inexpensive and quick to arrange, yet impose comprehensive personal liability. The most important thing is to get the right balance between debt and equity.

If you can fund the project from your own resources, there are attractions to doing so. Only in this way do all of the rewards of success flow to you. As soon as you bring in other sources of financing, they slice off some of the reward, be it interest, a share of the value on the sale of the business, or dividends. They may also constrain the business through the use of covenants, borrowing limits, and the placement of financial obligations on the business. By these means they are potentially not only carving off part of your rewards but also capping them by restricting your operation.

Most firms will, however, require outside financing to realize their full potential, if not at the outset then at some stage in their growth.

> *Be prepared to invest some of your own assets in your new business*

Most small firms confine their financial strategy to bank loans, either long term or short term, viewing the other financing methods as either too complex or too risky. In fact, in many respects the reverse is true. Almost every source of financing other than banks will, to a greater or lesser extent, share some of the risks of doing business with the recipient of the funds.

The great attraction to borrowing from the bank lies in the speed with which facilities can usually be arranged. Many small businesses operate without a business plan, so most events that require additional funds, such as sudden expansion or contraction, come as a surprise, either welcome or unwelcome. It is to this weakness in financial strategy that banks are ultimately appealing. Since the loan is often taken out in a hurry to solve a crisis, it is hardly surprising that many difficulties arise.

Reviewing the Financing Options

There are many sources of funds available to small firms, although not all are equally appropriate to all firms at all times. These different sources of financing carry very different obligations, responsibilities, and opportunities for profitable businesses. The differences have to be understood to allow for an informed choice.

Comparing Lenders and Investors

At one end of the financing spectrum lie shareholders, either individual business angels or corporate entities, such as venture capital firms. They share all the risks and vagaries of the business alongside the founder and

THE EXPECTATIONS OF LENDERS AND INVESTORS

LENDERS – RISK AVERSE	INVESTORS – RISK TAKERS
Interest paid on outstanding loan	No dividends paid, unless profits warrant it; frequently not even then
Capital repaid either at end of term or sooner if they have concerns	Capital returned with substantial growth by new shareholders
Security given either from assets or from personal guarantees	Security comes from belief in people and their business vision

ASSESSING THE RISK
Lenders, such as banks, are looking for safe ventures that will repay their capital on demand. By contrast, investors, such as venture capitalists or business angels, seek exciting and therefore risky prospects that will generate profits in the long term.

expect an equal share in the rewards if things go well. They are less concerned with a stream of dividends, which is just as well because few small companies ever pay them, and instead hope for a radical increase in the value of their investment. They expect to realize this value from other investors who want to take their places for the next stage in the firm's growth cycle, rather than from any repayment by the founder. Investors in new or small businesses do not look for the security of buildings or other assets to underpin their investment. Instead, they look to the founder's vision and the core management team's ability to realize it.

At the other end of the financing spectrum are the banks, who try very hard to take no risk, but who expect some reward irrespective of performance. They want interest payments on money lent to you, usually from day one. While they too hope that the management of the business is competent, they are more interested in securing a charge against any assets the managers own, either business or private, in the form of a personal guarantee. At the end of the day, and that day can be sooner than the borrower expects, a bank wants all its money back. It would be more prudent to think of banks as people who will help you turn a proportion of an illiquid asset, such as an unmortgaged property or life insurance policy, into a more liquid asset, such as cash, at a heavy cost, rather than as lenders.

KNOWING THE DIFFERENCES

To make the correct decision on which source of financing is appropriate, you need to understand the differences in expectation between lenders, who provide debt, and investors, who provide equity or share capital. This is central to a sound grasp of financial management. In between the extremes of shareholders and the banks lie myriad other financing vehicles, which have a mixture of lending or investing criteria.

A business needs to keep its finances under constant review, choosing the most appropriate mix of funds for the risks it plans to take and the economic climate ahead. The more risky and volatile the road ahead, the more appropriate it will be to take a higher proportion of risk capital. In times of stability and low interest, higher borrowings may be more acceptable to both borrower and lender.

Understanding Bank Loans

Banks are the principal and frequently the only source of financing for nine out of every ten new and small businesses. Bankers are looking for asset security to back their loan and the near certainty of getting their money back. They are not risk takers willing to gamble on your success. They will not consider risking their money in your business if you are not prepared to risk your own in it. They will also charge an interest rate that reflects both the current market conditions and their view of the risk level of the proposal.

Bankers like to speak of the five Cs of credit analysis, which are the factors they look at when they evaluate a loan request.

1 **CHARACTER** Bankers lend money to borrowers who appear honest and who have a good credit history. Before you apply for a loan, it makes sense to obtain a copy of your credit report and clean up any problems.

2 **CAPACITY** This is a prediction of the borrower's ability to repay the loan. For a new business, bankers look at the business plan. For an existing business, bankers

consider the business's financial statements and general industry trends.

3 **COLLATERAL** Bankers generally want a borrower to pledge an asset that can be sold, if necessary, to pay off the loan if the borrower lacks funds.

4 **CAPITAL** Bankers scrutinize a borrower's net worth, which is the amount by which assets exceed debts.

5 **CONDITIONS** Whether bankers give a loan or not can be influenced by the current economic climate as well as by the amount of money required.

When applying to a bank for a loan, be prepared to address the following points.

BANKING CRITERIA

These are a summary of the areas that a bank will consider when deciding to advance funds. They are all negotiable and all under your control. It follows that, the better your case is prepared, the better the terms you can negotiate.

LOAN AMOUNT

The amount of funds a bank will advance is determined by a number of conditions. First it will look to see how much money the owner and other shareholders have put into the business. Ideally it will want to see those investors put in as much as the bank is being asked for. If the bank's proportion gets too high, there is the danger that the owners end up seeing the business as virtually belonging to the bank. In these circumstances, bankers think the founders may not be motivated to give of their best and indeed may even put their energies elsewhere.

The bank will also look to see what level of profit is being made or is being forecast in the business plan. That is not because it wants to share in the firm's success; it simply wants to satisfy itself that the profit is more than sufficient to repay the principal and cover the interest charges that may be levied on the loan both now and in the future. Lenders, such as banks, are less interested in rapid growth and the consequent capital gain there will be than they are in a steady stream of earnings – for both the owner and them – almost from the outset.

SECURITY

The bank will also look for security to back the loan. The balance sheet details will show the bank what unencumbered assets there are in the business. Unmortgaged property is a most desirable asset but others include debtors (who surely one day will pay up), inventory, and work in progress, which will get sold. Intangible assets, such as patents, copyrights, and other intellectual property, may be the firm's most valuable assets, but they are unlikely to be of much interest to the bank as security for a loan because they are not actually "worth" anything.

CASE STUDY: How Lenders Treat Intangible Assets

RICHARD HOLDSWORTHY'S company, Holdworth Press, published a regional series of business magazines. He started the business some 15 years earlier, after a successful career as the editor of a national newspaper. He built up the production from just one black-and-white magazine concerned with local issues to 12 magazines in full color covering all the important business regions of the country. Each new magazine took four years to build up to a profitable proposition and each required an investment of $250,000. Once established in the marketplace, the magazine could look forward to at least seven years of profitable life ahead.

In his financial statements he agreed with his auditors to treat investment in new magazines as an intangible asset. The argument was that, if the property and equipment for printing the magazines could be treated as a capital investment, why not the equally substantial investment in the titles themselves?

In one year Holdsworthy ambitiously planned to launch four new magazines. He took his financial statements to the bank, showing an asset base of over $2 million as security for his proposed borrowings. The bank rejected the $1.75 million of intangible assets representing the investment in the magazines, allowing only $250,000 as the secure asset base of the company. The extra funds were eventually provided by a venture capital firm.

If, in the bank's view, the security available in the business is insufficient, it will look outside for personal guarantees. The first people it will turn to are the directors and their families and other business associates. Here the bank will seek to take a charge on any available assets, such as private property, shares in other companies, and so forth.

The main disadvantage of giving personal guarantees if you are running a company is that they negate the key advantage of limited liability, which is to allow entrepreneurs to take risks they might not otherwise take for fear of losing everything. The second disadvantage is that, once given, personal guarantees are extremely difficult to get back. Banks seek to hold on to personal guarantees even when the business assets have grown to be more than sufficient to cover any probable liability. You can see the bank's point of view – it gives cast-iron security – but for a business owner it can be seen as a Sword of Damocles hanging over them and their family for the whole of their working life.

INTEREST CHARGES

Banks usually make two charges (at least) for advancing funds. First, a setup charge is made for putting the arrangements in place. Banks often try to make this charge every year, despite the fact that your basic financing arrangements remain unchanged. You should resist this charge where you can. Second, an interest charge, usually pegged to U.S. Treasury bills, is made. Anything from 2 to 5 percent over the rate the government pays is fairly normal for small firms' bank borrowings, although the more risky the business proposition, the higher the rate.

It follows that you should do anything you can to make your proposition seem less risky so that you will be able to negotiate a better rate of interest. A well-prepared business plan usually helps greatly here, as does any evidence of how you have honored financial commitments in the past. Do not assume, however, that the bank you are dealing with will know about or remember your excellent repayment record on other loans such as your mortgage, a lease agreement, or personal overdraft. Tell them.

Types of Bank Funding

Asking a bank for a loan is not as simple as it may sound. There are loans and loans, and one may be far more suitable for your purposes than another. Make sure you know exactly what you want before you approach your bank manager.

OVERDRAFT

The principal form of short-term bank funding is an overdraft, secured by a charge over the assets of the business. Overdrafts were originally designed to cover the timing differences between, say, acquiring raw materials and manufacturing finished goods, which are later sold.

Starting out in a contract cleaning business with a major contract, you need sufficient funds initially to buy the cleaning equipment. This will have been paid for three months into the contract, so there is no point in getting a five-year bank loan to cover this, because within a year you will have cash in the bank and a loan with an early redemption penalty. An overdraft is the most suitable loan here.

If, however, your overdraft does not get out of the red at any stage during the year, then you need to reexamine your financing and consider a fixed-term loan. All too often companies utilize an overdraft rather than a loan to acquire long-term assets, and that overdraft never disappears, eventually constraining the expansion and profitability of the business.

Think carefully before giving a personal guarantee to a bank: it will be very hard to get it back

CASE STUDY: The Danger of Relying on an Overdraft

HENRY MERRYWEATHER'S printing company was experiencing some financial difficulties. After 20 years in business, the rules of the game were changing, and changing fast. New technology was the key now, and he had invested $200,000 in the very latest computer hardware and software out of cash flow. The trouble was that the payback from that investment was coming through more slowly than he expected. Teething problems had been expected, but losing his I.T. manager within weeks of the new equipment arriving was an unexpected and unwelcome setback. To make matters worse, the company was now coming into its traditionally slow period. Every printer was slack now.

At the limit of his $275,000 overdraft facility, Merryweather started holding back payments to suppliers until customers paid up. Eventually this approach became untenable because the company ran out of crucial supplies. Something radical had to be done in order to weather this storm.

The management produced a plan that would substantially lower the firm's cost base, quickly. It involved layoffs and so would, in the short term, require even more money than was now required, but it was the only viable strategy to allow the firm to operate through its present difficulties and secure the bank's position, too.

Merryweather and his team arranged an appointment with their bank manager. The meeting did not go well. The bank itself was the subject of a takeover bid and was not prepared to extend further borrowing facilities.

Merryweather and his team prepared for a difficult three months until the seasonal upturn came. What they were not prepared for was the bank's new strategy. As soon as customers paid up, the bank immediately cut Merryweather's overdraft facility back by a similar amount. First $25,000, then $50,000, and then another $30,000 was lopped of the overdraft in a matter of days. Within 10 days the bank had whittled the overdraft facility down from $275,000 to just $75,000. That remaining sum was covered by personal guarantees, which meant that the bank had effectively eliminated its risk exposure at the expense of ruining the business.

In order to preserve something of the business, Merryweather had to sell out to a competitor. The deal was quickly done on disastrous terms, reducing Merryweather's stake in the business from several million dollars to just $25,000.

BRINGING THE PRESSES TO A HALT
By reducing the printing company's overdraft facility at its most difficult trading time, the bank forced Merryweather to sell out to a competitor on poor terms.

The attraction of overdrafts is that they are very easy to arrange and take little time to set up. That is also their inherent weakness. The key words in the arrangement document are "repayable on demand," which leaves the bank free to make and change the rules as they see fit, with no consideration of your financial position. With other forms of borrowing, as long as you stick to the terms and conditions, the loan is yours for the duration. This is not so with overdrafts, as the case above illustrates.

TERM LOANS

If you are starting up a manufacturing business, you will be buying machinery to last probably five years, designing your logo, buying stationery, paying the deposit on leasehold premises, buying a vehicle, and investing funds in winning a long-term contract. The profits on this are expected to flow in over a number of years, so they need to be financed over a similarly long period of time, either through a bank loan or by inviting someone to invest in shares in the company – in other words, a long-term commitment.

Term loans, as these long-term borrowings are generally known, are funds provided by a bank for a number of years. The interest can be either variable, changing with general interest rates, or it can be fixed for a number of years ahead. In some cases, it may be possible to move between having a fixed interest rate and a variable one at certain intervals. It may even be possible to have a moratorium on interest payments for a short period, to give the business some breathing space while it is getting up and running. Provided the conditions of the loan are met in such matters as repayment, interest, and security cover, the money is available for the period of the loan. Its main advantage over an overdraft is that the bank cannot pull the rug from under your feet if their situation (or the local manager) changes.

Consider a term loan rather than an overdraft if you need a loan for more than a year or two

LOAN GUARANTEE PROGRAMS

These are operated in the United States, the United Kingdom, and elsewhere. The programs guarantee loans from banks and other financial institutions for small businesses with viable business proposals that have tried and failed to obtain a conventional loan because of a lack of security. Loans are available for periods between two and 10 years on sums between $5,000 and $250,000, or more. The government guarantees 70 to 90 percent of the loan. In return for this guarantee, the borrower pays a premium of 1 to 2 percent per year on the outstanding amount of the loan. The commercial aspects of the loan are matters to be agreed between the borrower and the lender.

Different countries have different conditions and these can change from year to year. But the basic concept of governments taking a hand to encourage banks to be a little bolder in their approach to new and small firm lending has been well entrenched for over two decades.

OTHER TYPES OF BANK LENDING

Banks are usually a good starting point for almost any type of debt financing. If you import raw materials, banks can provide you with Letters of Credit. If you have a number of overseas suppliers who prefer settlement in their own currency – for which you will need foreign currency checking facilities or buying forward – banks can make the necessary arrangements. They are also able to provide many of the other cash-flow and asset-backed financing products described below, although they are often not the only or the most appropriate provider.

CREDIT UNIONS

If you do not like the terms being offered by the traditional banks, you could consider forming your own bank. It is not quite as crazy an idea as it sounds. Credit unions formed by groups of small-business people, both in business and aspiring to start up, have been around for decades in the United States, the

MONEY SAVER

Term loans are the most secure form of bank financing because the funding is guaranteed for a number of years. A cash-flow forecast can predict how much money you will need, when, and for how long. That will allow you to use some overdraft funding and so pay interest only on the money you use.

United Kingdom, and elsewhere. They have been an attractive option for people on low incomes because they provide a cheap and convenient alternative to banks. Some self-employed people, such as taxi drivers, have also found it convenient to form credit unions. They can then apply for loans to meet unexpected capital expenditure for repairs, refurbishments, or technical upgrading.

The popularity of credit unions varies from country to country. In the U.K., for example, fewer than one in 300 people belong to one, compared with more than one in three in Canada, but they are slowly growing in the U.S. Certainly, few could argue about the attractiveness of an annual interest rate set 3 percent below that of the traditional banks, which is what credit unions aim for. Members have to save regularly to qualify for a loan, although there is no minimum deposit and, after 10 weeks, members with a good track record can borrow up to five times their savings, though they must continue to save while repaying the loan. There is no set interest rate, but dividends are distributed to members from any surplus, usually at a rate of about 5 percent a year. This, too, compares favorably with bank interest on deposit accounts.

Borrowing from Family and Friends

Those close to you can often lend you money or invest in your business. This helps you to avoid the problem of pleading your case to outsiders and enduring extra paperwork and bureaucratic delays. Help from friends, relatives, and business associates can be especially valuable if you have been through bankruptcy or had other credit problems that would make borrowing from a commercial lender difficult or even impossible.

Many types of businesses, for example organic farms or specialized bookstores, have loyal and devoted followers, people who care as much about the business as the owners do.

DOS AND DON'TS OF RAISING MONEY FROM FAMILY AND FRIENDS

✓ Do agree on proper terms.

✓ Do put the agreement in writing and, if it involves a guarantee or a change of legal entity, have a formal agreement drawn up.

✓ Do make an extra effort to explain the risks of the business and the possible downside implications to their money.

✓ Do make sure when raising money from parents that other siblings are compensated in some way, perhaps via a will.

✓ Do make sure you want to run a family business before raising money from them. It will not be the same as running your own business.

✗ Don't borrow from people on fixed incomes.

✗ Don't borrow from people who cannot afford to lose money.

✗ Don't make the possible rewards sound more attractive than you would to a bank.

✗ Don't offer jobs in your business to anyone providing money unless they are the best person for the job.

✗ Don't change the normal pattern of social contact with family and friends after they have put up the money.

Their decision to lend is driven to some extent by their feelings and is not strictly a business proposition. Their involvement brings a range of extra benefits, costs, and risks that are not a feature of most other types of finance. You must decide if these are acceptable before agreeing to accept the loan.

Some advantages of borrowing money from people you know well are that you may be charged a lower interest rate, may be able to delay paying back money until you are more established, and may be given more flexibility if you get into a jam. But, once the loan terms are agreed to, you have the same legal obligations as you would with, say, a bank or any other source of financing.

In addition, borrowing money from relatives and friends can have a major disadvantage. If your business does poorly and those close to you end up losing the money they lent you or invested in you, that may well damage some good personal relationships. So, in dealing with people close to you, be extra careful not only to establish clearly the terms of the deal and put it in writing but also to make an extra effort to explain the risks and not to accept money from people who cannot afford to lose it. In short, it is your job to make sure that your helpful friend or relative will not suffer a true hardship if you are unable to meet your financial commitments. If your business does run into trouble at some stage, your personal difficulties will only be compounded if you hurt other people too.

Financing Cash Flow by Factoring

Customers often take time to pay their bills. In the meantime, you have to pay the people who work for you and your less patient suppliers. So, the more you grow, the more funds you need. One way of solving this problem is to "factor" your creditworthy customers' bills to a financial institution, receiving some of the funds as your goods leave the door, hence speeding up cash flow and leaving you with more available funds.

HOW FACTORING WORKS

Factoring is generally available only to a business that invoices other business customers, either in their home market or internationally, for its products or services. It can be made available to all businesses, although it is usually of most value during the early stages of growth. It is an arrangement that allows you to receive up to 80 percent of the cash due from your customers more quickly than they would normally pay.

CASE STUDY: Financing Growth Using Factoring

GIBBS INTERNATIONAL, a luxury lingerie business founded by Mary Gibbs and her husband, Andrew, grew to having annual sales of $500,000 within three years. Its two-year business plan calls for sales of $5 million. The company already has sales in Europe and the U.S.

The company's growth has been financed by invoice factoring, which is about as unglamorous as their products are sexy. It does not have the risk associated with venture capital and does not require the sophisticated negotiating skills needed to borrow large amounts of money from a bank. However, invoice factoring, or invoice discounting, where banks lend against the sales and money owed by debtors, has become the company's preferred funding route.

Mary said: "I was reluctant to use invoice financing because I thought people only used it when their business was in trouble." But experience has convinced the Gibbses that invoice financing was right for them. From being strapped for cash, the company now has the money to invest in product development.

The factoring company in effect buys your business debts and can provide a debtor accounting and administration service. In other words, it takes over the day-to-day work of invoicing and sending out reminders and statements. This can be a particularly helpful service to a small, expanding business. It allows the management to concentrate on developing the business, with the factoring company providing expert guidance on credit control, protection against bad debts, and improved cash flow.

You will, of course, have to pay for the use of the factoring services. Having the cash before your customers pay will cost you a little more than normal overdraft rates. The factoring service will cost between 0.5 and 3.5 percent of each sale, depending on the volume of work, the number of debtors, the average invoice amount, and other related factors. You can get up to 80 percent of the value of your invoice in advance, with the remainder paid when your customer settles up, minus the various charges just mentioned.

If you sell direct to the public, sell complex and expensive capital equipment, or expect progress payments on long-term projects, then factoring is not for you. If, however, you are expanding more rapidly than other sources of financing will allow, this may be a useful service, at least while you find your business feet.

TIME SAVER

Cash-flow financing through a factor is available only to businesses selling to other businesses. The sale must leave few areas for potential disputes, and the customers must themselves be creditworthy. Take out credit references on customers before approaching a factor, because your customers may not meet their credit standards.

Asset-backed Financing

P hysical assets, such as cars, vans, computers, office equipment and the like, can usually be financed by leasing them, rather as a house or apartment may be rented. Alternatively, they can be bought on dealer or bank financing. Both these methods leave other funds free to cover the less tangible elements in your cash flow.

Leasing is a way of getting the use of vehicles, plant, and equipment without paying the full cost at once. Operating leases are taken out where you will use the equipment for less than its full economic life, for example a car, photocopier, vending machine, or kitchen equipment. The lessor takes the risk of the

USING CAPITAL WISELY
Buying a car ties up valuable capital that could be used for something else. Consider either leasing it or buying it on credit for a more efficient way of using your money.

equipment becoming obsolete, and in some cases assumes responsibility for repairs, maintenance, and insurance. You, the lessee, pay for this service, so it is more expensive than a finance lease, where you lease the equipment for most of its economic life and maintain and insure it yourself. Leases can normally be extended, often for fairly nominal sums, in the latter years.

The obvious attraction of leasing is that no deposit is needed, leaving your working capital free for more profitable use elsewhere. Also, the cost is known from the start, making forward planning more simple. There may even be some tax advantages over other forms of financing. However, there are some possible pitfalls, which only a close examination of the small print on the leasing agreement will reveal.

So, do take professional advice before taking out a lease on any equipment or vehicle.

Financing these asset purchases.also preserves your operating capital, but the unpaid portion shows up as a liability on your balance sheet.

Unearthing Business Angels

One likely first source of equity or risk capital will be a private individual, with their own funds, and perhaps some knowledge of your type of business. In return for a share in the business, such an individual will put in money at their own risk. These angels often have their own agenda and operate through managed networks.

CASE STUDY: Business Angels on the Net

Investing Angels.com is a new network for business angels operating via the internet. It filters business plans vigorously and then sends the best to prospective angels. This encourages e-mail exchanges between angels and companies seeking financing.

This use of the internet raises some interesting challenges to the traditional angel model. For example, angels are characterized as "invisible" people who value their privacy, yet on the firm's website there are a series of named would-be investors. Moreover, some of them are not merely wealthy individuals but are presidents, chairmen, and former CEOs. Although they are seeking to invest as individuals, it is clear from their willingness to be named that they are looking to encourage companies that may have need of their extensive industry experience to approach them.

Potential angels must meet strict U.S. Securities and Exchange Commission guidelines as accredited investors, have a net worth of at least $1 million, and show experience in start-ups.

The time and effort needed to close a deal could be considerably reduced by such a service, although the extent to which investing angels.com can replace face-to-face discussions

is debatable. The business seeks to raise $1 to $4 million – amounts that are too small for traditional venture capital firms.

Investing Via the Internet
Using the internet to send business plans to angels has opened up this formerly "invisible" world of financing. Angels can now receive details of businesses looking for investors and then decide whether they want to back them.

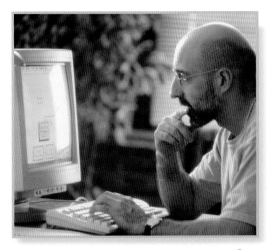

Angel networks operate throughout the world, and in some cases these networks operate on the internet (see case study, left). In the United Kingdom and the United States there are hundreds of angel networks with tens of thousands of individual business angels who, between them, are prepared to put up several billion dollars each year for investing in new or small businesses.

Business angels are more likely to invest in early-stage investments, where relatively small amounts of money are needed in areas close to their home base. They operate very quickly, often making decisions in a few days based on little hard data after only a few meetings with the person seeking finance. Their confidence in the owner-manager is a vital part of their decision.

Finding Venture Capital

Venture capital providers are investing other people's money, often from pension funds, in businesses. They have a different agenda than that of business angels and are more likely to be interested in investing more money in a business for a larger stake.

HOW VENTURE CAPITAL WORKS

Venture capital is a means of financing the start-up, development, expansion, or purchase of a business. The venture capitalist acquires an agreed proportion of the share capital (equity) of the company in return for providing the requisite funding. Venture capitalist firms often work in conjunction with other providers of financing in putting together a total funding package for a business. Worldwide, several hundred venture capital firms invest in businesses both small and large.

Venture capital is a medium- to long-term investment of not just money but time and effort. The venture capital firm's goal is to enable growth companies to develop into the major businesses of tomorrow.

FACTS YOU NEED TO KNOW ABOUT BUSINESS ANGELS

1 40 percent suffer partial or complete loss of their investment.

2 50 percent do not conduct research into prospective investments.

3 55 percent do not take up personal references, compared with only 6 percent of venture capital providers in general.

4 90 percent have worked in a small firm or owned their own business.

5 Business angels meet owners five times on average before investing, compared with venture capital providers who in general require 10 meetings.

6 10 percent of business angel investment is for less than $10,000, and 45 percent is for over $50,000.

7 Most business angels invest close to home. Up to 50 miles is usual, with 200 miles as the limit.

8 Angels rarely invest abroad.

9 Angels often flock together. Syndicated deals make up more than a quarter of all deals.

10 Angels are up to five times more likely to invest in start-ups and early-stage investments than venture capital providers in general.

DUE DILIGENCE

Venture capitalists go through a process known as "due diligence" before investing. This involves a thorough examination of the business and its owners. Past financial performance, the directors' track records, and the business plan will all come under close scrutiny by accountants and lawyers. Directors are then required to "warrant" that they have provided all the relevant information, under pain of financial penalties. The cost of

VENTURE FINANCE IN EUROPE AND THE U.S.

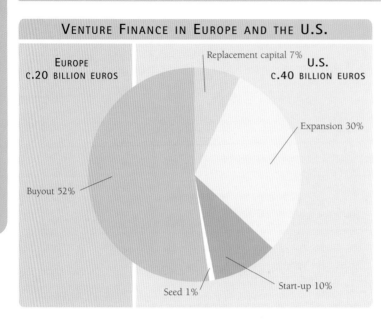

EUROPE
C.20 BILLION EUROS

U.S.
C.40 BILLION EUROS

Replacement capital 7%

Expansion 30%

Buyout 52%

Start-up 10%

Seed 1%

HOW VENTURE CAPITAL IS USED

Twice as much venture capital is available in the U.S. as in Europe. Just over 10 percent of that money goes into start-up businesses and seed financing for firms before they start to operate. The largest share goes into management buyouts and those firms seeking to expand.

this process must be borne by the firm raising the money, but the consolation factor is that it will be paid out of the money raised.

EXPECTATIONS

In general, venture capitalists would expect their investment to have paid off within seven years, but they are hardened realists. Three in every 10 investments they make are total write-offs, and six perform averagely well over the period. So, the one star in every 10 investments they make has to cover a lot of also-rans.

Venture capitalists have a target rate of return of 30 percent plus, to cover this poor success rate.

Raising venture capital is not a cheap option. The arrangement costs will almost always run to six figures. They are not quick to arrange, either. Six months is not unusual, and over a year has been known. Every venture capitalist has a deal done in six weeks in their portfolio, but that truly is the exception.

Venture capital providers will want to exit from their investment at some stage, and their exit route will be planned before they even start

CASE STUDY: Financing Growth Using Venture Capital

DENNIS HUME started his computer business some ten years ago with capital of $40,000. Within five years he had built up a substantial business with annual sales of over $10 million. Hume felt that the business needed more capital to allow it to reach its full potential. It needed development staff, more equipment, and larger premises.

Hume raised $5 million from a venture capital provider to finance growth, and the expansion was so successful that it needed a further $5 million just two years later. By the time the company made an initial public offering a few years later, it was worth over $250 million. Twenty employees were now millionaires and the venture capital firm's stakes were worth $80 million and $45 million respectively.

investing in a business. Their preferred route is via a public offering (see below), but a sale is more usual. Either way, they are not in it for the long haul.

Going for an Initial Public Offering (IPO)

There are two possible types of stock markets on which to gain a public listing. A listing on the New York Stock Exchange, the London Stock Exchange, or any other major country's exchange calls for a track record of making substantial profits with decent seven-figure sums being made in the year in which you plan to float, as this process is known. A full listing also calls for a large proportion of the company's shares to be put up for sale at the outset.

THE FLOTATION OPTIONS
The U.S. stock markets look like an attractive proposition because they value companies at a much higher rate than their European counterparts, but the flotation costs with the N.Y. Stock Exchange and NASDAQ are very high.

In addition, you would be expected to have 100 shareholders now and be able to prove that a further 100 will come on board as a result of the listing. Having such a large number of shareholders is rarely an appealing idea to entrepreneurs, who expect to see their share price rise in later years and so are loath to sell off so much of the business at what they believe to be a bargain-basement price. There is also the danger of a takeover in the inherent loss of power when so many of the shares are in so many other people's hands.

CHOOSING WHERE TO FLOAT
If an IPO still appeals, however, the U.S. market may be the best place to float. The value placed on new companies on those stock markets is between three and five times that of U.K. and European markets (see the chart below).

Junior markets, such as London's Alternative Investment Market (AIM) or the Nouveau Marché in Paris, are a much more attractive proposition for business entrepreneurs seeking equity capital. Formed toward the end of the 1990s specifically to provide risk capital for

WHERE TO FLOAT...AND WHY IT MATTERS					
MARKET	NUMBER OF STOCKS	FLOTATION COST	ENTRY REQUIREMENTS	MINIMUM MARKET CAPITALIZATION	COMPARABLE PRICE EARNINGS RATIOS (P/ES)
ALTERNATIVE INVESTMANT MARKET	350	$0.5m	Low	None	1
LONDON STOCK EXCHANGE	2,500	$1m+	High	$1m+	1
TECHMARK	200	$0.75m+	High	$50m+	x 3
NEW YORK STOCK EXCHANGE	2,600	$7m	Very high	$12m+	x 2
NASDAQ	5,500	$6m	Very high	$10m+	x 5

new rather than established ventures, these markets have an altogether more relaxed atmosphere than the major stock markets.

The AIM is particularly attractive to any dynamic company of any size, age, or business sector that has rapid growth in mind. The AIM market is the largest junior market in Europe. Over 300 firms are listed and some $2 billion of new equity capital has been raised. The smallest firm on the AIM entered at under $1 million capitalization, and the largest at over $330 million. The formalities are minimal, but the costs of entry are high, and you must have a nominated adviser, such as a major accounting firm, stockbroker, or banker.

> *Choose to go public in order to put a stamp of respectability on you and your company*

THE BENEFITS OF FLOATING

Going public will enhance the status and credibility of your business, and it will enable you to borrow more against the security provided by your new shareholders, should you so wish. Your shares will also provide an attractive way to retain and motivate key staff. If staff are given, or rather are allowed to earn, share options at discounted prices, they too can participate in the capital gains you are making, which gives them an added incentive to make the business a success.

With a public share listing, you can now join in the takeover and asset-stripping game. When your share price is high and things are going well, you can look out for weaker firms to gobble up. All you have to do is offer them more of your shares in return for theirs. You do not even have to find real money.

INTERNET-BASED DIRECT PUBLIC OFFERINGS (DPOs)

DPOs are a relatively new U.S. phenomenon that have the potential to change the face of financing for small firms. DPOs involve small companies offering their stock direct to would-be investors over the internet. There are two ways of doing this: one is to use a service; the other is for firms to use their own websites to go direct to the public. There are already some internet-based listing services for DPOs in the U.S.

■ **THE ACCESS TO CAPITAL ELECTRONIC NETWORK (ACE-NET)** This DPO was set up in 1997 by the U.S. Small Business Administration as a public–private

FLOATING AT FRANKFURT
Choosing to float your business on a major stock market brings financial risks and benefits. With so many new shareholders, your authority as owner does become less certain, but you are now in a position to buy up other companies and so expand your profit base.

partnership to lower the legal barriers for small businesses needing financing of up to $5 million. The filing form satisfies federal and many states' securities regulations, with 37 states recognizing it, and it is relatively cheap, at only $450 for an annual listing. The offering document can be completed on-line and can be changed in real time, allowing the entrepreneur the flexibility to modify the offer. Only accredited investors (with over $1 million to spend) are able to invest in this DPO.

▥ **DIRECT STOCK MARKET** Direct Stock Market is a similar, private service that was set up in 1993. A listing on this market costs between $2,000 and $4,000 for a 90-day listing. Firms have to file their own paperwork off-line with the states in which they wish their listing to be registered (unlike the ACE-NET service). It is clear, therefore, that potential investors from Europe cannot participate in companies listed under such programs. It is also almost certain that regulations mean that these internet services cannot sell securities in non-U.S. firms. However, this does not prevent European entrepreneurs from creating a U.S. company to exploit the fund-raising potential of such services.

▥ **GOING DIRECT** U.S. firms may also decide to go direct and battle their way through various state legislation hoops. The positive side for firms is that this method overcomes barriers of geography and information, and that small investors are unlikely to carry out due diligence or download prospectuses. DPOs allow small investors access to genuine possibilities without paying fees to either a matchmaking service or venture capital firm, and allow much smaller investments (from $500 upward).

The downside of internet DPOs is that they are time-consuming and high-risk for the business angel (or would-be angel), and it is difficult to distinguish between genuine companies and frauds. For the listed business, there are a raft of different state legislations in operation to

protect investors from scams, which can seriously disrupt the offer process. Not surprisingly, many people have already been charged with internet securities fraud, with dozens of cases involving entirely fictional deals.

What the difficulties in establishing this sort of service in the U.S. have amply demonstrated is the need for regulation at a federal level rather than at state level, if the service is to be successful. This suggests that, were such a service to be established in the future in Europe for potential European investors, it would be appropriate to regulate it at the European level rather than country level, in order to offer similar sums of money and geographic spread to the U.S. version.

Grants, Awards, and Competitions

Unlike debt, which has to be repaid, or equity, which has to earn a return for the investors, grants and awards are not refundable. So, although they are often hard to get, they can be particularly valuable. Almost every country has incentives to encourage entrepreneurs to invest in particular locations or industries.

GREEN CARDS

The U.S. has an allowance of green cards (work and residence permits) for up to several hundred immigrants each year. Each immigrant has to be prepared to put up sufficient funds to start a substantial business in the country.

GOVERNMENT AND INSTITUTIONAL GRANTS AND FUNDING

Federal, state, and local governments offer many incentives to small and new businesses, especially to those involved in exporting or in emerging technologies. These inducements include grants and awards, tax abatements and concessions, and marketing opportunities. On a federal level, these matters are often announced on the Commerce Business Daily, but the best source of information is the U.S. Small Businesss Administration website, www.sba.gov. The site not only includes the most timely news, but it also links to other federal and state sites, with information about funding, financing, and marketing opportunities.

Nationally, and even more so on a state and local level, much government funding is directed toward disadvantaged groups, or to distressed industries and localities. You cannot change your ethnic origin, but you can rent a warehouse in a targeted neighborhood, or hire a former recipient of public assistance who has been trained at government expense.

Another source of grants and awards, especially in high-tech fields, is research and development prizes in industry and trade groups.

BUSINESS COMPETITIONS AND AWARDS

If you enjoy publicity and like a challenge, then you could look out for a business competition to enter. Like government grants, business competitions are ubiquitous and, like national lotteries, they are something of a hit-or-miss affair. But one thing is certain: if you do not enter, you cannot win.

There are annual awards aimed at new or small businesses. For the most part these are sponsored by banks, the major accountancy bodies, chambers of commerce, and local or national newspapers, business magazines, and the trade press. Keep a look out in newspapers as well as trade publications for notices advising applicants how to apply.

Government departments may also have their own competitions as a means of promoting their initiatives for exporting, innovation, job creation, and so forth.

The nature and the amount of the awards change from year to year, as do the sponsors. But looking out in the press, or contacting one of the organizations mentioned above, should put you in touch with a competition organizer

CASE STUDY: Making Initial Exporting Arrangements

BRIAN WILSON started his business from a 1,200-square-foot converted baker's shop with only three staff. The objective was to produce ready-grated cheese for the retail and catering market. The initial sales target was three tons per week. The business was one of the first in the U.K. to grate cheese on a commercial scale.

Sales in the first year was $200,000, with supply to the growing pizza industry accounting for 80 percent of the sales. Three years after its start-up, with sales continuing to climb steadily, Wilson took the important step of moving the business to its second site, which provided 15,000 square feet of production, warehousing, and office space.

Within 10 years the annual sales had grown to $5 million. The business had again run out of space, so they followed a strategy of zero growth in sales while building up profit margins.

Throughout the business's history, Wilson had put considerable effort into securing grants and awards. They picked up six major awards, including the region's coveted Business Excellence Award two years running, as well as being nominated Best Business of the Year. This generated a good deal of favorable publicity, which had a positive effect on staff, customers, and the firm's bank. They also picked up some $50,000 in grant money.

Following the move to still larger premises, annual sales doubled to $15 million, and when Wilson (age 46) sold the business it was valued at $12.5 million.

quickly. Alternatively you could try going online for an internet search.

Money awards constitute a majority of competition prizes. But the most important value may be the prestige and the high reputation your business will gain in the business community, which is made up of your potential customers and clients. Other awards are for equally valuable goods and services, such as consultancy or accountancy advice, training, and computer hardware and software.

Keeping Your Options Open

Choosing which external source of financing to use is to some extent a matter of personal preference. One of your tasks in managing your firm's financial affairs is to keep good lines of communication open with as many of the sources outlined above as possible. The other task is to consider which is the most appropriate source for your particular requirements at any one time. The main issues you need to consider here are:

■ cost of setting up
■ ownership and control
■ length of time to arrange
■ management time involved
■ flexibility
■ additional expertise
■ security
■ personal liability

Not all of these issues will concern you at any one time. Your decisions will depend on your age, the financial state of your company, and your expectations for the future.

For example, if you are 60, ready to retire to Florida, your company is making superb profits, and you have a strong and experienced management team in place, management time and ownership will not feature high (if at all) among the issues that concern you.

Alternatively, if you are just setting out and are confident that your great new idea will be a

Grants and awards

Go to stock market

Venture capital and business angels

Factoring and leasing financing

Banks and trade credit

Family and friends

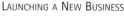

LAUNCHING A NEW BUSINESS
Using the analogy of a rocket blasting off, we can see the stages of "fuel" that a new business is likely to take on board as it struggles to get into orbit. Orbit is the point at which the firm has realized its founder's ambitions.

world-beater, then the prospect of selling 51 percent of the shares to a business angel who offers you the money may not be as appealing as buckling down to write a business plan to raise some bank financing, thereby keeping control of the business in your own hands.

CONSIDERING THE COSTS

Clearly, if a large proportion of the funds you need to expand your business is going to be consumed in actually raising the external financing itself, then your setup costs for this expansion are going to be very high indeed.

Raising new share capital, especially if the amounts are relatively small (under $500,000), is generally quite expensive. You will have to pay your lawyers and accountants, and those of your capital provider, to prepare the agreements and to conduct the due diligence examination (the business appraisal). It would not be unusual to find that between 10 and 15 percent of the first $500,000 that you raise will be used up in setup costs.

If you want sole control of your business, do not sell shares in it in order to raise external financing

An overdraft or factoring agreement would be relatively cheap to set up, costing usually a couple of percent or so. Long-term loans, leasing, and other financing agreements could involve some legal costs.

OWNERSHIP AND CONTROL

If you do not want to share the ownership of your business with outsiders, then clearly raising new share capital is not a good idea. Even if you do recognize that owning 100 percent of a small venture is not as attractive as owning 40 percent of a business 10 times as large, it may not be the right moment to sell off. This is particularly so if, in common with many business founders, long-term capital gain is one of your principal goals. If you can hold

---

CASE STUDY: Keeping in Touch with Financiers

BOLSOVER, A $2-MILLION IN ANNUAL SALES providing sales and marketing services to the chemical industry, had grown for some time without large amounts of outside money. However, the company's founder, Ian Benton, believed that the next stage of growth would need substantial funds, as strategies shifted from services to products. To this end, he regularly invited venture capitalists to sit in on board meetings or to attend training sessions with his top management team. This, he reckoned, would ensure he got off to a flying start with the money men when his plans were formalized. He also sent copies of business plans to his bank manager even when no changes were envisioned in financing arrangements. This kept the bank up-to-date on what Bolsover was doing and showed that strategy was planned rather than just a series of happy incidents.

Eventually, Ian saw a greater opportunity to turn his business into the only global player in his market. One of the financiers that Ian had been in close contact with for several years was eager to be involved, putting up the $2 million

required in a matter of a few weeks. Ian built his business up and sold it for $50 million eight years after raising the venture capital.

INVOLVING INVESTORS
Keeping prospective investors informed of your business's progress and plans for development can give you a head start when the time comes to ask for finance.

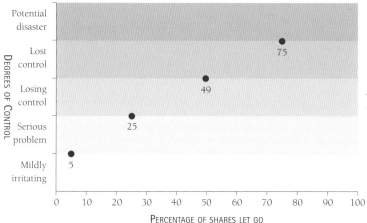

DEGREES OF CONTROL

Selling shares in your business inevitably results in a loss of control on your part. Once over the 75 percent level, you could find yourself voted out of your own business.

on to your shares until profits are reasonably high, you will realize more gain for every share sold than if you sell out in the early years or while profits are low.

Some capital providers, such as venture capitalists and Wall Street firms, take a hands-on approach by putting a nonexecutive director on your board who will have a view on how you should run the business. Generally speaking, though, providers of long-term loans will leave you alone, so long as you service the interest and repay the capital as agreed, much as your bank does if you pay the mortgage on time.

LOSING CONTROL BY DEGREE

Parting with shares inevitably involves some loss of control. Letting, say, 5 percent go may be just a mild irritation from time to time. However, once 25 percent has gone, outsiders could have a fair amount of say in how things are run. Nevertheless, as long as you have over 51 percent, you are still in control, if only just. Once you become a minority owner of your own business, however, things could get a little dangerous. Theoretically, you could be outvoted at any stage.

Things will start to get dangerous for you as a minority owner. Depending on the laws of the state in which your corporation is registered, relatively small groups of directors,

or even shareholders, could find it easy to call a special meeting and, if they so wished, put it to a vote to remove you from the board. You may then have little say in the running of your own business.

MOVING QUICKLY

Overdrafts can be arranged in just days, whereas raising venture capital can take months. It follows that very different amounts of scarce management time will be used, depending on the financing route taken. So, if speed matters, your funding options may be limited.

Venture capital providers have been known to string out negotiations with a finance-seeking business for long enough to see if the forecasts made in the business plan come to pass. After all, venture capital is there to help businesses grow faster, not just to keep them afloat.

TIME SAVER

While some sources of financing are less difficult to obtain than others, all will involve you in some cost and effort. Think your requirements through carefully before approaching finance providers, so you spend time only on sources that you are likely to use.

At the top of the timescale is any form of initial public offering. Not only can this take a year or so to arrange, but doing so requires you to take your place in the line of other firms wanting to float. As if that were not enough, the whole thing may have to be called off or postponed if market conditions change suddenly. This change in the market is particularly prevalent in internet-related businesses, where the market is inclined to great volatility.

MANAGEMENT TIME

Any source of financing that takes a considerable amount of time to arrange can be a problem for a business owner or manager already fully stretched. As we have seen, injecting new equity capital can take anything from six to 15 months, with the directors being required to prepare several versions of the business plan and make dozens of presentations to potential backers. Many companies experience a profit dip in the months following a share issue. This is brought about largely because management energy was drawn away from the day-to-day running of the business.

STAYING FLEXIBLE

As your plans change, the amount of money you actually need may alter during financing negotiations. Some sources of funds, such as leasing, equipment financing, and long-term loans, dictate the amount that has to be agreed upon at the outset. For new share capital there is some fluidity during negotiations, and for overdrafts it is possible to withdraw only what is needed at any one time, with the upper limit negotiated. This usually happens each year.

Once you have investigated and used a source of funds, you may want to be able to use that source again as your plans unfold. This will not always be possible, however. Share capital, loans, and leasing agreements are for a specific sum, and it can be difficult and expensive going back to the same source for more. Venture capitalists may also not be willing to offer more financing. They may already have a full portfolio of investments in your business sector and so may not be anxious to invest more, however successful your firm. In this case, further expansion might mean starting all over again with another venture capital firm, which would involve extra and highly unwelcome costs in time and money.

Assess all the funding options, and their terms and conditions, before deciding which to choose

It may pay to make sure that at least some of your financing comes from a source such as factoring (see pp. 58–59). This method, in contrast to the other methods outlined above, gives total flexibility to change the amount of money withdrawn, so that you can mirror the amount needed at any one time – both upward and downward.

POTENTIAL TO ADD VALUE

With some sources of financing you can get useful expertise as well as money. For example, with factoring you could get expertise in managing your home and overseas credit, which could result in better credit control, fewer bad debts, and less capital tied up in debtors. You will save time, and therefore money, by not having to deal with these aspects of credit control yourself.

With new share capital you may get a non-executive director placed on your board who has industry-relevant experience. While the

CLOSING THE DEAL
The final handshake marks the end of often long negotiations to receive the financing you want at the terms you consider reasonable. Your expansion can now begin.

director's principal task is to ensure that the capital provides interest, you will also get the benefit of his knowledge and expertise.

SECURITY AND CERTAINTY

For most sources of money, once you have agreed upon the terms and you comply with them, the future is reasonably predictable – in so far as that money is concerned. The exception to this rule is an overdraft. These are technically, and often actually, repayable on demand, and they are sometimes called in just at the precise moment when you need them most, with potentially disastrous consequences (see p. 54).

PERSONAL LIABILITY

As a general rule, most providers of long-term loans and overdraft facilities will look to the directors to provide additional security if the business assets are in any way inadequate. This may be in the form of personal guarantees, such as pledging specific assets, like your house. Only when you raise new share capital do you escape increasing your personal liability, although you may be asked to provide warranties to assure new investors that everything in the company's past history has been declared.

Hiding information can have costly results, as the following example demonstrates. One business founder was pursued for two years after the check for the sale of his business to another company had been banked. The reason was that he had failed to reveal that a wrongful dismissal case was working its way through the legal system. The case was lost, and the new owners were presented with a $20,000 bill, which they in turn claimed from the business founder under the directors' warranty.

TRACKING
the money

Every business needs reliable financial information both for decision making and accountability. The starting point for gathering such information is having a sound system for keeping the books. After the basic accounting transactions have been recorded, the profit and loss account and balance sheet have to be prepared. You will need to understand how these accounts are constructed and what they tell you about your business's performance.

KEEPING THE BOOKS

Every business needs reliable financial information for both decision making and accountability. Reliable information does not necessarily call for a complex bookkeeping system: simple is often best. If and when the business grows, more sophisticated information will be required. That is when using a computer and some of the relevant software packages may be the best way forward. Even with a computer, errors will occur, however, and a process for detecting and correcting them will have to be evolved.

To survive and prosper in business, you need to know how much cash you have and what your profit or loss on sales is. These facts are needed on at least a monthly, weekly, or occasionally even a daily basis, in order for your business simply to survive, let alone grow. Without these facts, your apparently thriving business could, in fact, be making a loss rather than a profit, and you will certainly never be in complete control of your business when you do not know exactly what is going on financially.

RECORDING FINANCIAL INFORMATION

While bad luck plays a part in some business failures, a lack of reliable financial information plays a part in most. However, all the information needed to manage well is close at hand. Between them, the bills to be paid, invoices issued, petty cash slips, and bank statements are enough to give a true picture of performance. All that needs to be done is for that information to be recorded and organized so that the financial picture becomes clear. The way in which financial information is recorded is known as bookkeeping.

WHO WILL READ THE BOOKS?

It is not only the owner who needs these financial facts. Bankers, shareholders, and tax officials will be unsympathetic audiences to anyone without well documented facts to back themselves up. If, for example, the tax office presents a business with a tax bill, the onus then lies with the businessperson, using their records, either to agree or to dispute the sum

CASE STUDY: The Dangers of Not Keeping Accounts

STARTING UP THEIR BUSINESS consumed all the cash Eleanor and her partner, Chris, had. So, to save money, Eleanor planned to do the accounts herself. Unfortunately, Eleanor and Chris were so busy they never had time to do the books. They sent out invoices, and when the bank complained that they had exceeded their overdraft limit they would call in a few favors and get some customers to pay up. They paid the bills when they had the money, or if they needed more supplies from someone they owed money to.

Eleanor and Chris thought that, since they were so busy, they must be making money. At the end of the first quarter, Eleanor realized that she would never get the accounts done, so she took her shoe boxes full of bills and receipts to an accountant. In addition to presenting them with a large bill for sorting out the mess, the accountant revealed that they had in fact lost money, not made it.

With a good accounting system, they would have seen where they were going wrong immediately, instead of waiting a full three months to find out their financial position.

owed. If you are unable to explain a bank deposit adequately, the tax official may treat it as taxable income.

Similarly, a bank manager faced with a request for an increased overdraft facility to help a small business grow needs financial facts to work with. Without facts, the bank will generally have to say no to the request, because the bank has a responsibility to invest other people's money wisely.

Single-entry Bookkeeping

No matter how small your business is or how few the number of transactions that are made, having some note of financial events is better than having none at all. Keeping even the simplest of records, perhaps just as little as writing down the source of the deposit on the slip or in your checkbook, and recording the event in a book or ledger, will make your relations with tax inspectors and bankers go much more smoothly.

Unfortunately, many small businesses let their financial affairs take a back seat. It is easy to see why this can happen. The excitement or pressure of selling and fulfilling orders is more attractive and interesting than doing the books, so any bookkeeping tends to be left until after normal business hours.

If you are doing your books by hand and do not have a lot of transactions, the single-entry method is the easiest acceptable way to keep business records. Single entry means that you write down each transaction in your records once, preferably on a ledger sheet. This written record will be known as your cash book.

You record the flow of income and expenses through your business by making a running total of money taken in (gross receipts) and money paid out (payments or, as they are sometimes called, disbursements). Receipts and payments should be kept and summarized daily, weekly, or monthly, as the business needs

REASONS FOR KEEPING PROPER RECORDS

1. To know the cash position of your business precisely and accurately.

2. To discover whether your business is profitable, and if so, by how much.

3. To know which of your activities are profitable and which are not.

4. To ensure a timely flow of information for decision making.

5. To give bankers and other sources of financing confidence that your business is being well managed.

6. To allow you accurately to calculate and agree upon your tax liability.

7. To help you prepare financial forecasts and projections.

8. To make sure you both collect and pay money owed correctly.

9. To keep accountancy and audit costs to a minimum.

require. At the end of the quarter, the three monthly summaries are totaled up. You are now ready to deal with your tax form.

For a more detailed account, you need to keep an analyzed cash book, where you break down the receipts and payments. Details and examples of both cash books are given overleaf.

KEEPING MORE DETAILED RECORDS

If you are taking or giving credit, then you will need to keep some more information as well as the cash book, whether analyzed or not.

You will need to keep copies of paid and unpaid sales invoices, paid and unpaid purchases, as well as your bank statements. The bank statements should then be reconciled to your cash book to tie everything together. For example, the bank statement for the simple cash book example (p. 76) should show $808.14 in the account at the end of June.

KEEPING A CASH BOOK

Shown below is an example of a simple cash book. This written record system uses the single-entry bookkeeping method.

■ You can see at a glance the receipts and payments both in total and by main category. This breakdown lets you see, for example,

how much is being spent on each major area of your business, and who your most important customers are.

■ In the left-hand four columns, the month's receipts are entered as they occur, together with some basic details and the amount of the sales. At the head of the fourth column is

A SIMPLE CASH-BOOK SYSTEM

		RECEIPTS				PAYMENTS	
DATE	NAME	DETAILS	AMOUNT ($)	DATE	NAME	DETAILS	AMOUNT ($)
JUNE 1	Balance	Brought forward	450.55	JUNE 4	Gibbs	Inventory purchase	310.00
JUNE 4	Anderson	Sales	175.00	JUNE 8	Gibbs	Inventory purchase	130.00
JUNE 6	Brown	Sales	45.00	JUNE 12	ABC Telecoms	Telephone bills	55.23
JUNE 14	Smith & Co	Refund on returned inventory	137.34	JUNE 18	Colt Rentals	Vehicle rental	87.26
JUNE 17	Jenkins	Sales	190.25	JUNE 22	W Mobiles	Mobile phone	53.24
JUNE 20	Hollis	Sales	425.12	JUNE 27	Gibbs	Inventory purchase	36.28
JUNE 23	Jenkins	Sales	56.89				
						Total payments	672.01
				JUNE 30	Balance	Carried down	808.14
		Total receipts	1,480.15				1,480.15
JULY 1	Balance	Brought down	808.14				

The amount of cash now in the business. This will be brought down to the next month

The difference between payments and receipts is carried down to the receipts side of the book the amount of cash brought forward from the preceding month.

■ In the right-hand columns, expenses are listed in the same way. The total receipts for the month are $1,480.15 and for expenses $672.01. The difference is the amount of cash now in the business. The business has brought in more cash than it has spent, and so the figure of $808.14 is higher than the amount that was brought forward at the beginning of the month ($450.55).

■ This figure of $808.14 is the amount to be brought forward to the next month. The total of the month's payments and the amount carried down equals the sum of the receipts.

ANALYZING YOUR CASH BOOK

Shown below is an example of the payments side of an analyzed cash book. (The receipts side is similar, but with different categories.)

■ Using the analysis side of the entry, you can now see at a glance how the payments break down: how much has been spent on inventory, vehicles, telephone bills, and any other expenses in any one month. The monthly totals for each category can then be totalled for the year. These are useful pieces of management information, because they tell you exactly what your money is being spent on. In addition, they are essential facts for the completion of your tax return.

AN ANALYZED CASH-BOOK SYSTEM

	PAYMENTS			ANALYSIS			
DATE	NAME	DETAILS	AMOUNT ($)	INVENTORY	VEHICLES	TELEPHONE	OTHER
JUNE 4	Gibbs	Inventory purchase	310.00	310.00			
JUNE 8	Gibbs	Inventory purchase	130.00	130.00			
JUNE 12	ABC Telecoms	Telephone bills	55.23			55.23	
JUNE 18	Colt Rentals	Vehicle rental	87.26		87.26		
JUNE 22	W Mobiles	Mobile phone	53.24			53.24	
JUNE 27	Gibbs	Inventory purchase	36.28	36.28			
TOTALS			672.01	476.28	87.26		108.47

Totaling down the amount column and across the analysis columns gives the same figure

Land line and mobile phone bills are both listed in the "telephone" column

Double-entry Bookkeeping

If you operate a partnership, are set up as a company, or plan to grow, then you will need a double-entry bookkeeping system. This system requires two entries for each transaction, which provides built-in checks and balances to ensure accuracy. Each transaction requires an entry as a debit and as a credit. This may sound a little complicated, but once you get started it will become second nature. The example from a double-entry ledger opposite will give you an idea of what is involved.

A double-entry system is more complicated and time-consuming if done by hand, since everything has to be recorded twice. Also, if it is done manually, this method requires a formal set of books, namely journals and ledgers. All transactions are first entered into a journal and then posted (written) on a ledger sheet; that is, the same amount is written down in two different places. Typical ledger accounts are titled income, expenses, assets, and liabilities (debts).

The types of records to be kept are:
- day books
- cash books
- purchase ledger
- sales ledger
- capital or asset ledger
- general ledger

DAY BOOKS

Day books, sometimes called journals or books of original entry, are where every transaction is initially recorded in date order. Each day book is used for one kind of transaction, so if there are enough transactions of a particular kind, you open a day book for it. For example, there are always enough cash transactions to warrant a cash day book. If a firm sells on credit, then there will be a sales day book.

CASH BOOKS

Many small businesses accept both cash and checks. For bookkeeping purposes these are all called cash, although initially a separate record

KEEPING GOOD RECORDS
A successful business is dependent upon a constant flow of money coming in from customers, which can then be used to pay suppliers. Keeping good records of which payments are due and which have been paid, which bills have been settled and which are pending, means that at any given time you can assess the financial state of your business.

A SIMPLE SYSTEM OF BUSINESS RECORDS

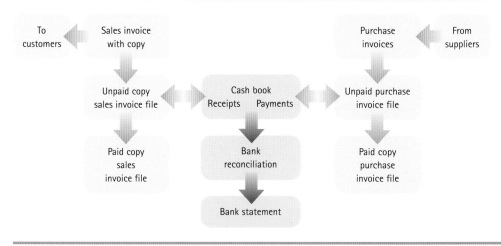

USING DOUBLE-ENTRY LEDGERS

Shown here is an example of a double-entry ledger. The debits in a double-entry ledger must always equal the credits. If they do not, you know there is an error somewhere.

■ In a double-entry system, a payment of rent would result in two separate journal entries: a debit for an expense of $250 and a corresponding credit of $250 – in other words, a double entry.

A DOUBLE-ENTRY LEDGER

DATE	DESCRIPTION OF ENTRY	DEBIT ($)	CREDIT ($)
JULY 10	Rent	250	
	Cash (rent account)		250

is kept of each: cash is recorded in the petty cash book, and checks are entered in the cash book.

The petty cash book is used to record actual cash transactions. Money in is recorded on the left-hand page and money out on the right. The money out could include such items as stamps or office coffee. Always keep receipts, even for inexpensive items, because one day you may have to verify these records. Once a week, or daily if the sums involved justify it, total the money in and out to get a cash balance. Check that it agrees with the actual cash in the cash register or petty cash box.

The cash book records all receipts and payments made by check. Once again, money coming in is on the left-hand page and money going out on the right. Every week, add up both pages to arrive at a cash in bank balance. This should be checked against your bank statement at least once a month to ensure that the basic information you are working with is correct.

PURCHASE AND SALES LEDGERS

If your business gives credit to customers, or takes credit from suppliers, you will need a sales and a purchase ledger. Each ledger should ideally have a separate page for every business with which you deal.

■ **PURCHASE LEDGER** On the right-hand side of the purchase ledger are listed the date, description, amount, and cost of each item bought on credit. On the left-hand side, a

record is kept of all payments made to the supplier, with the items for which the payments were made. Each month, by deducting the left-hand total from the right, you can see how much each supplier is owed. Check each statement against your own view of the financial situation, and dispute any discrepancy immediately.

■ **SALES LEDGER** The sales ledger deals with customers in much the same way. One important difference is that credit sales are shown on the left-hand side of the ledger, while customers' payments appear on the right-hand side. This is simply an accounting convention to deal with credits and debits.

It would also be very useful to keep a note of customers' (and suppliers') addresses, telephone numbers, and contact names with each entry in the ledgers. This will ensure that you have all the relevant information when it comes time to chase down late payments or deal with questions

MONEY SAVER

If you just pile your bills, receipts, and check stubs into an old shoe box and take it to an accountant at the end of the quarter, or when you run out of cash, it will cost a lot more to get your accounting done than if you keep good records.

Capital Asset Register

A capital asset register records capital items you own, such as land, buildings, equipment, and vehicles, showing the cost at date of purchase. It also records the disposal of any of these items and the cumulative depreciation.

The General Ledger

This ledger is usually kept by your accountant or bookkeeper. It brings together all the information from the primary ledgers, as these other basic records are called. Expenses from the cash books and purchase ledger are posted (entered) on the left-hand side of the nominal ledger. Income from sales (and any other income) is posted on the right. Normally, each type of expense or income has a separate page, which makes subsequent analysis easier.

▓ **The Trial Balance** Every month, each page in the general ledger is totaled and used to prepare a trial balance. In other words, the sum of all the left-hand totals should end up equaling the sum of all the right-hand totals. This is the basis of double-entry bookkeeping, and this balancing of the sums is what gives you confidence that the figures are correctly recorded. If the sums do not balance, then an error has crept in. Advice on remedying this situation is given on pp. 81 and 82.

Using a Computer for Record Keeping

There are many advantages to using a computer. It reduces the chances of arithmetic errors, saves time in adding and subtracting columns, and makes the calculations in an analyzed cash book that much easier to do. If you use a computer you

can choose between using an accounting program (recommended if you have more than 50 transactions a month) or, if your business is small, a spreadsheet.

Using an Accounting Program

If you use an accounting program for keeping your records, double-entry bookkeeping becomes a much simpler affair: each entry needs to be recorded only once; the computer does the rest. Specific plus points are:

▓ It is not possible to make any simple arithmetic errors.

▓ You will achieve better inventory control.

▓ You will be able to fill in your tax return quickly and accurately.

▓ You will achieve better control of your payments.

▓ You will save money on your accountant's fees.

▓ **No Arithmetic Errors** As long as the information is entered correctly on the computer, it will be added up correctly. For example, with a computer, the $250 rent expenditure in the example given on p. 79 is entered as an expense (a debit), and then the

Bookkeeping on a Computer
Double-entry bookkeeping becomes a much simpler operation on a computer. There is also less margin for error, as long as you enter the amounts correctly.

computer automatically posts it to the rent account as a credit, thereby providing the double entry. In effect, the computer eliminates the extra step or the need to master the difference between debit and credit yourself.

■ **BETTER INVENTORY CONTROL** If your business is concerned with inventory holding, an accounting program can help you to match inventory levels to demand. It could even provide you with profit margin information quickly by product, so that you can discover which products are selling well and are therefore worth promoting and which are less attractive, and so might need to be discontinued.

■ **FASTER TAX RETURNS** Routine tasks, such as filling in your tax return (and VAT in Europe and sales tax in the United States), take minutes to complete if you use a computer rather than days if you do not. In addition, the system can ensure that your returns are accurate and fully reconciled.

■ **CONTROL OF PAYMENTS** With an accounting program, invoices will always be accurate. You can also see at a glance which customers are regularly taking too long to pay their bills. Reminder statements of payments for late payers can be automatically prepared on the computer.

■ **SAVING MONEY** Your quarterly and annual accounts preparation and, where appropriate, audit will be greatly streamlined if you use a computer to do your accounts. This will save time and money, particularly on accountant's fees, and allow you to monitor profits and cash flow accurately.

USING A SPREADSHEET

If your business has relatively few transactions each month – say, no more than 20 or 30 items of receipt and payment to record – instead of using a double-entry accounting system you may be able to use a simple spreadsheet. This will provide an accurate, if minimal, record of your payments and receipts. It will not give you the advantages of a double-entry accounting system, but then with this number of records the chances are that you do not need one. Using a spreadsheet will, however, give you the other advantages of using a computer.

CORRECTING ERRORS

While using a computer will eliminate arithmetic errors, this does not mean that your computerized bookkeeping will always be perfect. There are, in fact, quite a few things that can still go wrong.

Aim for accuracy – computers are only as foolproof as the person entering the figures

Most errors show up in the trial balance, when you will see a difference between the sum of credits and debits. The difference between the two is what you need to look for. You need to discover whether that sum has been entered incorrectly or has simply been omitted. By using the "find" facility on the computer for that specific number, you may be able to locate the error.

If the error is very small, say $30 or so, and it has proved difficult to trace, you can put the missing amount into a suspense account. Removing the sum in this way means that you can get on and complete the accounts. Then, when you locate the error, you can make the necessary correction. Do not deduct the amount in order to make the figures agree, because you will then have to readjust the books when you do find the error.

MONEY SAVER

With the cost of basic accounting software starting at barely $50, and more sophisticated programs costing between $200 and $500, it makes good sense to plan to use such an accounting system from the outset.

COMMON BOOKKEEPING ERRORS

When the books do not balance it could be due to any one of a number of different errors inadvertently made when doing the books. Check for any of the following to find the source.

■ **ERRORS OF OMISSION** A transaction has been omitted altogether.

■ **ERRORS OF COMMISSION** A transaction has been posted to the wrong account, though to the right side. For example, it has been posted to the "John Brown" account instead of the "James Brown" account.

■ **COMPENSATING ERRORS** Different errors of the same value, made on opposite sides of the ledger. The effect of one is hidden by the equal effect of the other, so that the trial balance still balances. There could even be more than two errors involved, with the total debit errors matching the total credit errors.

■ **ERRORS OF PRINCIPLE** Where a payment item has been posted to a receipt account; for example, if you entered a bill to be paid as money due from one of your customers.

■ **ERRORS OF ORIGINAL ENTRY** The original entry was wrong. Perhaps the source document, such as an invoice, has been added up incorrectly or misread.

■ **ERRORS OF REVERSAL** Both aspects have been posted to the wrong sides: the debit aspect to the credit side, and the credit aspect to the debit side of the books.

■ **OMITTING ONE SIDE OF DUAL POSTING** Errors due to complete omission of one side of the dual posting. (A computerized system would not allow this to happen.)

■ **ERRORS OF SUMMATION** Sometimes known as "casting errors." Columns have been added up incorrectly, and the wrong balance carried down. Computerized accounts eliminate this problem.

■ **ERRORS OF TRANSPOSITION** A figure has been accidentally reversed in writing. For example, 32 has been written as 23, or 414 as 441. This error is always a multiple of 9, and if the error is one of transposition it can be spotted fairly easily.

Dealing with Incomplete Records

Sometimes a business gets started without having a bookkeeping system in place, or accurate and timely recording has been neglected for a period. There is no cause for despair here, because the incomplete record process can still help you to produce reliable books from unreliable data.

If you have been so imprudent as to have been operating your business without records, and a tax bill has come in, all is not completely lost. With the help of your accountant you should be able to produce a profit figure from the information in your incomplete records.

If you kept no records to begin with, resolve to start reliable bookkeeping for the future

To do this, use what records you have got to add up all the assets, such as cash, inventory, equipment, money owed by customers, and so forth, at the end of the period. Do the same for the liabilities, such as money owed to the bank or creditors. Then deduct the sum of the assets from the sum of the liabilities: the difference is the profit made in the period, and so the amount to be taxed.

This is undoubtedly not the most accurate way to keep track of your finances, and it certainly lacks any detail, but if incomplete records are all that you have, this method has the advantage of allowing you to draw a line under the past financial year. You can then decide to make a fresh start for the future by using a sound and reliable bookkeeping system.

WORKING OUT YOUR PROFIT FROM INCOMPLETE RECORDS

ASSETS		($)
CASH IN HAND		150
MONEY OWED BY CUSTOMERS		355
FIXED ASSETS (CAR, COMPUTER, ETC.)		1,080
TOTAL		1,585
MINUS LIABILITIES	Overdraft	500
	Money owed to suppliers	735
TOTAL		1,235
DIFFERENCE BETWEEN ASSETS AND LIABILITIES		350
TO WHICH ADD OWNER'S DRAW FOR PERIOD		4,000
TAXABLE PROFIT		4,350

OVERALL PICTURE
These accounts lack the detail of a double-entry system and the breakdown of an analyzed cash book, but they are sufficient to produce a figure for the profit made during a certain period.

The Profit and Loss Statement

The purpose of bookkeeping is to provide yourself with the data needed to run your business efficiently. It also helps you to work out how much you owe in taxes. The way to calculate these matters is to prepare a profit and loss statement, which uses the figures for the income of the business, the cost of providing the goods or services being sold, and the cost of running the business to provide a detailed picture of your financial affairs.

In carrying out any business activity, two very different actions go on: producing goods or services at a cost to yourself, then selling these goods or services to your customers.

In order to secure your customers and give them the product or service they want, you will incur necessary costs, such as raw materials, salaries, rent, and so forth. These costs are also known as expenses.

When you sell your goods and services, the money may not come in immediately, but eventually the cash will arrive. This money goes by a variety of names including revenue, income, and sales income.

By deducting the expenses from the income, you end up with the profit (or loss) for the particular period under review.

Creating a Detailed Statement

A simple profit and loss statement is certainly better than nothing, but it does provide only the skeleton facts about the business' financial standing. You can, however, use the basic bookkeeping information to give a much richer picture of events within the business if you set up the right analysis headings. To develop a basic profit and loss statement into a more detailed and informative one is simply a matter of including more information.

Basic Profit and Loss Statement for Safari US	
Year 1	($)
Total Income	1,416,071
Total Expenses	1,389,698
Profit	26,373

Basic Statement
At its simplest, the profit and loss statement has at its head the period covered, followed by the income, from which all the expenses of the business are deducted to arrive at the profit (or loss) made in the period.

The following pages show how you can build up a basic profit and loss statement to give a more complete picture of the events of a year. The statements of a fictional company named Safari US, which sells package vacations, will be used to show the development of a very basic profit and loss statement into a detailed one for any service industry. For a manufacturing, rather than a service, business, this development differs in the way gross profit is calculated (see p. 86).

Calculating Gross Profit

Whatever the business activity, you have to buy certain raw materials. These will include anything on which you have to spend money to produce the goods and services you are selling. So, if you sell cars, the cost of purchasing the cars you sell will be one such cost. In Safari US's case, the cost of airline tickets and hotel rooms is the raw material of the package vacations they provide.

What you have left from your sales revenues after deducting the cost of sales, as these costs of production are known, is the gross profit. For Safari US, the difference between the income of $1,416,071 and the cost of the goods (vacations and insurance) they have sold is just $160,948. That is the sum with which the management has to run the business, not the much larger headline-making income figure of nearly $1.5 million.

Calculate your gross profit to find out how much money you can spend

THE IMPORTANCE OF GROSS PROFIT

The gross profit is one of the most important figures in the profit and loss statement. It represents the only money coming into the business about which you can have much say in how it is spent, because it is not needed actually to produce the goods or services. It will, instead, be used to pay for all the running costs of the business, and any money remaining after all the bills have been settled and all the employees paid may either be taken as earnings by the owner or used to expand the business. It follows, therefore, that those products or services that produce the highest gross profit

(that is, they have the largest difference between cost of sale and selling price) are a business's most valuable asset.

The gross profit, not the much larger income sum, is the figure to use when taking out a loan or making plans for expansion. To use the income figure would probably be disastrous.

INCLUDING BUSINESS EXPENSES

The expenses that are likely to arise in a business need to be itemized in the profit and loss statement. These expenses are listed after the gross profit has been calculated. They

GROSS PROFIT CALCULATION FOR SAFARI EUROPE		
YEAR 1		(£)
INCOME	TOURS SOLD	1,402,500
	INSURANCE AND OTHER SERVICES	13,571
	NON-OPERATING REVENUE	0
TOTAL INCOME		1,416,071
LESS COST OF GOODS SOLD	Tours bought	1,251,052
	Insurance and other services	4,071
TOTAL COST OF GOODS SOLD		1,255,123
GROSS PROFIT		160,948

GROSS PROFIT

Safari US has two sources of income: one from tours and one from insurance and other related services. The company also, of course, has the costs associated with buying vacations and insurance policies from suppliers.

A MANUFACTURER'S GROSS PROFIT

To calculate the gross profit in a manufacturing business the process is quite different, as the example below shows.

■ In the first instance, the basic accounting for a manufacturing business is the same as for a service business. The difference comes when you take into account the raw materials needed for manufacturing. You will be holding raw materials in stock, but you want to count into the cost of goods sold only the materials that are actually used. You do this by noting the inventory at the start of the period, adding in any purchases made, and deducting the closing inventory figure.

■ To arrive at the gross profit, you also need to build in the indirect labor cost in production, in addition to any overhead, such as workshop usage, with its inherent costs of heat, light, and power.

GROSS PROFIT SUMMARY

	($)
SALES	100,000
COST OF GOODS SOLD	65,000
GROSS PROFIT	35,000

EXPANDED GROSS PROFIT CALCULATION

YEAR 1		($)	($)	($)
SALES				100,000
MANUFACTURING COSTS	Raw materials opening inventory	30,000		
	Purchases in period	25,000		
MINUS RAW MATERIALS CLOSING INVENTORY		15,500		
COST OF MATERIALS USED			39,500	
DIRECT LABOR COST			18,000	
MANUFACTURING OVERHEAD COSTS	Indirect labor	4,000		
	Workshop heat, light, and power	3,500		
TOTAL MANUFACTURING COSTS			7,500	
COST OF GOODS SOLD				65,000
GROSS PROFIT				35,000

GROSS PROFIT SUMMARY
By deducting the cost of goods sold from the sales income, you are left with the gross profit. At this level of accounting there are few differences between a service business and a manufacturing one.

EXPANDED ACCOUNTS
By giving more detail in the financial statements, you can see which figures (the manufacturing overhead costs, labor costs, and the cost of the inventory used in the production of the items sold) need to be deducted from the income to give the gross profit figure.

include all costs associated with running the business, such as rent, telephone, marketing, and so forth.

In Safari US's case, the business expenses include not only the basic services, such as telephone, electricity, and gas, which will be paid for on a monthly basis, but also annual bills, such as memberships and subscriptions, and irregular events, such as staff training (see table right). There is also a sum for the depreciation of equipment, which your accountant will help you to calculate (see pp. 98–100). While all these expenses are correctly included, they are not necessarily allowable for tax purposes in all countries (see pp. 159–165).

The heading "total expenditure" in the table is not exactly accurate because, although all the most obvious forms of expenditure have been taken into acount, there are some other expenses associated with running a business. These are treated in a slightly different way, for reasons that will become apparent when you look at the different types of profit.

APPRECIATING THE DIFFERENT TYPES OF PROFIT

The figures on p. 89 are the full profit and loss statement for Safari US. It is clear from this that profit can be measured in several ways, each one a step on from the last. They are:
▓ gross profit
▓ operating profit
▓ net profit before tax
▓ net profit after tax
▓ **GROSS PROFIT** This is the profit that remains after all the costs related to making what you sell have been deducted.
▓ **OPERATING PROFIT** After you have deducted from the gross profit the expenses, or expenditure, you are left with what is

ACCOUNT INCLUDING EXPENSES

The gross profit calculation has now been taken to the next stage, where all the costs of actually running the business are taken into account. The gross profit minus the total expenditure is known as the operating profit.

BUSINESS EXPENSES FOR SAFARI US		
YEAR 1		($)
INCOME	Tours sold	1,402,500
	Insurance and other services	13,571
	Nonoperating revenue	0
TOTAL INCOME		1,416,071
MINUS COST OF GOODS SOLD	Tours bought	1,251,052
	Insurance and other services	4,071
TOTAL COST OF GOODS SOLD		1,255,123
GROSS PROFIT		160,948
EXPENDITURE	Rent	18,000
	Heat, light, and power	3,500
	Telephone system lease	2,000
	Computer lease	5,000
	Marketing and promotion	12,500
	Postage and stationery	3,250
	Telephone	3,575
	Insurance and legal	3,500
	Employee's wages	36,000
	Consultancy services	25,000
	Membership and subscription	1,500
	Travel and entertainment	4,250
	Training and staff development	6,000
	Depreciation of equipment	5,500
TOTAL EXPENDITURE		129,575

Levels of Profit for Safari US		
Year 1		**($)**
Income	Tours sold	1,402,500
	Insurance and other services	13,571
	Nonoperating revenue	0
Total Income		1,416,071
Minus Cost of Goods Sold	Tours bought	1,251,052
	Insurance and other services	4,071
Total Cost of Goods Sold		1,255,123
Gross Profit		160,948
Expenditure	Rent	18,000
	Heat, light, and power	3,500
	Telephone system lease	2,000
	Computer lease	5,000
	Marketing and promotion	12,500
	Postage and stationery	3,250
	Telephone	3,575
	Insurance and legal	3,500
	Employee's wages	36,000
	Consultancy services	25,000
	Membership and subscription	1,500
	Travel and entertainment	4,250
	Training and staff development	6,000
	Depreciation of equipment	5,500
Total Expenditure		129,575
Operating Profit		31,373
Minus Bank Interest and Charges		5,000
Net Profit Before Tax		26,373
Tax		5,474
Net Profit After Tax		20,899

The Final Account

The accounts have now been taken to their last stage, where the operating profit has had interest charges and tax deducted from it, to produce the final figure of the net profit after tax.

known as the operating profit. When it comes to valuing the business, it is the operating profit that is generally used as the multiplying factor in the "xxx times earnings" valuation.

■ **Net Profit Before Tax** Next, any financing costs must be deducted. The reasoning here is that the business manager can have little influence over the way in which the business is financed (no borrowings means no interest expenses, for example; high borrowings mean high expenses) or over the interest rates, which are regulated at a macroeconomic level. In the case of Safari US, once you have deducted the financing costs ($5,000 in interest charges), you are left with a net profit before tax of $26,373.

■ **Net Profit After Tax** Tax is deducted to leave the net profit after tax. This is the sum that belongs to the owners of the business. In the case of a corporation, this is the sum from which dividends are paid.

The Projected Profit and Loss Statement

A profit and loss statement for the first year in business can be used as a basis for creating a projected account for the future. Here Safari US's accounts have been estimated for the following two business years on the basis of the first year's accounts.

A projected profit and loss statement forms a vital part of your business plan when you are seeking financing for expansion. A new business seeking financing will have to project all three years.

Looking into the Future
The accounts for the first year of business can be used as a means to estimate the figures for the next two years. A total profit of just over $500,000 is foreseen by Safari US by the end of year 3.

THREE-YEAR PROFIT AND LOSS STATEMENT FOR SAFARI US
(INCLUDING PROJECTED FIGURES FOR YEARS 2 AND 3)

		YEAR 1 ($)	% OF SALES	YEAR 2 ($)	% OF SALES	YEAR 3 ($)	% OF SALES
INCOME	Tours sold	1,402,500		3,085,500		4,502,025	
	Insurance and other services	13,571		29,856		43,563	
	Nonoperating revenue	0	0	0	0	0	0
TOTAL INCOME		1,416,071	100	3,115,356	100	4,545,588	100
MINUS COST OF GOODS SOLD	Tours bought	1,251,052		2,732,557	1,251,052	3,941,594	
	Insurance and other services	4,071		8,956		13,068	
TOTAL COST OF GOODS SOLD		1,255,123	89	2,741,513	88	3,954,662	87
GROSS PROFIT		160,948	11	373,843	12	590,926	13
EXPENDITURE	Rent	18,000		18,000	18,000	24,000	
	Heat, light, and power	3,500		3,500		4,000	
	Telephone system lease	2,000		2,000		2,000	
	Computer lease	5,000		5,000		5,000	
	Marketing and promotion	12,500		18,000		25,000	
	Postage and stationery	3,250		5,000		7,500	
	Telephone	3,575		4,750		6,500	
	Insurance and legal	3,500		5,500		10,000	
	Employee's wages	36,000		40,500		58,000	
	Consultancy services	25,000		10,000		10,000	
	Membership and subscription	1,500		2,500		5,000	
	Travel and entertainment	4,250		10,500		18,500	
	Training and staff development	6,000		10,000		21,000	
	Depreciation of equipment	5,500		5,500		5,500	
TOTAL EXPENDITURE		129,575	10	140,750	5	202,000	5
OPERATING PROFIT		31,373		233,093		388,926	
MINUS BANK INTEREST AND CHARGES		5,000		5,000		5,000	
NET PROFIT BEFORE TAX		26,373	2	228,093	7	383,926	8
Tax		5,474		45,619		87,276	
NET PROFIT AFTER TAX		20,899	1	182,474	6	296,650	7
CUMULATIVE PROFIT/LOSS		20,899		203,373		500,023	

THE BALANCE SHEET

To sum up the current financial position of your business you need to draw up a balance sheet. The balance sheet is the primary reporting document of the business. It contains evidence of all the financial events over the entire life of the business, showing where money has come from and what has been done with that money. Logically, the two sums must balance. A balance sheet is also a useful tool for ordering your personal financial affairs. This chapter demonstrates how to compile both types of balance sheet.

When important financial issues are at stake it is always helpful to draw up a balance sheet, whether the subject of concern is personal or business. Before deciding whether to move to a new house or buy a new car you need to size up your financial situation. This could be formalized into a personal balance sheet.

The Personal Balance Sheet

The first step in the process of drawing up a personal balance sheet is to summarize your basic financial position. To demonstrate the entire process, consider the finances of Amanda Smith. A basic summary of her current financial situation is shown in the table on the right. To understand her true position, the information needs to be reorganized and more detail added.

DEFINING LIABILITIES AND ASSETS
In money matters everything divides neatly into two: things you have and things you owe, with the latter usually exceeding the former. Using this concept and slightly different words, the same basic financial information could be presented in the manner of the table shown at the top of page 91. On the right-hand side is a

list of Amanda's assets: what she has done with the money she has had. On the left is listed where she got the money from to pay for these assets: the liabilities and claims against her.

Things get a little more complicated at the bottom of the left-hand column. She has acquired $159,035 worth of assets and so must have provided an identical sum from one source or another to pay for these assets. She owes only $45,650 to other people, so it is likely that Amanda must have put in the balance over the past years. In other words, she has put her past salary toward buying the assets, to which was added an increase in her house value.

AMANDA SMITH'S BASIC FINANCIAL POSITION	
	($)
CASH	50
HOUSE	150,000
MORTGAGE	45,000
MONEY OWED BY SISTER	135
OVERDRAFT	100
CAR	7,000
CREDIT CARDS	50
JEWELLERY/PAINTINGS	350
FINANCE BALANCE (ON VARIOUS GOODS)	500
FURNITURE	1,500

BASIC ACCOUNTS
This very limited information reveals the basics of Amanda's financial situation, such as the value of her house and what loans she has.

LONG- AND SHORT-TERM POSITIONS

This presentation still does not tell the whole story. Even though she appears to have a fairly dazzling $159,035 of assets, Amanda knows that she is short of cash for day-to-day living. She would like to be able to see at-a-glance both long- and short-term aspects of her current financial position. To do this, the information needs to be restructured in the manner of the table shown at the foot of this page.

Amanda's short-term financial position is dominated by the money that her sister owes

AMANDA SMITH'S ASSETS AND LIABILITIES				
LIABILITIES & CLAIMS	($)	ASSETS	($)
OVERDRAFT	100	CASH	50
MORTGAGE	45,000	HOUSE	150,000
FINANCE BALANCE	500	CAR	7,000
CREDIT CARDS	50	JEWELRY/PAINTINGS	350
TOTAL CLAIMS BY OTHER PEOPLE	45,650	MONEY OWED BY SISTER	135
		FURNITURE	1,500
MY CAPITAL	113,385		
TOTAL OF MY AND OTHER PEOPLE'S MONEY	159,035	MY ASSETS	159,035

LIABILITIES AND ASSETS
Adding more detail gives a fuller account of Amanda's financial position. Her liabilities and claims (that is, where she got her money) equal her assets (that is, what she has done with her money).

AMANDA SMITH'S LONG- AND SHORT-TERM POSITIONS			
LIABILITIES (LONG-TERM)	($)	ASSETS (LONG-TERM)	($)
MY CAPITAL	113,385	HOUSE	150,000
MORTGAGE	45,000	CAR	7,000
FINANCE BALANCE	500	FURNITURE	1,500
		JEWELRY/PAINTINGS	350
TOTAL	158,885	TOTAL	158,850
LIABILITIES (SHORT-TERM)	($)	ASSETS (SHORT-TERM)	($)
OVERDRAFT	100	MONEY OWED BY SISTER	135
CREDIT CARDS	50	CASH	50
TOTAL	150	TOTAL	185

LONG AND SHORT TERM
Breaking down her liabilities and assets into long term (fixed) and short term (current) makes Amanda's financial situation clearer. The bottom line tells her that she owes $150 and has assets of $185

her. If that is safe, then all current liabilities can be met. If it is unsafe, and so unlikely to be repaid quickly, the position is not so good. "Current" is used in financial language to mean something that is going to be realized or consumed within one year. So current liabilities are those that have to be paid within a year, and current assets will turn into cash within a year.

THE NET POSITION

Only one more adjustment to the information is needed to turn Amanda's short- and long-term position into a balance sheet (see table right). Having broken down her liabilities and assets into long- and short-term categories, it is now vital to ensure that both these financial positions are readily visible to the examiner. In other words, Amanda's day-to-day assets and liabilities need to be clearly highlighted.

What Amanda needs to see is the net position. "Net" means a position after the relevant liability has been taken away. So Amanda's net current assets are how much she currently owes subtracted from how much she has. The resulting sum is also referred to as working capital.

You will note that underneath the heading of "fixed assets" in the balance sheet to the right the term "book value" has been used. This means the cost of any fixed assets minus the amount of depreciation charged up to that date. (For more on depreciation see pp. 98–100.)

By redrafting the financial position, you can see the whole picture more clearly. Starting with the items that have a long life or will be around for several years, you can deduce that $158,885 is tied up in fixed assets (her house, car, furniture, jewelry, and paintings). Turning next to items with a relatively short life, you can see that a further $35 is tied up in net current assets (that is, current assets minus current liabilities).

All these have been financed by $113,385 of Amanda's capital and $45,500, which has been provided by a mortgage and a finance company, which are Amanda's long-term liabilities. The sum of these two figures also comes to $158,885, and so her balance sheet can be seen to balance correctly.

AMANDA SMITH'S BALANCE SHEET – THE NET POSITION

ASSETS AND LIABILITIES		($)
FIXED ASSETS	House	150,000
	Car	7,000
	Furniture	1,500
	Jewelry/paintings	350
	BOOK VALUE	158,850
CURRENT ASSETS	Money owed by sister	135
	Cash	50
TOTAL CURRENT ASSETS		185
MINUS CURRENT LIABILITIES	Overdraft	100
	Credit cards	50
TOTAL CURRENT LIABILITIES		150
NET CURRENT ASSETS		35
NET TOTAL ASSETS		158,885
FINANCED BY	My capital	113,385
	Mortgage	45,000
	Finance balance	500
TOTAL		158,885

THE NET POSITION
Amanda's balance sheet is now displayed in a vertical format for clarity. You can see that her total assets of $158,885 balance her capital and long-term liabilities.

BALANCE SHEET FORMAT

The balance sheets shown here are displayed in a vertical format rather than the horizontal form used for the two preceding charts. The vertical format is the convention for a balance sheet in the U.K., whereas the U.S. uses the horizontal form.

The Business Balance Sheet

The information collected so far is all that is needed for a balance sheet depicting Amanda's personal affairs. To convert this personal balance sheet into one that could be used in a U.K. business, however, requires a few small adjustments (see table right). The long-term borrowings – in this case the mortgage and finance charges – are now renamed as "creditors, amounts falling due in over one year." They are deducted from the total assets to show the net total assets being employed by her business.

The bottom of the business balance sheet shows how Amanda has supported these assets; in this case, by her own funds. She could also have invested the profit made in earlier years back into the business (see Understanding Reserves, p. 95).

A final change that has been made is to assume that her house is now a business premises owned by her company. (This assumption has wider implications, but none that is relevant to the balance sheet.)

Categorizing Business Assets

Accountants describe assets as valuable resources, owned by a business, that were acquired at a measurable money cost. Assets can be categorized in three ways:

- cash assets
- possessed assets
- owned assets

BUSINESS BALANCE SHEET

Adapting Amanda's personal balance sheet into a business one involves renaming her long-term liabilities and making the assumption that her home is now used as a business premises and so is owned by her company.

AMANDA SMITH'S BUSINESS BALANCE SHEET			
ASSETS AND LIABILITIES		($)	($)
FIXED ASSETS	Premises	150,000	
	Car	7,000	
	Furniture	1,500	
	Jewelry/ paintings	350	
	BOOK VALUE		158,850
CURRENT ASSETS	Money owed by sister	135	
	Cash	50	
TOTAL CURRENT ASSETS		185	
MINUS CURRENT LIABILITIES	Overdraft	100	
	Credit cards	50	
TOTAL CURRENT LIABILITIES		150	
NET CURRENT ASSETS			35
TOTAL ASSETS			158,885
MINUS	Creditors, amounts falling due in over one year		45,500
NET TOTAL ASSETS			113,385
FINANCED BY	My capital	113,385	
TOTAL OWNER'S FUNDS			113,385

Cᴀsʜ Assᴇᴛs

To be valuable, the resource must be cash, or of some use in generating current or future profits. For example, a debtor (someone who owes a business money for goods or services provided) usually pays up. When the debtor does pay the debt, the repayment becomes cash and so meets this test. If there is no hope of getting payment of a debt in the foreseeable future, then you can hardly view the sum as an asset of any kind.

Possᴇssᴇᴅ Assᴇᴛs

Ownership, in its legal sense, can be seen as different from possession or control. The accounting use of the word is similar but not identical. In a business, possession and control are not enough to make a resource an asset. For example, a leased machine may be possessed and controlled by a business but be owned by the leasing company. So, not only is it not an asset, it is a regular expense. However, had the same piece of machinery been bought outright, then it would be treated as an asset of the business. No one but the accountant could detect the difference.

Oᴡɴᴇᴅ Assᴇᴛs

Most business resources are bought for what is termed by accountants as a measurable money cost. Often, this test is all too painfully obvious. If you pay cash for something, or promise to pay at a later date, it is clearly an asset. Any goods manufactured by your business involved money being paid in wages, materials, etc. during that process, and so these too are assets. There may be problems in deciding exactly

Fᴀᴄᴛ Fɪʟᴇ

The asset "goodwill" is one important gray area of particular interest when buying or selling a small business. It constitutes the value placed upon the reputation (for example, the brand name) of the business.

what money figure to put down, but there is no problem in seeing that money has been spent.

Rᴀɴᴋɪɴɢ ᴀssᴇᴛs

There is a useful convention that recommends listing assets in the balance sheet in their order of permanence; that is, starting out with the most difficult to turn into cash and working down to cash itself. Using this convention in current assets, inventories are purchased and would appear before debtors, because goods have to be sold to customers, who then pay up, eventually releasing the cash back into the business.

This structure is very practical when you are looking at someone else's balance sheet for information, or comparing balance sheets. It can also help you to recognize obvious information gaps quickly.

Accounting for Liabilities

These are the claims by people outside the business that one day will have to be met. Liabilities include items that can be easily identified and measured, such as loans and money due to suppliers, as well as those that are less easy to quantify. Accountants have their own rules on how figures are to be arrived at for these gray areas, but they do not pretend to give anything more than an approximation. Common business liabilities are:

▪ Tax
▪ Accruals
▪ Deferred income
▪ Overdrafts
▪ Loans
▪ Financing agreements
▪ Money owed to suppliers

Every measuring device, including financial controls, has inherent inaccuracies. To make things more complicated, not all financial events are equally easy to measure. Seek advice from your accountant about liabilities.

AMANDA'S RESERVES
The revenue reserve ($50,000) and the capital reserve ($38,385), together with the capital introduced ($25,000) represent all the money invested by Amanda in this venture.

DEALING WITH BAD DEBTS

Some liabilities can be less easy to identify and even harder to put a figure on, bad debts being a prime example. The difference between the average order placed by your biggest and smallest accounts will provide some idea of the spread that could encompass a bad debt figure. Also, there is no certainty that only one bad debt will occur in each year. In practice, you will probably settle for last year's bad debt figure, extrapolating up to reflect any growth in sales.

Understanding Reserves

In the final version of Amanda Smith's business balance sheet on p. 93 her capital was shown as being the sole support for the liabilities of the business. The implication was that she had put this whole sum in at once. In practice, this is much more likely to have happened over time, and in a variety of ways.

Perhaps she started out in business, since that is how we must now look at her affairs, with a sum of, say, $25,000. Since then she has made a net profit after tax of $50,000, which she has reinvested into her business to finance growth. In addition, the business premises that she bought a few years ago for $111,615 has

AMANDA SMITH'S RESERVES			
FINANCED BY		($)	($)
CAPITAL INTRODUCED			25,000
RESERVES	Revenue reserve	50,000	
	Capital reserve	38,385	88,385

just been revalued at $150,000, providing a paper gain of $38,385. The bottom portion of her business balance sheet could now be recast as shown in the table above.

REVENUE RESERVES

The profit of $50,000 plowed back into the business is called a revenue reserve, which means that the money actually exists and could be used to buy inventory or more assets, for example. A revenue reserve is usually created when a business makes a profit and all or a portion of that profit is left in the business and not paid out in dividends.

CAPITAL RESERVES

The increase in value of the business premises, on the other hand, is a paper increase, which means that the $38,385 increase in capital reserves that it represents could not be used to buy anything, because it will not be in money form until the business premises are sold. However, that paper reserve could be used to underpin a loan from the bank, thus turning a paper profit into a cash resource.

ACCOUNTING RULES

Finance has a language of its own. Some of the terms, while sounding like familiar everyday English, can have quite different meanings when used in accountancy. In addition, some rules can appear alien to common sense and become obvious only when you remember that the goal of the accounting reports is stewardship rather than value. Stewardship means accounting for where money came from and what was done with it. This chapter covers the most important rules of the financial game.

A particularly prudent sales manager once said that an order was not an order until the customer's check had cleared; the customer had consumed the product and had not died as a result; and, finally, the customer had shown every indication of wanting to buy the product again. By contrast, most of us know quite a different kind of salesperson who, usually as a result of vast optimism (or overconfidence), expects to achieve the most unlikely volume of sales in the most uncertain conditions.

In finance you should, and indeed ought to, count your chickens before they hatch

Realizing Income from Customers

Common sense suggests that you should wait until customers pay up before calculating your sales figure. After all, anything could happen: they may reject the product, change their mind, or go bust before they pay you. In finance, however, you need to look ahead and to assume that sales will convert into cash. When it comes to bookkeeping and tax returns, income is usually recognized as having been earned when the goods are dispatched, or service rendered, and the invoice sent out. This has nothing to do with when an order is received, or how firm an order is, or how likely a customer is to pay promptly.

So the sales income figure that is seen at the top of a profit and loss account is the value of the goods dispatched and invoiced to customers during the period in question. It in no way reflects the amount of money actually received during that same period.

THE MATCHING PRINCIPLE

The reasoning behind this lies in what accountants call the matching principle. This states that income and expenditure have to be related to the relevant and same time period. So a profit and loss account is actually measuring economic activity, not cash. It is not that cash is unimportant, it is just that there is another account for measuring it: the cash-flow forecast (see pp. 22–35).

According to the matching principle, if raw materials are purchased and worked on, rent

MONEY SAVER

One element that can consume money for no reward is dealing with returns caused by sending the wrong goods or the wrong quantities. Making sure the right goods in the correct quantities are shipped in the first place is an investment that will result in lower costs and more satisfied customers.

RETURNED GOODS
Allowing for returned goods means that you can provide a more accurate figure for your net sales. Here, $1,000 of goods are expected to be returned each year.

ALLOWING FOR RETURNS		
	($)	**($)**
GROSS SALES INCOME	100,000	
RETURNS	1,000	
NET SALES INCOME		99,000

paid, telephone calls made, and so forth, in one month, then alongside those expenses must be matched the income from the sales actually executed in that month.

ALLOWING FOR RETURNS

The matching principle assumes that expenses and income are matched against time. This does not mean, however, that you can ignore the possibilities of bad debts occurring or of products being returned. If such events occur infrequently or at a very low level, then you can allow for these in your financial calculations.

For returns, if you know from experience that they are a certain percentage of sales, then you can allow for that in your calculation by introducing the terms "gross sales income," meaning the figure before returns, and "net sales income," meaning the figure after the allowance has been made.

In the example shown above, the returns are expected to average 1 percent of sales, and so the rest of the expenses in the profit and loss account are deducted from $99,000 rather than the full $100,000.

ALLOWING FOR BAD DEBTS

For bad debts you can make a similar provision in the accounts, allowing for a certain amount each month. In most months there will be no bad debts, but once in a while one will occur and use up all the provisions made earlier, thus leaving no funds for future occurrences.

If either returns or bad debts are common in an industry, then separate rules will need to be made for dealing with them. Mail order companies, for example, will handle large quantities of returned goods. Rather than treat these returns as infrequent and unwanted events, they will regard them as an everyday part of their business.

Accruing for the Future

The profit and loss statement sets out to match a business's income and expenditure to the appropriate time period. It is only in this way that the profit for the period can be realistically calculated. However, not all of these financial events will leave a clear and traceable trail, and this is when you need to introduce the method of accruing. If you do not accrue, your accounts will not reflect your current position.

WHEN TO ACCRUE

The basic transactions, such as sales, purchases, and salaries, will be easy to deal with because the amounts will all be recorded in your books. But suppose, for example, that you are calculating one month's profits when the quarterly telephone bill comes in. The picture might be as follows: sales income for January of $4,000, minus telephone bill (last quarter) of $800, giving a profit of $3,200.

This is clearly wrong. In the first place, three months' worth of telephone calls have been

FACT FILE

Accruing is the general term used to describe making a provision for something for which there is no documentary evidence, but which nevertheless has an impact on profit or loss.

THE PRINCIPAL METHODS OF DEPRECIATION USED IN BUSINESS

Described below are three of the most common of many ways of depreciating fixed assets. In choosing which method of depreciation to use – and in practice you may have to use different methods for different types of asset – it is useful to remember what you are trying to do. You are aiming to allocate the cost of buying the asset as it should apply to each year of its working life.

■ **THE STRAIGHT LINE METHOD** This method assumes that the asset will be consumed (that is, used) evenly throughout its life. In the example below it has been assumed that a computer is being bought for $1,200 and sold at the end of five years for $200. The amount to be written off is therefore $1,000. Using 20 per cent as the depreciation, or write-down, rate, you can work out the book value for each year.

■ **THE DIMINISHING BALANCE METHOD** This method works in a similar way, but

instead of an even depreciation each year you assume that the drop will be faster in the beginning. Some assets, motor vehicles for example, will reduce more sharply in their first year than later on. So while at the end of year one both these methods of depreciation will result in a $200 fall, in year two the picture starts to change (see below). The straight line method takes a further fall of $200, while the diminishing balance method reduces by 20 per cent (the agreed depreciation rate) of $800 (the balance of $1,000 minus the $200 depreciation so far), which equals $160.

■ **THE SUM OF THE DIGITS METHOD** This is a more commonly used method in the U.S. than in the U.K. While the diminishing balance method applies a constant percentage to a declining figure, the sum of the digits method applies a progressively smaller percentage to the initial cost. It involves adding up the individual numbers in the expected lifespan of the asset to arrive at the denominator of a fraction. The numerator is the year number concerned, but in reverse order.

For example, if the computer asset bought for $1,200 had an expected useful life of five years, then the denominator in the sum would be $1 + 2 + 3 + 4 + 5$, which equals 15. In year one it would depreciate by $\frac{5}{15}$ times the initial purchase price of $1,200, which equals $400. In year two it would depreciate by a further $\frac{4}{15}$ (which would take it to $480), and so on.

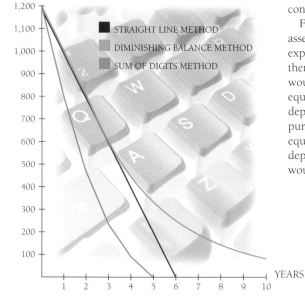

ASSET WORTH ($)

- ■ STRAIGHT LINE METHOD
- ■ DIMINISHING BALANCE METHOD
- ■ SUM OF DIGITS METHOD

YEARS

DEPRECIATION RATES
These three methods – straight line, diminishing balance, and sum of the digits – are used to assess the rate of depreciation of goods and property.

matched against one month's sales. Equally wrong is the fact that the quarterly telephone bill for October to December has been charged against the following January's income.

Unfortunately, bills reflecting the current month are rarely available when you are preparing the monthly accounts, so in practice the telephone bill is accrued for. This means that a figure (which, thanks to metering, should be absolutely correct) is put into the profit and loss statement as a provision to meet this liability when it comes due.

Taking Account of Depreciating Assets

Assets are usually entered into the accounts at cost. In reality, the real worth of an asset will probably change over time. Usually, it decreases in value, but in some cases it will increase. Knowing how an asset is likely to change its value is important when dealing with depreciation.

The worth, or value, of an asset is a subjective estimate on which no two people are likely to agree. This is made even more complex, and artificial, because the assets themselves – property, equipment, computers, and so forth – may not be for sale.

ASSESSING DEPRECIATION
Calculating depreciation values is not an accurate science. Here depreciation of a $10,000 machine has been set at a notional $5,000, leaving a book value of $5,000.

RECORDING COST
In the search for objectivity, the accountants have settled for cost as the figure to record. This inevitably means that a balance sheet does not actually show the current worth or value of a business, but then that is not the intention of a balance sheet.

This recording of the cost of an item does not mean that accountants assume that this figure remains unchanged forever. For example, a machine costing $10,000 with a useful working life of four years may, after two years, have a book value of just $5,000.

ALLOCATING COST OVER TIME
The recording of depreciation is how you show the asset being consumed, or used, over its working life. It is simply a bookkeeping method to allow the allocation of some of the initial cost of an asset to the appropriate time period. This time period will be determined by such factors as how long the likely working life of the asset is.

CALCULATING DEPRECIATION
Depreciation can be calculated using different methods. Three of the most common methods are outlined on p. 98.

Depreciation is not a method of providing for new equipment to replace old. It is simply a bookkeeping event. For example, the machine mentioned above has been bought and paid for. The only real events that have occurred are the machine being paid for ($10,000) and it becoming the property of the company buying

DEPRECIATING ASSETS		
	($)	($)
FIXED ASSETS	10,000	
CUMULATIVE DEPRECIATION TO DATE	5,000	
BOOK VALUE		5,000

VALUING A GOING CONCERN			
GOING	($)	GONE	($)
FIXED ASSETS (AT COST)	100,000	FIXED ASSETS (AT COST)	100,000
MINUS DEPRECIATION	20,000	MINUS RESALE VALUE	5,000
NET BOOK VALUE	80,000	NET BOOK LOSS	95,000

GOING OR GONE

A going concern with fixed assets worth $100,000 has a net book value of $80,000 (after depreciation has been deducted). If the business were soon to close down, the assets' resale value of just $5,000 would leave a net book loss of $95,000.

it. The depreciation is a notional figure put in for the reasons given. It follows that the book value of the machine of $5,000 after two years is also a notional figure. The machine could be worth next to nothing (as in the case of a computer) or it could even be worth more (as with a vintage vehicle, for example).

Other assets, such as land and buildings, will be revalued occasionally, and inventory is entered in the books at cost, or market value, whichever is the lower, in line with the principle of conservatism (see below).

TAX RELIEF

Tax assessors usually do not allow depreciation as a business expense but do allow tax relief on the capital expenditure. This is covered in more detail on pp. 160–162. The proportion of capital purchase allowed by the Internal Revenue Service to be offset against taxes is called the writing-down allowance.

Valuing Going Concerns

A "going concern" is a term that has a ring of confidence about it. It seems to imply that all is well. An accountant has looked the business over and given it the all clear by signing off the year-end accounts with that affirmation. In other words, the accounts have been prepared on the going concern basis. In fact, accounting reports always assume that a business will continue to operate indefinitely into the future, unless there is good evidence to

the contrary. This means that the fixed assets of the business are looked at simply as profit generators and not as being available for sale.

Once a business closes, you cannot realistically look at the assets in the same way because they are no longer being used in the business to help generate sales and profits. The most objective figure is what they might realize in the marketplace. The same amount of fixed assets have now been given a resale value of just $5,000, resulting in a $95,000 net book loss.

Using Accounting Conventions

The rules described in this chapter provide a useful framework, but they are open to a range of possible interpretations. Over time, however, a generally accepted approach to how the rules are applied has been arrived at. This approach hinges on the use of the following three accountancy conventions:
- conservatism
- materiality
- consistency

CONSERVATISM

Accountants are often viewed as harbingers of gloom, always prone to taking a pessimistic point of view of the state of your business finances. The fact that a point of view has to be taken at all is the root of the problem. The convention of conservatism means that, given a choice, the accountant takes the figure that will result in a lower end profit. This might mean, for example, taking the higher of two possible expense figures. This approach is taken on the basis that few people are upset if the profit figure at the end of the day is higher than earlier estimates. The converse is, understandably, rarely true.

MATERIALITY

A strict interpretation of depreciation (see pp. 98–100) would lead to all sorts of trivial paperwork. For example, miscellaneous office supplies, such as pencil sharpeners, staplers, and paper clips, all theoretically items of fixed assets, should be depreciated over the course of their working lives. This is obviously a useless exercise with such low-cost items, however, and in practice such items are written off at the time at which they are bought.

Clearly, the level of materiality is not the same for all businesses. A multinational may not keep meticulous records of every item of equipment under $1,000, but this may represent all the equipment a small business has.

CONSISTENCY

Even with the help of these rules and conventions, there is a fair degree of latitude in how you can record and interpret financial information. If you depreciate your assets over two years, you will produce a lower figure for profit than if you chose a longer period.

While it might be appealing to change your depreciation policy to suit your changing needs, you should choose the method that gives the fairest picture of how the company is performing, and stick firmly with that one.

Also, if you use one method this year and another one next year, it becomes more difficult for you and your accountant to evaluate your business. The same should apply to all your other accounting policies. This is because it is very difficult for both you and your accountant to keep track of events in a business that is always changing its accounting methods.

Changing accounting policies may also confuse prospective investors, who may just walk away to the next opportunity.

This does not mean that you are stuck with one method forever. If trading or financing circumstances change, your policy may have to change, too. Any change in accounting policy, however, should not be taken lightly.

View your accountant's approach as conservative rather than pessimistic

CONTROLLING the numbers

Rather as the instruments on a car dashboard tell you different things about its performance – speed, engine temperature, fuel level, and so on – a business too has its own set of gauges. These are known as ratios. Different ratios can be used to highlight how well a business is doing from every conceivable angle. This chapter examines the key measures that reveal the innermost workings of every business, showing how well or badly they are performing.

WATCHING THE BIG PICTURE

Gathering and recording financial information is all a matter of preparation for analyzing a business's performance. Only when you have all the figures in front of you can you see how well (or how badly) your business is doing. The analytical process requires tools, in this case ratios, and their usefulness and limitations need to be understood before they can be used to good effect.

All analysis of financial information involves comparisons: a business may be more/less profitable, may have more/fewer creditors/debtors, or a higher/lower working capital than last year.

A business is constantly changing, and so the most useful way to measure its activity is through ratios. A ratio is simply one number expressed as a proportion of another. For example, traveling 100 miles may not sound too impressive, until you realize that it was done in one hour. The ratio here is 100 miles per hour. If you knew that the vehicle in question had a top speed of 120 miles per hour, you would have some means of comparing it to other vehicles, at least with respect to their speed.

Analyzing with Ratios

In finance, too, ratios can turn sterile data into valuable information in a wide range of different ways, and this can help you to make crucial choices. The chart on the right presents some basic financial information about two businesses that are in very much the same line

of work. Some of the information, such as working capital, capital employed, and bank loans, comes from the balance sheet, while the sales (turnover), gross profit, and net profit come from the profit and loss account.

At first glance, Company B looks in better shape than Company A: its sales, gross profit, and net profit are all higher than company A's. But once you begin to apply some ratios, a slightly different picture starts to emerge.

COMPARING GROSS MARGINS

Turning now to the chart above right, you can see that the gross margin, that is, the gross

FIRST IMPRESSIONS
Company B's sales figures look most impressive compared to Company A's: its sales, gross profit, and net profit figures are all higher. But a more detailed look at this information reveals that all is not well with Company B.

WHO LOOKS IN THE BEST SHAPE FOR FINANCIAL GROWTH?		
	COMPANY A ($)	COMPANY B ($)
SALES	356,000	545,000
GROSS PROFIT	195,000	255,000
WORKING CAPITAL	27,500	100,025
CAPITAL EMPLOYED	60,000	200,000
BANK LOANS	20,000	150,000
NET PROFIT	30,000	40,000

WHO IS IN THE BEST SHAPE FOR FINANCIAL GROWTH?

	COMPANY A ($)	COMPANY B ($)
SALES	356,000	545,000
GROSS PROFIT	195,000	255,000
WORKING CAPITAL	27,500	100,025
CAPITAL EMPLOYED	60,000	200,000
BANK LOANS	20,000	150,000
NET PROFIT	30,000	40,000

	COMPANY A (%)	COMPANY B (%)
ROA	50	20
GEARING	33	75
NET PROFIT	8.4	7.3
SALES/CAPITAL EMPLOYED	($)6	($)3
GROSS MARGIN	54.7	46.7

profit expressed as a percentage of sales, is nearly 55 percent for Company A, while Company B's is only nearly 47 percent. These figures were reached as follows: Company A = 195/356 x 100 = 54.7; Company B = 255/545 x 100 = 46.7. There is a similar disparity in net profit margins.

RETURN ON CAPITAL EMPLOYED/ASSETS (ROA)

The most serious differences show up, however, when information is brought in from the balance sheet. For example, Company B is using $200,000 of capital, tied up in equipment, inventories, premises, and the like, to make just $40,000 in profit. This represents a 20 percent

ANALYSIS USING RATIOS

Despite producing a larger profit, Company B is in a worse shape than Company A. Its gross margin and net profit margin are both lower, and its ROA is only 20 percent.

return on the capital employed (ROA). By comparison, Company A's slightly lower profit of $30,000 is being produced using $60,000 of capital. You do not have to be a financial genius to see that this is less than a third of the capital of Company B. So, Company A's ROA – a ratio that could be considered similar to the interest you might get from a bank on any money deposited – is more than double that of its rival at a rate of 50 percent.

The more you look, the more successful Company A turns out to be. It has much lower bank borrowings, so it would be safer if the economic climate turned sour, and its sales per dollar tied up in capital is double that of Company B. In summary, Company A may sell fewer products and make less profit, but it is much more profitable, makes more efficient use of its resources, and is unlikely ever to be at the mercy of its bankers.

To use a personal illustration, would you rather have $200,000 of your money invested with someone giving you a return of $40,000, or $60,000 invested with someone giving you a return of $30,000? The choice is not a difficult one to make.

The financial ratios used in this example are more fully explained in *Going into Detail* (see pp. 112–129).

MONEY SAVER

Sophisticated accounting software has "report generator" programs that provide analysis of the ratios. This is like having an accountant advising on any problems in interpreting the ratios. Such software may be more expensive but will save money in the long run by improving the quality of your decisions.

Some Problems with Ratios

There is a natural feeling with financial ratios to think that high figures are good ones and that an upward trend represents the right direction. Unfortunately, there is no general rule on which way is right for financial ratios. In some cases, a high figure is good; in others, a low figure is best. Indeed, there are even circumstances in which ratios of the same value are not as good as each other. These occur when taking into account the following:

■ different financial situations
■ the sizes of different businesses
■ seasonal factors
■ changes in inflation

THE FINANCIAL DIPSTICK
In general, business performance as measured by ratios is best thought of as lying within a range, rather like the oil level that is indicated on the dipstick of a vehicle. So, for example, if liquidity (current ratio) stays between 1.5:1 and 2.5:1, it would be acceptable. Any move outside that range would be a cause for concern, albeit different concerns.

DIFFERENT FINANCIAL SITUATIONS

Looking at the two working capital statements in the chart below, you can see that the amount of working capital in each example is the same

at $16,410, as are the current assets and current liabilities, at $23,100 and $6,690 respectively. It follows that any ratio using these factors would also be the same. For example, the current ratios (current assets divided by current liabilities) in these two examples are

DIFFICULT COMPARISONS		COMPANY A ($)	COMPANY B ($)
CURRENT ASSETS	Inventory	10,000	22,990
	Owed by debtors	13,000	100
	Cash	100	10
	TOTAL CURRENT ASSETS	23,100	23,100
MINUS CURRENT LIABILITIES	Overdraft	5,000	90
	Owed to creditors	1,690	6,600
	TOTAL CURRENT LIABILITIES	6,690	6,690
NET CURRENT ASSETS		16,410	16,410
CURRENT RATIO		3.4:1	3.4:1

BEYOND THE SIMILARITIES
Company A and Company B are identical in their total current assets, total current liabilities, and net current assets, but that does not mean that they are in the same financial shape. Company A's higher number of debtors and lower levels of inventory put it in a more favorable position than Company B.

identical at 3.4:1. What must be looked at now are the differences.

For Company A there is a reasonable chance that some cash will come in from debtors, certainly enough to meet the modest creditor position. For Company B, however, there is no possibility of useful amounts of cash coming in from business, with debtors owing only $100; while creditors, who are owed the relatively substantial figure of $6,600, pose a real threat to financial stability.

The inventory figure for Company B of nearly $23,000 is valuable only if the inventory is salable, and in any event the cash will be a long time coming in. Customers have to be found and sold to, and then there is a wait until they pay. Both these examples show that although the current ratios are identical, the businesses are by no means in identical situations.

As a general rule, a higher working capital ratio is regarded as a move in the wrong direction. The more money a business has tied up in working capital, the more difficult it is to make a satisfactory ROA, simply because the larger the denominator, the lower the ROA.

In some cases, the right direction is more obvious. A high ROA is usually better than a low one, but even this situation can be a danger

Look at average results for a realistic view; do not be misled by low or high sales figures.

signal, warning that higher risks are being taken. And not all high profit ratios are good: sometimes a higher profit margin can lead to reduced sales volume and so to lower overall profits.

SIZES OF DIFFERENT BUSINESSES

There can also be problems in trying to compare one business's ratios with another. You would not, for example, expect a Focus to be able to cover a mile as quickly as a Jaguar. A new small business can achieve quite startling sales growth ratios in the early months and years. Expanding from $10,000 sales in the first six months to $100,000 in the second would not be unusual, yet to expect a mature business to achieve the same rate of growth would be unrealistic. So be careful to make sure that like is being compared with like. Allowances must also be made for differing circumstances in the businesses being compared (or, if the circumstances are the same, then the industry/ economic environment of the years compared).

A MATURE BUSINESS
Growth has to be relevant to the size of the business and the size of the market. For example, if BP grew from sales of $5 billion to $25 billion, it would wipe out every other oil company in the world.

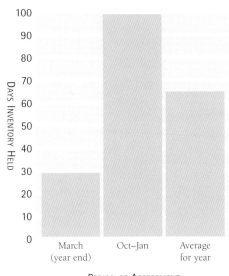

PERIOD OF ASSESSMENT

SEASONAL VARIATIONS
As this chart shows, taking inventory levels at any one time as being indicative of performance would be a mistake. The average figure is the one that gives a true picture.

Using either of these stock figures could give a false picture, but the average of the two might be nearer the mark.

In the example on the left you can see that the year-end inventory figure from the accounts is barely a third of the high sales level later in the year. Basing any calculations on either figure would be a mistake. An average of somewhere between the high and low figures would be a more representative figure on which to work.

CHANGES IN INFLATION

Financial ratios all use money as the basis for comparison, and historical money at that. This would not be so bad if all these monies were from the same date in the past, but that is not so. You have to acccept that comparing one year with another may not be very meaningful unless you account for the change in the value of money caused by inflation.

In recent years, inflation has been relatively low in the developed world, ranging between 3 and 6 percent. But it has not always been low, and if inflation increases again you will have to allow for it in your ratio analysis. Even at 4 percent inflation, a figure of $1,000 from a four-year-old set of accounts would equate to just $855 today.

You may, for example, have calculated from their accounts that a competitor has been growing at 8 percent on average over the past four years, without taking inflation into account. If inflation has been running at an average of 4 percent, however, then the company's real growth has been only 4 percent. Furthermore, if the economy has also been growing at 4 percent, then it is possible that the company, far from growing healthily, as you had believed, has in fact been doing no more than drifting along with the current and achieving little growth.

It is also important to check that one business's idea of an account category, for instance current assets, is the same as yours. The concepts and principles used to prepare accounts do leave some scope for differences, and apparent variations may not, in fact, really exist. The notes to the accounts will help clarify this matter and explain any anomalies you may find. These are to be found at the end of the financial statements.

SEASONAL FACTORS

Many ratios make use of information in the balance sheet. However, balance sheets are prepared at one particular moment in time and so may not represent the average situation.

For example, seasonal factors can cause a business's sales to be particularly high once or twice a year. A balance sheet prepared just before one of these seasonal upturns might show very high inventory levels, bought in specially to meet this demand, with accompanying very low cash, as a result of this inventory purchase and a slack business period. Conversely, a look at the balance sheet just after the upturn might show very high cash and rather low inventory levels.

FACTORS THAT AFFECT ROA

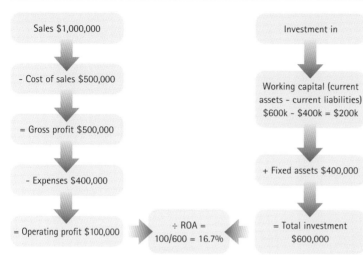

Sales $1,000,000

- Cost of sales $500,000

= Gross profit $500,000

- Expenses $400,000

= Operating profit $100,000

÷ ROA = 100/600 = 16.7%

Investment in

Working capital (current assets - current liabilities) $600k - $400k = $200k

+ Fixed assets $400,000

= Total investment $600,000

Deciding on Financial Objectives

Before you can compare a business's performance using ratios, you need to have some idea of what that business wanted to, or should have been able to, achieve. Achieving a 15 percent increase in sales might sound good, but if 25 percent has been set as a realistic target, then the lower figure does not impress.

All well-managed businesses share some common objectives in the area of finance, and it is regarding performance in those areas that measurement is required. To make a satisfactory return on the capital or resources employed (ROA), be it money or people, firms need to keep idle assets (or people) to a minimum. In the long run all businesses have to produce a satisfactory return on the money invested in them, or the money will simply go elsewhere.

FACTORS AFFECTING ROA

Most, although not all, ratio analysis is about probing the various effects of a range of different actions on ROA.

A useful generic model to help understand the factors affecting ROA is shown in the chart above. The left-hand side of the chart is a cut-down profit and loss account and the right-hand side is a slice of the balance sheet, showing how the money is tied up. The numbers included show a return of $100,000 on capital employed of $600,000, which equates to 16.7 percent.

■ **INCREASED SALES OR DECREASED COSTS** Either of these could result in an increase in profit. If the working capital, inventories, and debtors, for example, and the fixed assets (buildings, equipment, etc.) do not rise, then the ROA will improve. For

TIME SAVER

When deciding on your financial objectives, you should do some research to find out how other businesses similar to your own have performed. You can do this by obtaining copies of their accounts, which usually come with key profit ratios already calculated.

FINANCIAL MATURITY

The maturity of a business is often reflected in its accounting system. A newly set-up business may keep no records at all, but by its second year it should have a basic bookkeeping system up and running. During its third year of operation, the business should be keeping a full set of accounts, and in its fourth year it can use these accounts to plan budgets and analyze ratios.

example, if the profit rises to $120,000, while the capital employed stays at $600,000, the ROA rises to 20 percent (120/600 x 100).

▧ **A REDUCTION IN INVESTMENT** The same result can be achieved by reducing investment in fixed assets and working capital required to produce a given level of profit. In this example, if you could trim the stock holding down and employ less equipment, thereby reducing the capital employed from $600,000 to $500,000 (while still getting the same output and profit), the ROA would once again be 20 percent (100/500 x 100).

MAINTAINING A SOUND FINANCIAL POSITION

Businesses also want to maintain a sound financial position, achieve a healthy rate of growth, and exhibit signs of financial maturity. Achieving these objectives may require carrying more rather than less inventory, for example, in addition to having cash in hand for the unexpected. Those actions may appear to make the business look less efficient in the short run, but they will allow it to weather storms and so become more successful.

Some stability in ratios will be seen as a sign of financial maturity by banks and other financial institutions, and will lend some credibility to your projections. This in turn will improve your creditworthiness and make borrowing easier and perhaps less costly.

For example, a business that has consistently collected its money from customers in under 40 days will look more soundly run than one

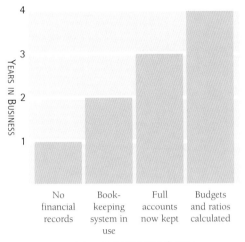

LEVEL OF ACCOUNTING SYSTEM

that took 45 days one year, 30 the next, followed by a return to 45 days. The average is the same, but in one case it looks as though the business has policies and procedures for collecting money that work, while in the other it looks more as though panic measures were introduced to deal with a cash-flow problem, then promptly dropped when cash became easier.

Applying the Yardsticks

In addition to deciding which areas to examine, you need to know what standards to compare performance against. There are four generally accepted yardsticks that you can use. You can compare this year's results with:
■ last year's performance
■ self-imposed targets
■ a competitor's performance
■ industrywide performances (benchmarking)

COMPARING THIS YEAR WITH LAST YEAR

First, you might want to see how well you are doing this year compared with last, comparing performance against a historical standard. This is the way in which growth in sales or profits is often measured. There are, however, several limitations to this sort of comparison.

If accounting methods change from year to year, perhaps in the way depreciation is dealt with, then you are not comparing like with like. Also, the monies in one year are not the same as the monies in another, simply because inflation has changed them. An even more fundamental weakness with using historical comparisons alone is that your business may be quite different over time. Customers, products, staff, and equipment all change, so comparing one year with another may highlight a difference without telling you much about why it occurred.

For example, if sales and profits of a business last year were $100,000 and $20,000 respectively, and this year they are $200,000 and $40,000, at first glance you would think that the business had done twice as well. But if you knew that all of that increase came from a special onetime order of a product that had been bought in from outside, so that the business acted only as a middleman, you might not be so impressed.

COMPARING THIS YEAR WITH A SET TARGET

A second type of comparison would be more revealing in these circumstances. Here you compare performance against the standards set for yourself. For example, you may want to double sales or add 25 percent to profits, enter a new market, or launch new products and services. These objectives are set out in a budget that says, in effect, that you plan to spend this amount of money to achieve that particular result in this time period. Comparisons can then be made between actual results and the budget (see pp. 130–135).

COMPARING THIS YEAR WITH A COMPETITOR'S RESULTS

You may also want to see how well you are doing compared with someone else's business, perhaps a local competitor or someone in a similar line of business elsewhere. This may provide useful pointers to where improvements can be made or to new business opportunities. For this type of analysis you need external information. There is a wealth of readily available financial data on companies and industries to be found through credit-rating agencies and in U.S. Securities and Exchange Commission filings.

USING BENCHMARKING

A fourth yardstick you can use is benchmarking. Some business sectors, such as the hypothetical example given in the chart below, submit information in an anonymous form to industry or trade groups. Then information, often in the form of ratios, is distributed so that people can see how well their business is doing compared with the best or average of their peers.

In the example below, if your delivery reliability was less than 85 percent and your employees were absent for more than 5 percent of the time, then your performance is worse than average and falls far below the best.

PEER COMPARISONS
Benchmark ratios allow you to compare your performance with that of the best in your industy. A below average performance should act as a warning signal that all is not well with your business.

BENCHMARKING SMALL ENGINEERING FIRMS		AVERAGE	TOP 25%	TOP 10%
DELIVERY RELIABILITY		87%	98%	100%
TRAINING ON THE JOB	Existing employees	5 days	8 days	10 days
	New employees	12 days	20 days	28 days
ABSENTEEISM		3.2%	2%	1%

GOING INTO DETAIL

Rather as the various instruments on a car's dashboard tell you different things about its performance, such as speed, engine temperature, fuel level, and so on, so various ratios are used to reveal the different aspects of how a business is performing. Understanding how to interpret these ratios is a necessary first step before you can decide on areas for improvement in your business. The ratios will also tell you essential information about competitors, customers, and suppliers, and how successfully, or otherwise, their businesses are performing. In this chapter the key measures are examined that reveal the innermost workings of every business, including your own, showing how well or badly it is performing and how safe or risky it is.

For your own business you should have all the information readily at hand, as long as you have kept your bookkeeping up-to-date and prepared balance sheets and profit and loss accounts. Businesses that are incorporated have to file their accounts, which are then in the public domain and, as such, available to everyone.

Financial ratios (many of which are expressed as percentages – a type of ratio in which everything is based against 100) can be clustered under a number of headings, each of which probes a different aspect of a business's performance. The areas covered in this chapter are the following:
▓ profitability
▓ liquidity
▓ solvency
▓ growth
▓ value
▓ safety

A set of sample accounts for an imaginary company named Fast Food Inc. is shown on pp. 113–114. Analyses of these accounts are used throughout the chapter to illustrate the use of financial ratios. These are much simplified accounts, and not everything you would expect to see in a set of accounts has been included, but they provide enough information to illustrate the key ratios.

Measuring Profitability

The usual ratios to measure profitability or the efficient use of resources comprise:
▓ gross margin percentage
▓ operating margin pecentage
▓ net margin percentage
▓ Return on Assets (ROA)
▓ Return on Investment (ROI)
▓ profits per employee

GROSS MARGIN PERCENTAGE
To arrive at this figure, you need to deduct the cost of sales from the sales revenue, and then express the result as a percentage of sales. The higher the percentage, the greater the value added to the goods and services produced.

$$\text{Gross margin} = \frac{\text{Gross profit} \times 100}{\text{Sales}}$$

In this case, the gross margin percentage for Fast Food in year 1 is:

$$\text{Gross margin} = \frac{50{,}000 \times 100}{100{,}000} = 50\%$$

For year 2 the gross margin percentage for Fast Food has moved down slightly to 48 percent.

THE PROFIT AND LOSS STATEMENT FOR FAST FOOD INC. FOR PAST TWO YEARS		YEAR 1 ($)	%	YEAR 2 ($)	%
SALES		100,000	100	130,000	100
COST OF SALES	Materials	30,000	30	43,000	33
	Labor	20,000	20	25,000	19
	COST OF GOODS SOLD	50,000		68,000	
GROSS PROFIT		50,000	50	62,000	48
EXPENSES	Rent	18,000		20,000	
	Wages	12,000		13,000	
	Advertising	3,000		3,000	
	Depreciation			2,000	
	TOTAL EXPENSES	33,000		38,000	
OPERATING PROFIT		17,000	17	24,000	18.5
DEDUCT INTEREST ON	Borrowings	2,150		2,050	
NET PROFIT BEFORE TAX		14,850	14.8	21,950	16.8
TAX PAID AT 20%		2,970		4,390	
NET PROFIT AFTER TAX		11,880	11.88	17,560	13.5
NUMBER OF EMPLOYEES		2		4	

FAST FOOD'S PROFIT AND LOSS STATEMENT
The information provided here on sales, expenses, and borrowings enables Fast Food's accountant to calculate their net profit after tax. This is the money that can be used to pay dividends to shareholders or can be invested in the business.

Some possible causes for this downward shift include: lower selling prices, higher material or labor costs, wastage, and theft. In addition to these, a change in the types of products or services being sold can be a cause for such a downward movement.

OPERATING MARGIN PERCENTAGE
In this case you deduct not only the cost of sales but also expenses (other than finance charges, such as interest, and taxes).

This is a measure of how well the management is running the business. It is

BALANCE SHEET FOR FAST FOOD INC. FOR PAST TWO YEARS

		YEAR 1	YEAR 2
NET ASSETS EMPLOYED		$	$
FIXED ASSETS	Furniture and equipment	12,500	30,110
	Minus depreciation		2,000
	BOOK VALUE		28,110
CURRENT ASSETS	Inventory	10,000	12,000
	Owed by debtors	13,000	13,000
	Cash	100	500
	TOTAL CURRENT ASSETS	23,100	25,500
MINUS CURRENT LIABILITIES	Overdraft	5,000	6,000
	Owed to creditors	1,690	5,500
	TOTAL CURRENT LIABILITIES	6,690	11,500
NET CURRENT ASSETS		16,410	14,000
TOTAL ASSETS		28,910	42,110
MINUS CREDITORS OVER ONE YEAR	Long-term bank loan	10,000	10,000
NET TOTAL ASSETS		18,910	32,110
FINANCED BY	Shareholders' funds	10,000	18,940
	Profit retained (reserves)	8,910	13,170
TOTAL SHAREHOLDERS' FUNDS		18,910	32,110

FAST FOOD'S
BALANCE SHEET
Deducting all of Fast Food's liabilities from its fixed and current assets produces the figure for its total assets. This figure also represents the amount of capital the owner has invested in the business.

usually assumed that financing decisions are taken by the business owner rather than the manager (although obviously in a small business the owner and manager are usually one and the same). It is also assumed that interest and tax rates are influenced by macroeconomic factors, thus taking decisions concerning these matters out of management control and accountability.

$$\text{Operating margin} = \frac{\text{Operating profit}}{\text{Sales}} \times 100$$

In this case, the operating profit percentage for Fast Food in year 1 is:

$$\text{Operating margin} = \frac{17,000 \times 100}{100,000} = 17\%$$

In year 2 this percentage is up slightly to 18.5 percent, which is for the most part the result of total expenses being only $5,000 higher ($38,000 compared to $33,000) while sales were $30,000 higher.

NET MARGIN PERCENTAGE

This is the bottom line figure. It can be shown either before tax (EBIT – earnings before interest and tax) or after tax. In its after tax form, which is used here, it represents the sum available to be either distributed as dividends or retained by the business owner to invest in the future of the business.

$$\text{Net margin} = \frac{\text{Net profit}}{\text{Sales}} \times 100$$

In this example, the calculation for Fast Food in year 1 is:

$$\text{Net margin} = \frac{11,880 \times 100}{100,000} = 11.88\%$$

This would generally be considered a respectable figure, the range being between 5 and 25 percent for most businesses.

In year 2 it is up to 13.5 percent, which is largely brought about by the same reasons that led to the increase in operating profit. The fact that the cost of borrowing did not go up,

because the growth was financed by retained profits, also helped to achieve this increase in the net margin percentage.

RETURN ON ASSETS (ROA)

This is the primary measure of performance for most businesses. If, for example, $10,000 invested in a bank earned you $500 interest in a year, then the return on your capital employed would be 5 percent ($500 ÷ $10,000 x 100 = 5%).

In a business, this ratio is calculated by expressing the operating profit (that is, profit before interest and taxes) as a percentage of the total capital employed – both in fixed assets and in working capital (called net current assets in the balance sheet).

$$\text{ROA} = \frac{\text{Operating profit}}{\text{Fixed assets} + \text{Working capital}} \times 10$$

Note that the bottom part of the equation (the fixed assets + working capital) will equal the return on the shareholders' funds plus the long-term loans, that is, the figure you will find in the "financed by" part toward the bottom of the balance sheet.

In year 1 at Fast Food the ROA is:

$$\text{ROA} = \frac{17,000}{12,500 + 16,410} \times 100 = 59\%$$

In year 2 it is much the same, at 57 percent. Both figures represent excellent results.

RETURN ON INVESTMENT (ROI)

The shareholders are usually most interested in the net return on their investment. So in this case you are concerned with the profit left after the interest has been paid on any loans to the business and after the taxman has had his slice. The shareholders have invested not only their initial stake but also any profits left in the business for future growth.

$$\text{ROI} = \frac{\text{Net profit after tax and interest}}{\text{Total shareholders' fund}} \times 100$$

In this example, in year 1 the calculation of the

ROI for Fast Food is:

$$ROI = \frac{11,880}{18,910} \times 100 = 63$$

For small firms in general this ratio can be anywhere between a few percentage points and upward of 35 percent. Results such as those in this example are excellent.

Profit Per Employee

If, as in most cases, your principal "assets" are people rather than capital assets, such as machines, then you will need to monitor what value your employees are contributing.

$$\text{Profit per employee} = \frac{\text{Net profit (after interest, but before tax)}}{\text{Number of employees}}$$

In Fast Food's case, the ratio for year 1 is:

$$\text{Profit per employee} = \frac{14,850}{2} = \$7,425$$

The figure drops sharply during the following year to $5,487 profit per head. This is not very unusual because small businesses tend to move forward in a jerky fashion. For a firm employing 30 people, taking on two more members of staff would be a relatively small step that would not affect their finances too much. But for Fast Food such a move would represent a doubling of their workforce and therefore a huge increase in their fixed costs.

It can be useful to calculate the sales per employee too, to give you a feel for activity levels. As you can see from the table on the right, things at Fast Food are slowing down, with profits per employee dropping from $7,425 to $5,487.

You could then go on and benchmark Fast Food against others in the industry (see p. 111 for information on benchmarking). The table on p. 117 compares the average performance of

Measuring Performance
By bringing together all the different ratios calculated so far, a profitability chart can be drawn up. You can now see at a glance how Fast Food is performing.

all small firms in the region, by sector, with that of Fast Food for sales per employee and ROA. such comparisons can be helpful to a business.

Were Fast Food your business operating in the retail market, you would see opportunities for improvement in terms of sales per employee. The ROA performance, however, is above average. The message here is that perhaps the capital investment in good new equipment is paying off, but you need to get a better result from your people. Incentive programs, with rewards worth striving for, could be a way of achieving this.

Measuring Liquidity

Liquidity is a measure of a firm's ability to meet its current financial obligations as and when they fall due. But keeping sufficient financing, or working capital, available to meet these obligations is not necessarily the sound idea it would appear to be. The higher the level of working capital, the higher the overall

FAST FOOD'S PROFITABILITY AT A GLANCE		
	YEAR 1	YEAR 2
GROSS MARGIN	50%	48%
OPERATING MARGIN	17%	18.5%
NET MARGIN	11.88%	13.51%
RETURN ON ASSETS (ROA)	59%	57%
RETURN ON INVESTMENT (ROI)	63%	55%
PROFIT PER EMPLOYEE	$7,425	$5,487

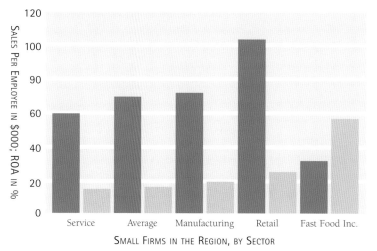

BENCHMARKING FAST FOOD

Comparing Fast Food's sales per employee and ROA with figures for small businesses in the same region is a very informative exercise. While the ROA is well above average, sales-per-employee leave much to be desired.

■ SALES PER EMPLOYEE $000

▨ ROA %

SMALL FIRMS IN THE REGION, BY SECTOR

amount of capital that is being used. That, in turn, means that profits have to be that much higher to make the same (or better) return on the capital employed.

The following measures all help to assess liquidity, or the lack of it:

■ current ratio
■ quick ratio
■ credit control ratios
■ aging debtors
■ average collection period
■ average payment period
■ inventory control
■ circulation of working capital

All of these measures are analyzed below, with reference to Fast Food's performance, so that you can understand how they are calculated and what their relevance is.

CURRENT RATIO

To identify the current ratio, you need to do the following calculation:

$$\text{Current ratio} = \frac{\text{Current assets}}{\text{Current liabilities}}$$

In the accounts for Fast Food, the first year's picture on the balance sheet shows $23,100 current assets to $6,690 current liabilities.

Therefore, for Fast Food, the calculation is:

$$\text{Current ratio} = \frac{23,100}{6,690} = 3.4$$

This shows current liabilities to be covered 3.4 times, and the ratio is usually expressed in the form 3.4:1. In the second year this has come down to 2.2:1 (25,500 ÷ 11,500 = 2.2).

At first glance, this last figure may look worse than the first year's position. Certainly, current liabilities have grown faster than current assets, but up to a point this is in fact a desirable state of affairs, because it means that the business is having to find less money to finance its working capital.

There is really only one rule that you need to remember about the level of a current ratio: it should be as close to 1:1 as the safe conduct of the business will allow.

This will not be the same for every type of business, however. A store buying finished goods on credit and selling them for cash could run safely at 1.3:1. A manufacturer, with raw materials to store and customers to finance, may need over 2:1. This is because the period between paying out cash for raw materials and receiving cash from customers is longer in a manufacturing business than in a retail business.

QUICK RATIO

In this ratio, only assets that can be realized quickly, such as debtors and cash in hand, are related to current liabilities. Note that the term "debtors" refers to the amount owed by debtors.

$$\text{Quick ratio} = \frac{\text{Debtors} + \text{Cash}}{\text{Current liabilities}}$$

In the Fast Food example, looking at year 1 only, you would exclude the $10,000 stock because, before it could be realized, you would need to find customers to sell it to, and then collect the cash. All this might take several months. Fast Food's ratio would therefore be:

$$\text{Quick ratio} = \frac{13,100}{6,690} = 1.9$$

In the second year this has dropped to 1.2:1 (13,500 ÷ 11,500). A quick ratio of 0.8:1 would be acceptable for most businesses.

CREDIT CONTROL RATIOS

Any small business selling on credit knows just how quickly cash flow can become a problem. This is particularly true if the customers are big companies, which often pay their bills more slowly than do smaller companies.

Surprisingly enough, bad debts (those that are never paid) are rarely as serious a problem as slow payers. Many companies think nothing of taking three months' credit, and it is important to remember that, even if your terms are net 30 days, it will often be nearer 45 days, or possibly longer, before you are actually paid.

TIME SAVER

A simple way to keep track of liquidity is to total the amount of money you are owed by customers and compare that with the money you owe to suppliers. If the numbers are broadly similar, you are likely to be able to pay bills as they fall due. The higher the favorable margin, the better.

This to some extent depends on how frequently invoices are sent out. Assuming they do not go out each day, and, perhaps more importantly, that your customer batches bills for payment monthly, then that is how things will work out. Help is at hand, though, with the following two control methods.

AGING YOUR DEBTORS

The first method of monitoring debts is to prepare a schedule of all your debtors ranked by age of debt. The table shown above right gives some idea of how this might be done. This method has the merit of focusing attention clearly on specific problem accounts. Once you have gotten the system going, it will pay dividends.

AVERAGE COLLECTION PERIOD

The second technique for monitoring debtors is using the ratio of average collection period. This ratio is calculated by expressing a business' debtors as a proportion of its credit sales, and then relating that figure to the days of the operational cycle in the period in question.

$$\text{Average collection period} = \frac{\text{Debtors}}{\text{Sales}} \times 365$$

Let us suppose that all Fast Food's sales are on credit and the periods in question are both 365-day years (that is, no leap years). In year 1, the ratio would be:

$$\text{Average collection period} = \frac{13,000}{100,000} \times 365 = 47$$

In year 2, the collection period is 36 days (13,000 ÷ 130,000 x 365 = 36). In this second year, therefore, Fast Food is collecting its cash from debtors 11 days sooner than in year 1. Their total debtors are the same, but the relative amount is lower in year 2. Fast Food's sales have grown by 30 percent to $130,000, and their debtors have remained at $13,000.

This is a good control ratio, which has the merit of being easily translatable into a figure anyone can understand, showing how much it is costing a business to give credit to customers.

FAST FOOD'S DEBTORS' SCHEDULE – END OF YEAR 1

DEBTOR	2 MONTHS OR LESS ($)	3 MONTHS ($)	4 MONTHS ($)	OVER 4 MONTHS ($)	TOTAL ($)
SMITH & CO	1,000				
BROWN & SON	1,000				
BARNES		3,000			
ELLIOTS		2,500			
RUTLINS			500		
LARKIN & CO			2,500		
BRIGHT INC				2,500	
TOTAL	2,000	5,500	3,000	2,500	13,000

RANKING DEBTORS BY AGE

Listing all your debtors by how long their bills have remained unpaid will enable you to keep track of the money that is owed to you.

If, for example, Fast Food is paying 10 percent for an overdraft, then giving $13,000 credit for 36 days will cost $128.22 (10 percent x $13,000 x 36 ÷ 365 = $128.22).

AVERAGE PAYMENT PERIOD

Of course, the credit world is not all one-sided. Once a small business has established itself, it too will be taking credit. You can usually rely

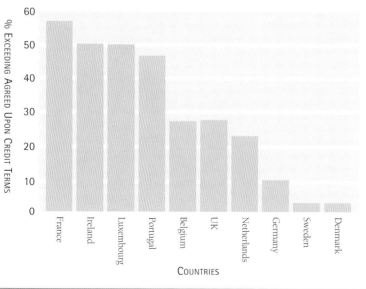

% EXCEEDING AGREED UPON CREDIT TERMS

Countries: France, Ireland, Luxembourg, Portugal, Belgium, UK, Netherlands, Germany, Sweden, Denmark

COUNTRIES

VARIATIONS IN PAYMENT TIMES

This chart shows the percentage of companies exceeding agreed upon credit terms in selected European countries. If you are selling into overseas markets, the practice of punctual payments can vary widely.

on your suppliers to keep you informed of your indebtedness, but only on an individual basis. To get the overall picture, it would be prudent to calculate how many days' credit, on average, are being taken from suppliers, using a very similar sum to average collection period. Note that the term "creditors" in the ratio means the amount of money you owe to creditors.

$$\text{Average payment period} = \frac{\text{Creditors}}{\text{Materials}} \times 365$$

For Fast Food, in year 1, the ratio would be:

$$\text{Average payment period} = \frac{1,690}{30,000} \times 365 = 21 \text{ days}$$

In year 2, this ratio would be 47 days (5,500 ÷ 43,000 x 365 = 47). The difference in these ratios probably reflects Fast Food's greater creditworthiness in year 2 (the amount for purchases assumes that all materials were purchased in the period in question). The longer the credit period you can take from your suppliers, the better, provided that you still meet their payment terms.

There are two other useful techniques to help the business manager keep track of these events: relating credit given to credit taken and aging your creditors.

RELATING CREDIT GIVEN TO CREDIT TAKEN

One technique is simply to relate days' credit given to days' credit taken. If they balance out, then you are about even in the credit game.

In year 1, Fast Food gave 47 days' credit to their customers and took only 21 days from their suppliers, so they were a loser. In the second year they got ahead, giving only 36 days while taking 47.

AGING YOUR CREDITORS

The other technique is to age your creditors in exactly the same way as the debtors (see p. 118). In this way it is possible to see at a glance which suppliers have been owed what sums of money, and for how long

INVENTORY CONTROL

A manufacturing, subcontracting, or assembling business, such as a picture framer, will have to purchase raw materials and work on them to produce finished goods. It will have to keep track of three sorts of inventory: raw materials, work in progress, and finished goods. A business such as a building contractor may hold no inventory at all, buying materials only as and when needed for each job. A retailing business, such as a store, will probably be concerned only with purchasing finished goods on credit and selling them for cash. If you assume that all of Fast Food's inventory is in finished goods, then the control ratio you can use is as follows:

$$\text{Days' finished goods inventory} = \frac{\text{Finished goods inventory}}{\text{Cost of sales}} \times \text{days in period}$$

Note that the cost of sales is used because it accurately reflects the amount of inventory, whereas the sales figure includes other items, such as the profit margin. If you are looking at the accounts of another company, it is probable that the only figure available for your calculations will be that for sales. In this case, it can be used as an approximation.

For Fast Food in year 1, this ratio is:

$$\text{Days' finished goods inventory} = \frac{10,000}{50,000} \times 365 = 73 \text{ days}$$

In year 2, the ratio is 64 days (12,000 ÷ 68,000 x 365 = 64).

It is difficult to make rules about inventory levels. A business has to carry enough inventory to meet demand, and a retail business must have it on display and on hand. However, if Fast Food's supplier can always deliver within 14 days, it would be unnecessary to carry 73 days' stock.

The same basic equation can be applied to both raw material and work-in-progress inventory, but to calculate raw materials inventory you should substitute raw materials consumed ("materials" on the profit and loss statement) in the equation for cost of sales.

Once again, the strength of this ratio is that a business can quickly and easily calculate how much it is costing them to carry a given level of inventory, in just the same way as customer credit costs are calculated. Another way to look at inventory control is to see how often your inventory is turned over each year.

$$\text{Inventory turnover} = \frac{\text{Cost of sales}}{\text{Inventory}}$$

So, for Fast Food this ratio would be:

$$\text{Inventory turnover} = \frac{50,000}{10,000} = 5$$

CIRCULATION OF WORKING CAPITAL

While the current ratio calculated previously gives an overall feel for a business' ability to pay its creditors, this is of less interest to the manager of a business, who is more concerned with how well the money tied up in working capital is being used.

From Fast Food's balance sheet for the last two years (see p. 114) you can see that net current assets – another name for working capital – have fallen from $16,410 to $14,000. This fall is not too dramatic in itself, but now look at these figures in relation to the level of business activity in each year and you will see them in a different light.

The ratio for calculating the circulation of working capital is:

$$\text{Circulation of working capital} = \frac{\text{Sales}}{\text{Working capital}}$$

For year 1 for Fast Food this is:

$$\text{Circulation of working capital} = \frac{100,000}{16,410} = 6x \text{ (times)}$$

In other words, each $1 of Fast Food's working capital produces $6 of sales. For year 2, the ratio is now 9 times, or $9 ($130,000 ÷ $14,000 = 9).

You can see from this calculation that not only has Fast Food got less money tied up in working capital in its second year of operation than in its first, but also that it has used its working capital more efficiently. In other words, it has circulated its working capital faster. Each $1 of working capital now produces $9 of sales, as opposed to only $6 in the first year, and because each $1 of sales makes profit, it follows that the faster the working capital is turned around, the higher the profit level will be.

The chart at the top of p. 122 illustrates what happens to a business' profits when its working capital circulation is increased step by step from a basic one times up to an impressive 10 times.

CONTROLLING INVENTORY
Any retail business must ensure that it carries enough inventory to keep the shelves filled to meet demand at all times. An efficient inventory control system is essential to maintain the right levels.

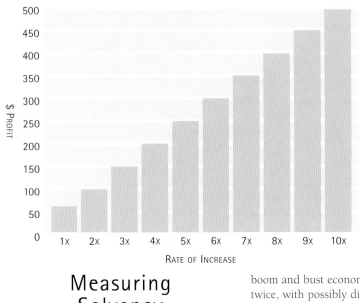

INCREASING WORKING
CAPITAL CIRCULATION
*This chart shows the effect
on profits of increasing the
rate of circulation of
working capital in a
business that makes $50
gross profit per $100 sales.*

Measuring Solvency

Just as liquidity is concerned with the short-term position, "solvency" is the term used to describe a business' long-term financial position. Operating while insolvent is a serious matter, and business owners who knowingly do so may find themselves being held personally accountable for debts so incurred.

The long-term financial position consists of looking at two things: the proportion of a business' funds that is borrowed, as opposed to being put up by the shareholders, and how well the business is able to meet any interest costs associated with such borrowing.

LEVERAGING

The more borrowed money a business uses, as opposed to that put in by the shareholders (through initial capital injection or by reinvesting profits in the business), the more highly leveraged the business is.

Highly leveraged businesses can be vulnerable either when sales dip sharply, as in a recession, or when interest rates skyrocket, as in a boom. If one follows the other, as can happen in a boom and bust economy, they may be hit twice, with possibly disastrous consequences.

$$\text{Leveraging} = \frac{\text{Debt (Long-term borrowings)} \times 100}{\text{Debt} + \text{Shareholders' funds}}$$

(Debt is listed under minus creditors over 1 year.)

For Fast Food, the ratio for year 1 is:

$$\text{Leveraging} = \frac{10,000}{(10,000 + 18,910)} \times 100 = 35\%$$

This means that 35 percent of the money used in the business was borrowed in the first year. In the second year, that drops to 24 percent $(10,000 \div [10,000 + 32,110] \times 100 = 24)$.

Small firms' leveraging levels on average range from 60 down to 30 percent. But many small firms are probably seriously overleveraged, especially as they go into the first stages of growth. This puts them in a vulnerable position.

INTEREST COVER

While leveraging is important, it is equally important to look at a company's ability to service the interest on that borrowing. If you were fortunate enough to inherit $250,000, you could buy a substantial house for $500,000 million and only be 50 percent leveraged.

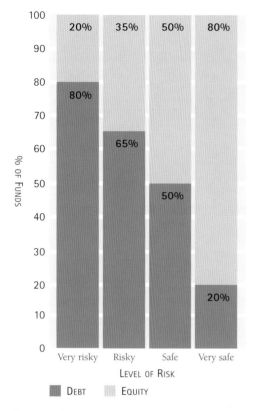

100
90
80
70
60
50
40
30
20
10
0

% OF FUNDS

| 20% | 35% | 50% | 80% |
| 80% | 65% | 50% | 20% |

Very risky   Risky   Safe   Very safe

LEVEL OF RISK

■ DEBT   ■ EQUITY

FINANCIAL RISK

Overleveraged businesses run at high risk because the proportion of their funds that are borrowed is very high. A safer position is reached once debt and equity are balanced, and any further decrease in debt adds to the safety of the business.

What may be difficult is to find the $2,000 per month required to pay the interest on the loan for the remaining $250,000.

$$\text{Interest cover} = \frac{\text{Operating profit}}{\text{Interest on long-term debt}}$$

So, Fast Food's interest cover for year 1 is:

$$\text{Interest cover} = \frac{17,000}{2,150} = 8x$$

In year 2, it increases to nearly 12 times (24,000 ÷ 2,050).

Anything upward of four times interest cover would be viewed as respectable; below three times might be worrying.

Measuring Growth

The most common measures of growth are sales turnover and the number of employees (popular yardsticks with owners and governments, respectively), but neither is of much use unless profit is taken into account. Many businesses rapidly aspire to growing turnover with little regard to profitability. Healthy growth, however, requires both sales turnover and profits being grown in proportion.

There are five styles of growth that small businesses gravitate toward. Only two have particular merit, two are potentially dangerous, and one seems to make being in business for yourself something of a pointless exercise.

CHAMPIONS

This is a term that would describe companies that grow their profits and turnover by at least 25 percent each year. Fewer than 6 percent of companies regularly achieve this goal. This growth strategy gives you a strong position in the market, with a growing sales presence and the profit to develop new products and services without needing to borrow.

Fast Food is an example of a champion. Profits are growing at 41 percent, while sales are growing at 30 percent.

PROFIT ENHANCERS

These companies concentrate on growing profits alone. This equally small proportion of the small business population can become vulnerable, because they are building on a fairly static customer base.

GRAZERS

These businesses move forward steadily at a pace that reflects their markets in general, rather like

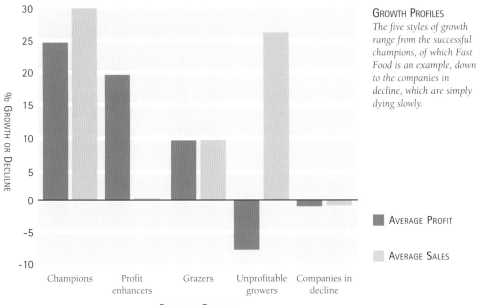

■ AVERAGE PROFIT

▨ AVERAGE SALES

STYLES OF GROWTH

a boat being swept along with the tide. The danger here is that although the boat is on an even keel in calm conditions, the tide may turn, bringing with it dangerous conditions.

UNPROFITABLE GROWERS

These are firms whose sales move forward sharply, while their profits are either fairly static or even going down. This is a particularly dangerous course to follow. With sales growth come all sorts of additional costs for producing, distributing, and selling the goods – for example, more inventory, more equipment,

more staff – which all have to be supported from a static revenue base. Just one bad debt or quality problem causing delays in payments is enough to sink such a business.

COMPANIES IN DECLINE

These companies are going backward by both measures. Their market positions are getting weaker, with a smaller sales base, and they are not making enough profit to do anything new.

It may be instructive to position your business and that of any competitors on the growth chart above to see how you compare.

TIME SAVER

A quick way to arrive at the approximate value of your business is to research how much comparable businesses have been sold for. By making an allowance for any difference in size, you can work out how much your business would have been worth to that buyer.

Measuring Value

You may not be thinking about selling your business yet, because your business is perhaps your most valuable asset, but you may want to assess its value from time to time.

If you are thinking of selling, you have a number of options. You may sell to the

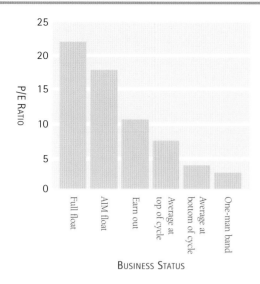

P/E RATIO (y-axis)

25
20
15
10
5
0

Full float
AIM float
Earn out
Average at top of cycle
Average at bottom of cycle
One-man band

BUSINESS STATUS

EFFECTS OF BUSINESS STATUS ON P/E RATIO

The price/earnings(P/E) ratio will be affected by whether the business is publicly traded and whether it is a one-man band. A publicly traded company will have a ratio up to a third higher than a private company, and a sole proprietor has the lowest P/E ratio of just 4.

management, pass it on to family members, or sell to another business. But whatever route you take will involve placing a value on the business. There are two options for valuing a business: assessing the value of the assets on the open market or calculating the price/earnings ratio.

VALUE OF ASSETS

One way to measure value is to work out what the various assets of the business would be worth on the open market. So, vehicles, premises, equipment, and any other assets could be professionally valued. From that sum you would take any outstanding liabilities to creditors, banks, the tax authorities, and severance payments due. This assessment might make sense if the business were actually going to go out of business, but it is unlikely to produce the best value.

PRICE/EARNINGS RATIO

Part, perhaps even all, that a small business has to sell, in the final analysis, is its capacity to make a profit. At any rate that is where the debate about value will start. The ratio most commonly used here to calculate the capacity for profit is price/earnings (P/E).

The P/E ratio is the number of times its annual profits at which a business is valued. If you look up a company's performance in the stock tables, you will see a P/E ratio calculated in the following way:

$$\text{P/E ratio} = \frac{\text{Market price per share}}{\text{Earnings per share}}$$

To arrive at this ratio, you must first calculate the earnings per share by dividing the net profit by the number of shares issued. For example, if a company had made $80,000 net profit and had issued 100,000 shares, the earnings per share would be 80¢. If the share price of the business in question was $10 and the share price was 80¢, then the P/E ratio is 12.5. This is another way of saying that the company is worth 12½ years' profits.

If you look up another company, in the internet sector for example, you might find a quite different multiple in force; 203 years' earnings is an all-time record in this sector.

If your business is in the food sector, and average P/E ratios there are 12, then that is where outsiders will start when they think about valuing your business. To reach a final figure, any valuer would also need to take the following into account:

■ any discount for a private business
■ unnecessary running costs
■ the economic cycle

DISCOUNT FOR A BUSINESS NOT ON THE STOCK MARKET

The first seriously negative event is the discount that will be applied because your business is not on the stock market. Private businesses are generally viewed as being worth at least a third less than a publicly traded company. This is from $96,000 (4 x $24,000) up to, say, $296,000 (8 x [$24,000 + $13,000 wages]). Perceptions are at least as important as figures when it comes to valuations.

ECONOMIC CYCLE

One last factor that affects private business valuations is the economic cycle. At the bottom of the cycle (a downturn), small private firms sell on average on multiples of between six and eight. At the top of the cycle (a boom), the same firm may sell for between 10 and 12.

All these figures are illustrative only. Every business sale and every circumstance has unique elements to it that can greatly affect the final outcome, and therefore the valuation.

Measuring Safety

because shares in a public company are much more liquid. There are more shares, and more buyers and sellers, for quoted rather than for unquoted businesses' shares. So Fast Food could find itself being valued in this way:

$$\text{P/E ratio} = \frac{12.00}{1.50} = 8$$

If the private company is a one-man band, or is seen as such, that ratio might be halved to a P/E of 4. The reasoning here is that the customers are probably loyal to the business owner and may not come over to any new owner. There is no certainty that the business will have a profitable life without the owner.

UNNECESSARY RUNNING COSTS

On the positive side, any expense seen as being unnecessary to running the business will be added back into profits before the calculation is done. So if you have three family members on the payroll who are performing no useful purpose, or who are taking out more than a new owner would have to pay to have the business run, then that sum would go back to swell the profits.

Operating profit is the figure used in this ratio, alongside the P/E ratio of 4 or 8 (see p. 125). Depending on how good you are at persuading a potential buyer that Fast Food is not a one-man band, and that the boss is currently overpaid, it could be worth anything

A particular volume of sales is required to cover the overhead and the cost of any materials and labour involved in your product or service. The point at which these different areas balance is known as break-even. Once a business passes the break-even point – in other words, when sales are greater than the overhead, materials, and labor costs – profits start to be made.

Your new business needs to become profitable relatively quickly, or it will run out of money

Any business operating at, or close to, break-even, exposes itself to unnecessary risks, because there is simply no room for error. A small drop in sales could be disastrous.

Obviously the more output, be that hours to sell, spare seats in a restaurant, or extra capacity in a factory, that you have available beyond the break-even volume, the better. The relationship between total sales capacity and the break-even point is called the margin of safety, which is usually expressed as a percentage. The business needs to be kept at a safe percentage margin of safety.

BREAK-EVEN POINT

The break-even analysis is an important tool to be used both in preparing a business plan and in the day-to-day running of a business. Understanding the danger of high fixed costs and the different characteristics of fixed and variable costs are important steps toward calculating the break-even point for your business.

THE DANGER OF HIGH FIXED COSTS

While some businesses have difficulty raising start-up capital, paradoxically one of the main reasons why small businesses fail in the early stages is that too much of the start-up capital is used to buy fixed assets.

Some equipment is clearly essential at the start, but other purchases could be postponed. This may mean that desirable and labor-saving devices have to be borrowed or leased for a specific period. This is obviously not as convenient as having them on hand all the time, but if, for example, color photocopiers, laptop computers, and even delivery vehicles are brought into the business at the outset, they become part of the fixed costs.

The higher the fixed-cost plateau, the longer it usually takes to reach break-even and then profitability. Becoming profitable quickly is essential for the survival of any business.

THE CHARACTERISTICS OF COSTS

Difficulties in calculating break-even usually begin when people become confused by the different characteristics of costs.

Some costs do not change, however much you sell; these are known as fixed costs. If you are running a store, the rent is a fairly constant figure, independent of the sales volume.

The cost of the products sold by the store, however, is completely dependent on volume: the more you sell, the more it costs to buy inventory. These are known as variable costs, or costs of production. Assumptions about sales will have to be made before you can add these to the fixed costs and so arrive at total costs.

CALCULATING BREAK-EVEN

The method of calculating break-even is:

$$\text{Break-even point} = \frac{\text{Fixed costs}}{\text{Contribution}}$$

The term "contribution" refers to the amount of money left over from the sales value after costs of production have been deducted. In Fast

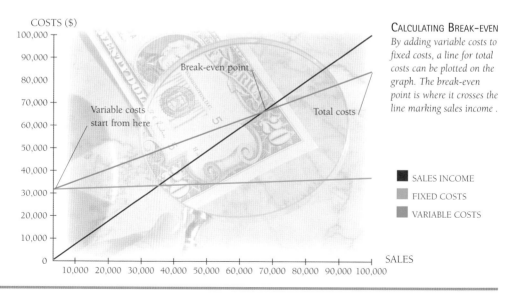

CALCULATING BREAK-EVEN
By adding variable costs to fixed costs, a line for total costs can be plotted on the graph. The break-even point is where it crosses the line marking sales income .

■ SALES INCOME
▨ FIXED COSTS
▩ VARIABLE COSTS

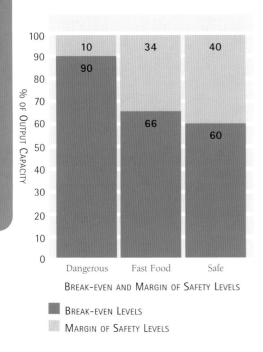

% OF OUTPUT CAPACITY

	Dangerous	Fast Food	Safe
top	10	34	40
bottom	90	66	60

BREAK-EVEN AND MARGIN OF SAFETY LEVELS

■ BREAK-EVEN LEVELS
▒ MARGIN OF SAFETY LEVELS

Food's case, this would be 50¢ in the pound or 0.5 dollars ($100,000 sales minus $50,000 costs of production, or variable costs):

$$\text{Break-even point} = \frac{33,000}{0.5} = \$66,000$$

BREAK-EVEN POINT FOR FAST FOOD

By recalculating Fast Food's break-even point step by step, you can see how this simple calculation is done. To make the calculations as comprehensible as possible, they have been displayed in graph format (see p. 127). In this case the assumption has been made that the theoretical limit of sales in year 1 is $100,000.

First the line for fixed costs is put in on the graph. In this case these are the $33,000 of expenses. These costs do not vary whether $1 or $100,000 worth of goods is sold.

The next line put in is for variable costs. In Fast Food's case they are the $50,000 cost of goods sold. The variable cost line starts from the fixed cost line (at $33,000) to give the total costs. The variable costs of material and labor

PLAYING SAFE

Fast Food's break-even point of $66,000 gives it a just about acceptable margin of safety of 34 percent. Any improvement on that would make the business a safer one. Had its break-even point been $90,000, it would have had a dangerously low 10 percent margin of safety.

for Fast Food are $50,000 to achieve $100,000 sales, so the line must climb by $50,000 from the $33,000 starting point by the time it reaches $100,000 worth of sales. The total costs are therefore $83,000.

The sales income line starts from zero. If you sell nothing, you get no income, but if you sell everything, you get $100,000.

Now you can see that the break-even point – the point at which the sales income line crosses the total costs line – is $66,000. So when Fast Food achieves $66,000 worth of sales, it has broken even. When it gets beyond this level of sales, it is in profit.

MARGIN OF SAFETY

The output available after break-even has been reached is known as the margin of safety. It is usually expressed as a percentage. The higher the percentage, the greater the margin. A low margin leaves little room for profitable operating.

Fast Food has $34,000 ($100,000 minus $66,000) out of a total capacity of $100,000 left after break-even. This equates to a 34 percent margin of safety, which is on the border of acceptability (see chart above).

Suppose, however, that the break-even point for Fast Food was $90,000, not $66,000. If the limit of its output was still $100,000, then it would have only $10,000 of sales capacity left on which to make the year's profit. This represents a dangerously low 10 percent margin of safety.

MAKING AN ACTION PLAN

Calculate key ratios for your business, both for the current year and for last year (if you were in business). See how much better or worse your performance is year to year. Now get those ratios for your main competitor and see how much better or worse your performance is by comparison. Finally, identify the areas that need improving and decide on an action plan.

KEY RATIO SUMMARY AND PERFORMANCE IMPROVEMENT ACTION PLAN

	LAST YEAR	THIS YEAR	% BETTER OR WORSE PERFORMANCE	MAIN COMPETITORS	% BETTER OR WORSE THAN OUR PERFORMANCE	ACTION TO BE TAKEN
PROFITABILITY						
GROSS MARGIN PERCENTAGE						
NET MARGIN PERCENTAGE						
PROFIT PER EMPLOYEE						
RETURN ON ASSETS (ROA)						
LIQUIDITY						
CURRENT RATIO						
QUICK RATIO						
AVERAGE COLLECTION PERIOD						
AVERAGE PAYMENT PERIOD						
SOLVENCY						
LEVERAGING						
INTEREST COVER						
GROWTH						
SALES GROWTH PERCENTAGE						
PROFIT GROWTH PERCENTAGE						
SAFETY						
BREAK-EVEN POINT						
MARGIN OF SAFETY PERCENTAGE						
OTHER KEY RATIOS FOR YOUR BUSINESS						

SETTING OUT YOUR BUDGET

As we have seen, the gold standard for measuring our achievement is how close we are to meeting or exceeding the objectives we have set for our own performance. A budget makes you think ahead, set objectives, allocate responsibility for key tasks, and get commitment from management. It sets the goals you intend to achieve, and by comparing your progress with your budget you will know when action is needed to keep the business on course. The budget brings a measure of predictability into an uncertain world.

While the business plan sets the strategic direction and purpose of the business, it is the budget that fleshes out exactly how each step of that plan will be implemented.

The budget sets out, line by line, in much the same format as the profit and loss statement, the major sources of income and expenditure for the period of the budget. The year is broken down into weeks or months, depending on the dynamics of your business.

WHEN TO BUDGET

The best way to budget is to look one year ahead and review the whole budget each quarter. At that review, add a further quarter to the end, so that you always have a one-year budget horizon. This is known as a rolling quarterly budget.

It may seem like hard work at first, but the sooner budgeting becomes a business routine, the more accurate your forecasts will become. This not only makes the whole planning process more easy and reliable, but it can also have the positive effect of making your business more creditworthy and valuable. Any business that consistently meets or exceeds its targets will have its profit targets accepted more readily than one that doesn't.

If, at the end of a quarter, you are 25 percent off budget, take heart from the fact that this means that you have been 75 percent successful.

CASE STUDY: Budgeting for Growth

ALISTAIR HOLMES visited a craft trade show every year in order to sell his work. After a few years he was approached by a foreign buyer, who placed a significant order. This made Alistair think about exporting, because he felt he was by now sufficiently well established. He had spoken at some length to this buyer and thought there was scope to sell even more of his products in that particular country. Unfortunately, the buyer wanted an exclusive arrangement, so Alistair had to consider other territories.

He wrote to the overseas buyer confirming his terms, and he decided to add that the exclusive arrangement would be for an initial two years. The agreement depended on the buyer's company placing enough regular orders for an agreed minimum quantity, and paying on time. Alistair felt confident enough to increase his production budget for the forthcoming year. He also decided to assign his most experienced salesperson to the new customer. He also gave this account a target 10 percent higher than the minimum order quantity.

HOW TO BUDGET

When setting out and using a budget there are a number of guidelines it is prudent to follow. They can be summarized as follows:

▪ **SET REALISTIC BUT STRETCHING GOALS** The budget must be based on realistic but challenging goals. Those goals are arrived at by both a top-down aspiration and a bottom-up forecast of what seems both possible and likely. So, for example, if sales have been growing at 10 percent a year for the past couple of years, that seems a possible and likely outcome for next year, and one that your sales force might go for. However, your business plan may involve trying to grow at a faster rate than in the past, in which case a goal of 15 percent could be seen as challenging but realistic.

▪ **ASK THE RIGHT PEOPLE** The budget should be prepared by those responsible for delivering the results. So the salespeople should prepare the sales budget and the production people should prepare the production budget. You need to manage the communication process so that everyone understands what the other departments are planning.

▪ **GET AGREEMENT** Agreement to the budget should be explicit. During the budgeting process, several versions of a particular budget will be discussed. For example, you may want to achieve a sales figure of $2

REASONS FOR BUDGETING

1 Ensures you make financial projections and plans, and keep them up-to-date.

2 Provides you with a standard against which to measure your performance.

3 Highlights areas of your business that need attention or improving.

4 Allows you to delegate responsibility for certain aspects of revenue generation and cost control.

5 Makes it more likely that you will not unexpectedly run out of cash.

---

million, while your sales team's initial forecast is for $1.75 million. After some debate, $1.9 million may be the figure accepted. Once agreed, a virtual contract exists, declaring a commitment to achieve on one hand (the sales team) and a commitment both to allocate resources and to be satisfied with the team's best efforts on the other (you). It makes sense for this commitment to be put in writing.

▪ **COMPLETE IN TIME** The budget needs to be finalized at least a month before the start of the year, and not weeks or months into the year. The reason for this is that the sooner people know their goals, the sooner they can start to achieve them.

▪ **REVIEW REGULARLY** The budget should be reviewed fundamentally at intervals during the year, in order to make sure that all the basic assumptions that underpin it still hold true. For example, the market itself may be growing much faster than you expected, thus rendering your goals too easy a target. Conversely, hard times in the market may mean that you have to reduce your targets.

▪ **COLLATE PROMPTLY** You need timely and accurate information to make the process worthwhile. Figures should be ready for review within seven to 10 working days of the month end.

FACT FILE

Overextended describes a business that is expanding beyond its financial resources. As sales expand, the money tied up in inventory and customers' credit grows rapidly. Presssure also comes from suppliers who want payment for the ever-increasing supply of raw materials. The natural escape valve for pressures on working capital is an overdraft (or a substantial increase in the current one).

SIMPLE BUDGET LAYOUT				
	MONTH		YEAR TO DATE	
	ACTUAL ($)	BUDGET ($)	ACTUAL CUMULATIVE ($)	BUDGET CUMULATIVE ($)
SALES	8,288	7,500	24,960	23,250
DIRECT COST OF SALES — Materials	2,475	2,250	7,527	6,825
Labour	2,063	1,950	6,248	5,925
Direct overheads	675	650	2,071	1,950
TOTAL SALES	5,213	4,850	15,846	14,700
GROSS MARGIN	3,075	2,650	9,114	8,550
EXPENSES — Factory	1,140	1,100	3,527	3,375
Selling	375	400	1,201	1,170
Technical	308	300	963	915
Accounting	245	240	757	735
Administrative	335	345	1,080	1,050
TOTAL EXPENSES	2,403	2,385	7,528	7,245
CONTRIBUTION TO ANNUAL PROFIT	672	265	1,586	1,305

BUDGET LAYOUT

This example of a simple budget shows figures for one month as well as cumulative figures for the year to date. You can see that sales of $8,288 have exceeded their budget of $7,500. This increase in sales results in higher than budgeted figures for just about every other aspect of the budget, with the exception of selling and administrative costs.

Monitoring Performance

Performance against budget needs to be carefully monitored as the year proceeds, and corrective action should be taken, where necessary, to keep you on track. This has to be done month by month (or at shorter time intervals if required), showing both the period in question and the cumulative year to date.

Looking at the fixed budget example (see above right) you can see at a glance that the business is behind on sales for this month but ahead on the year to date. The convention is to put all unfavorable variances in brackets, so a higher than budgeted sales figure does not have brackets, but a higher material costs figure does.

You can also see that, while profit is running ahead of budget, the profit margin is slightly behind (-0.3 percent). This is in part because other direct costs, such as labor and direct overhead in this example, are running well ahead of the targets set in the budget.

When monitoring performance against budget, take into account variations in performance and make allowances for increased capital expenditure if sales are higher than expected.

THE FIXED BUDGET

HEADING	MONTH			YEAR TO DATE		
	BUDGET ($000)	ACTUAL ($000)	VARIANCE ($000)	BUDGET ($000)	ACTUAL ($000)	VARIANCE ($000)
SALES	805	753	(52)	6,358	7,314	956
MATERIALS	627	567	60	4,942	5,704	(762)
MATERIAL MARGIN	178	186	8	1,416	1,610	194
DIRECT COSTS	74	79	(5)	595	689	(94)
GROSS PROFIT	104	107	3	820	921	101
PERCENTAGE	12.92%	14.21%	1.29%	12.90%	12.60%	(0.30%)

ANALYZING THE FIXED BUDGET
The fixed budget compares performance with the targets originally set. Sales in this example were $52,000 less than expected for the month, but $956,000 more than expected for the whole year.

VARIATIONS IN PERFORMANCE

The budget is based on a particular set of sales goals, only a few of which are likely to be met exactly in practice. In the example of a fixed budget (see chart above), you can see that $762,000 more material has been used than budgeted. In addition, more goods ($956,000 worth) have been sold, so this is not surprising.

The way to handle these variations in performance is to alter the fixed budget by flexing it. In this way you can show what you would expect to happen to expenses, given the increase in sales that actually occurred. You do this by applying the budget ratios to the actual data. So, for example, materials were planned to be 22.11 percent of sales in the budget. By applying this same percentage to the actual month's sales, you get a material cost of $587,000 rather than the $627,000 shown in the fixed budget.

When this new figure is entered in the flexed budget (see chart below), you can see that the overspending on the materials you would have expected to buy, given the level of sales actually achieved, is in fact only $19,000, a much more comforting figure than $762,000.

ANALYZING THE FLEXED BUDGET
By altering the sales figures from the fixed budget to reflect what actually happened in the preceding month, the relative costs of materials is changed. The variance is reduced from minus $762,000 to minus $19,000.

THE FLEXED BUDGET

HEADING	MONTH			YEAR TO DATE		
	BUDGET ($000)	ACTUAL ($000)	VARIANCE ($000)	BUDGET ($000)	ACTUAL ($000)	VARIANCE ($000)
SALES	753	753	–	7,314	7,314	–
MATERIALS	587	567	20	5,685	5,704	(19)
MATERIAL MARGIN	166	186	20	1,629	1,610	(19)
DIRECT COSTS	69	79	(10)	685	689	(4)
GROSS PROFIT	97	107	10	944	921	(23)
PERCENTAGE	12.92%	14.21%	1.29%	12.90%	12.60%	(0.30%)

The same argument holds for other direct costs, which appear to be running $94,000 over budget for the year. When you take into account the extra sales in the flexed budget, you discover an overspend of only $4,000 on direct costs. While this is still a serious amount, it is a small fraction of the figure that the unflexed, or fixed, budget was suggesting.

The flexed budget therefore allows you to concentrate your actions on dealing with true variances in performance.

TRENDS AND SEASONAL FACTORS

The figures shown for each period of the budget are not the same. For example, a sales budget of $1.2 million would not translate into sales of exactly $100,000 a month. The exact figure for each month would depend on two factors: trend and seasonality.

The projected trend, which may be market-driven, may mean that sales at the start of the period are $80,000 a month and those at the end are $120,000. The average will be $100,000, so making the $1.2 million total.

By virtue of seasonal factors, each month may also be pulled up or down from the trend.

You would expect the sales of heating oil, for example, to peak in the fall and tail off in the late spring because of variations in the weather (see graph below). Other examples of seasonal fluctuations are increased sales of patio furniture and barbecues in summer and toys and luxury items before Christmas.

ALLOWING FOR CAPITAL EXPENDITURE

The budget will have not only profit and loss implications. If the sales goals are high, there may be a requirement for more money to buy machinery to produce the product. This will have capital implications, because more funds may have to be found to increase the production rate.

There may also be cash-flow implications. Rapidly expanding the sales of manufactured products has the immediate impact of large amounts of cash being used for raw materials and labor and to finance debtors until they pay. For as long as sales growth is accelerating, cash consumption grows. This is not always harmful, but it must be budgeted for in a cash-flow forecast based on the budget.

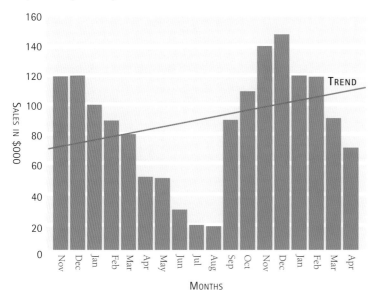

SEASONAL VARIATIONS OF TRENDS
A company selling heating oil would expect to sell considerably higher quantities during fall and winter months than during spring and summer. From the combined peaks and valleys, you can calculate average sales. You can also see the general trend of sales, which in this case is moving steadily higher.

BUDGET PROFIT AND LOSS ACCOUNT MODEL

		MONTH			YEAR TO DATE		
		BUDGET ($)	ACTUAL ($)	VARIANCE	BUDGET ($)	ACTUAL ($)	VARIANCE
SALES							
COST OF SALES							
GROSS PROFIT							
MINUS EXPENSES	Administration						
	Sales						
	Marketing						
	Distribution						
	TOTAL EXPENSES						
OPERATING PROFIT							

SUMMARY OF MAIN REASONS FOR IMPORTANT VARIANCES AND PROPOSED ACTIONS

1

2

3

Building a Budget Model

Setting a budget requires discussion with key staff in the different departments of a business. As a result of this, several different sets of figures may have to be produced.

A budget model, built using a spreadsheet, is the ideal way to accomplish this. By using a spreadsheet, the effect of changing any figure or figures can be seen on the whole budget automatically and instantly, without any tedious calculations. All that is required is to decide on the relationship between the various elements of the budget.

For example, you may decide that on your balance sheet debtors will be valued at 45 days' sales (in other words, you assume that they will

BUDGET MODEL

A model such as this is a template onto which you can impose figures for any period. Once you have decided on how the different aspects of your budget relate to each other, you can construct a model to set the budget.

take that long to pay their bills), or that on the profit and loss statement gross profit should be 50 percent. Thereafter, changes in sales levels as the budget is formulated will just roll down the model to produce revised profit and loss statements and balance sheets.

The model will also prove itself extremely useful for carrying out budget updates and revisions throughout the year, thereby keeping you fully up-to-date. If you possess a computerized bookkeeping system, you will find that it includes a budgeting model framework that you can use.

IMPROVING YOUR PERFORMANCE

You may identify areas of poor or declining financial performance while you are monitoring the performance of your business. Do not be overly alarmed – even the best-run companies have areas that do not perform as well as others – but make up your mind to improve these areas as quickly as possible. Involve your colleagues in your decisions so that the business can work together for greater profit and achievement.

If you suspect that your business is not doing as well as it could, then you need to find out which areas are failing. The most fruitful places to look for better results are:
▪ prices
▪ costs
▪ capital employed in the day-to-day running of the business

Small firms are often guilty of getting their prices wrong at first. The misconception that new and small firms can undercut established competitors is usually based on ignorance of either the true costs of a product or service or of the true value of an overhead.

The overhead argument usually runs like this: "They [the competition] are big, own plush offices, and have lots of overpaid marketing executives spending the company's money on expense-account lunches. I don't, and so I must

Systematically identify areas of improvement by analyzing past performance

be able to undercut them." The errors with this type of argument are, first, that the plush office, far from being an overhead in the derogatory sense of the word, is actually a fast-appreciating asset, perhaps even generating more profit than the company's main products. (Shops, restaurants, and hotels typically fit into this category.) The plush office, especially if accompanied by a prestigious address such as Fifth Avenue or Rodeo Drive, can also contribute to creating an image for the product or service in such a way as to enhance its price.

Second, the marketing executives may well be paid more than you, but if they do not deliver a constant stream of new products and strategies, they will be replaced by people who can.

Clearly, you have to take account of what your competitors charge, but remember that

---

CASE STUDY: The Dangers of Pricing Low

ADRIAN PATTERSON decided that after graduating from college he would prefer to start his own business rather than go to work for someone else. He had worked in a bagel shop during the vacation period and decided that this was something he would be able to do for himself. He decided that he could

undercut his previous employer and so assure himself of a good flow of business from the outset. When his accountant helped him to prepare projections, however, he found that at the price he proposed charging, he would never recover his overhead or break-even. Indeed, "overhead" and "break-even" were alien terms to Adrian before he discussed his plans with his accountant.

price is the easiest element of the marketing mix for an established company to vary. They could follow you down the price curve, forcing you into bankruptcy, far more easily than you could capture their customers with a lower price.

Pricing for Profit

While most small firms – 80 percent according to some reports – set their price with reference to costs, using either a cost-plus formula (for example, materials plus 50 percent) or a cost multiplier (for example, three times material costs), all customers buy with reference to value, and increasingly (and often via the internet) with competitive pricing. That can leave a lot of scope for managing your prices up. Price is, after all, the element of the marketing mix that is likely to have the greatest impact on your profitability.

In fact, it is often more profitable for a new company to sell fewer items at a higher price while the owner-manager gets the organization and product lines figured out. Once the business is established, it can then increase its line of products and lower its prices. The key is to concentrate on obtaining good margins, often with a range of prices and quality in your products.

THE EFFECTS OF RAISING PRICES

The chart on the top of p. 138 shows the effect of changing prices on your level of gross profit if the volume of customers remains the same or alters by 5 percent increments. To take the example of Fast Food, you can see what might have happened had it raised its prices, rather than grown its sales from $100,000 to $130,000. Assume that all this growth came from selling more to more customers.

Had it raised its prices by 5 percent and lost no customers, it would have made $5,000 more gross profit. Since the expenses have all been met, you can assume that all of this profit will drop to the bottom line of the accounts.

If the price increase had resulted in a loss of 5 percent of its customers, the sum would look like this. Sales would go down

---

PRICE IS IN THE EYE OF THE BEHOLDER

Many consumers see price as a reliable guide to the quality they can expect to receive. The theory is that the more you pay, the more you get. It follows that, had James Dyson priced his revolutionary vacuum cleaner, with its claims of superior performance, below that of its peers, then some potential customers may have questioned those claims.

In its literature, Dyson cites as the inspiration for the new vacuum cleaner the inferior performance of existing products in the same price range. A product at six times the Dyson price is the one whose performance Dyson seeks to emulate.

The message conveyed is that, although the price is at the high end for general household electrical appliances, the performance is disproportionately greater than the cheaper models. The runaway success of Dyson's vacuum cleaner, in an already busy market, would tend to endorse this argument.

How Changing Prices Affect Gross Profit

A price rise of 5 % accompanied by no drop in customers would result in a 5 % increase in the gross profit. A similar rise accompanied by a 15 % fall, however, would result in 3.25 % less gross profit.

to $95,000 in volume terms, but the gross margin would rise from 50 to 55 percent, because the company would be charging more. That would produce a gross profit of $52,250 ($95,000 x 55 percent). Expenses would remain at $33,000, leaving an operating profit of $19,250. That figure is $2,250 higher than the $17,000 that would have been made on the higher volume of sales made at the original lower price.

Working through the rest of the figures in the same way, you can see that, unless you think that you would lose more than 10 percent of your business by putting your prices up by 5 percent, you will not have a problem. In fact, increasing prices by 15 percent will deliver higher profits even if you lose more than 15 percent of your business. In Fast Food's case this was 50 percent. The lower your gross profit, the less business you can afford to lose for any given price increase.

There are other benefits that are not shown. Putting the pressure on price rather than volume means carrying less inventory, having fewer bills to chase, using less capital, and wearing out equipment less quickly.

Effects of Raising Prices

Change in Price	Change in Volume of Customers			
	0%	-5%	-10%	-15%
+5%	5%	2.25%	-0.5%	-3.25%
+10%	10%	7%	4%	1%
+15%	15%	11.75%	8.5%	5.25%

Reducing Your Costs

Costs are associated with activity. But, since activity is often misallocated, as the 80/20 rule (or Pareto principle) demonstrates (see chart far right), it follows that the opportunities for cost reduction are almost always greater than you think.

Look at the table below and the two charts above right for examples of the effects on your business of reducing costs.

Write a spreadsheet or build into your acounting software a function that ranks the main items of cost in your business and compares them with a previous period. The costs that are both large and rising are the ones to concentrate your efforts on reducing. The cost of this will be small in comparison to the potential savings.

Cost Savings Matter

	Before		After 2% Cost Saving		Extra Performance	
	$000	%	$000	%	$000	%
Sales	1,000	100	1,000	100	–	–
Costs	950	95	930	93	-20	-2
Profit	50	5	70	7	+20	+40

Reducing Costs

For a business making a 5% net profit, reducing costs by just 2% will raise profits by 40%, from $50,000 to $70,000. The business may have needed to find 10 or even 20% more customers to have the same effect on profit.

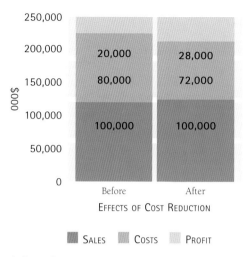

EFFECTS OF COST REDUCTION

■ SALES ░ COSTS ▨ PROFIT

TYPE OF CUSTOMERS

■ CUSTOMERS ▨ PROFIT

A SMALL REDUCTION CAN HAVE A BIG EFFECT

What makes cost reduction so powerful is the disproportionate effect on profits that even a small reduction in costs can have. By reducing costs by just 10%, this business has raised profits by an impressive 40%.

THE 80/20 RULE

A close examination of your client list will show that 20% of them account for the vast majority of your business and perhaps all of your profit. Yet you spend as much time servicing unprofitable customers as you do profitable ones.

Squeezing Working Capital

Once you have bought your store, set up your factory, or bought your delivery vehicle, the funds you have used are sunk costs. The items you bought may not be what you now need, but you will have to make do with them, for now at any rate, because the capital is tied up. You do, however, have discretion over your working capital. The more you squeeze that, the less money you have tied up in the business, which means lower borrowing costs.

WAYS TO MAKE BETTER USE OF YOUR WORKING CAPITAL

1 If you sell on credit, set out your payment terms clearly on your invoices. Customers need to know when you expect to be paid; this has advantages for both of you.

2 Find out when your biggest customers issue payments for invoices, and make sure your bills reach them in time.

3 Send out statements promptly to chase down late payers, and follow up with a phone call.

4 Always ask for business references when giving credit to new customers, and check credit reports to see how sound they are.

5 Have accurate inventory records and monitor slow-moving inventory.

6 Have an accurate sales forecasting system so that you can match inventory and work in progress to likely demand.

7 Take credit from your suppliers up to the maximum time allowed. Try to negotiate extended terms with major suppliers once you have a good track record.

8 Make any cash you have work harder. Overnight money markets via an internet bank could allow you to get interest on cash, rather than having it sitting in the bank doing nothing – for you, that is.

9 Work out if it makes sense to pay bills quickly to take advantage of early payment discounts offered by suppliers (see overleaf).

USING WORKING CAPITAL

The evidence points to small firms being inefficient users of working capital. The smaller they are, the less efficient they are, as these charts show. A very small firm is likely to be paid later by debtors and to have a slower turnover of inventory than a medium-sized business. Both of these areas result in lost income.

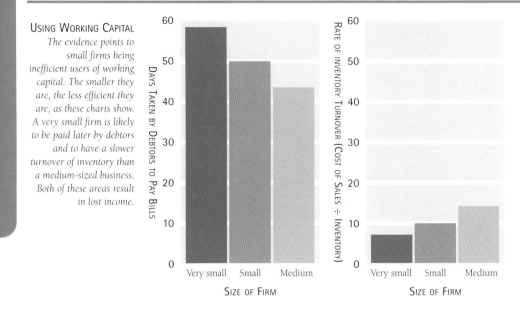

Sometimes suppliers offer high-interest discount rates for prompt settlement. If you are offered 2.5 percent to pay up now rather than in two months' time, that is equivalent to an annual rate of interest of 15 percent (12 ÷ 2 x 2.5 percent).

10 Deposit checks and cash promptly. This is not only the safest option for cash and checks, but the sooner you get your money into the banking system, the sooner you are either saving interest costs on loans or earning some interest income.

WORKING CAPITAL DOWN, PROFITABILITY UP

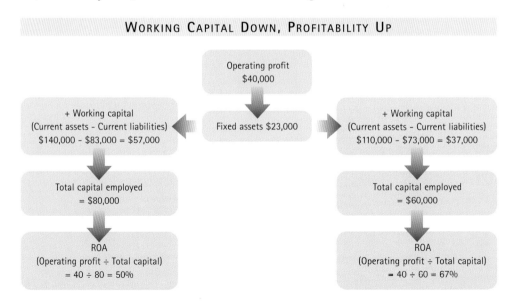

HOW TO EVALUATE A DISCOUNT OFFER

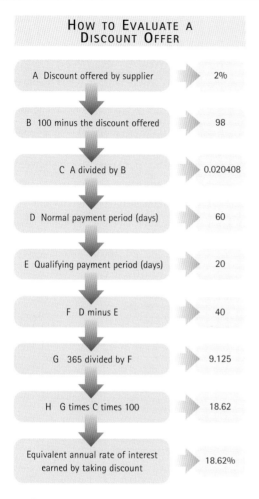

A Discount offered by supplier	2%
B 100 minus the discount offered	98
C A divided by B	0.020408
D Normal payment period (days)	60
E Qualifying payment period (days)	20
F D minus E	40
G 365 divided by F	9.125
H G times C times 100	18.62
Equivalent annual rate of interest earned by taking discount	18.62%

Changing Leveraging in Your Business

H ighly leveraged describes the situation of a business that has a high proportion of borrowed money. High leveraging has considerable attractions to a business that wants to make high returns on the shareholders' capital. (Look back at pp. 115–116 to remind yourself about interest cover and how to calculate the ROI.)

The table on p.142 illustrates the effects of changing the level of leveraging on return on

EVALUATING A SUPPLIER'S EARLY PAYMENT DISCOUNT
By following the steps shown here, you can see whether paying your bills early will suit you financially. Here settling your bills 40 days earlier than usual for a year is the equivalent of earning an annual rate of interest on your money of 18.62%.

investment. The business is assumed to need $60,000 capital to generate $10,000 operating profits. Four different capital structures are considered. They range from all share capital (no leveraging) at one end to nearly all loan capital at the other. The loan capital has to be serviced, and it is assumed that an interest of 12 percent has to be paid. The loan itself can be relatively indefinite, simply being replaced by another one at market interest rates when the first loan expires.

Following the table through, you can see that ROI grows from 16.6 to 30.7 percent by virtue of the changed leveraging. If the interest on the loan were lower, the ROI would be even more improved by high leveraging, and the higher the interest, the lower the relative improvement in ROI. So, during times of low interest, businesses tend to increase borrowings rather than raise equity (money from shareholders).

PROBLEMS WITH LEVERAGING

At first sight, high leveraging looks like a perpetual profit-growth machine. Naturally, business owners would rather have someone else lend them the money for the growth of their business than put it in themselves, if they could increase the return on their investment.

The problem comes if the business does not produce $10,000 operating profits. Very often, in a small business, a drop in sales of 20 percent means profits are halved. If profits were halved in this example, the business could not meet the interest payments on its loan. That would make the business insolvent, and so not in a sound financial position.

Bankers tend to favor 1:1 leveraging as the maximum for a small business, although they have been known to go much higher.

THE EFFECT OF LEVERAGING ON RETURN ON INVESTMENT (ROI)

		NO LEVERAGING ($)	AVERAGE LEVERAGING 1:1 ($)	HIGH LEVERAGING 2:1 ($)	VERY HIGH LEVERAGING 3:1 ($)
CAPITAL STRUCTURE	Share capital	60,000	30,000	20,000	15,000
	Loan capital (at 12%)	–	30,000	40,000	45,000
	TOTAL CAPITAL	60,000	60,000	60,000	60,000
PROFITS	Operating profit	10,000	10,000	10,000	10,000
	Minus interest on loan	–	3,600	4,800	5,400
	NET PROFIT	10,000	6,400	5,200	4,600
RETURN ON INVESTMENT (ROI)		10,000/60,000	6,400/30,000	5,200/20,000	4,600/15,000
EQUALS		16.6%	21.3%	26%	30.7%
TIMES INTEREST EARNED		N/A	10,000/3,600	10,000/4,800	10,000/5,400
EQUALS		N/A	2.8x	2.1x	1.8x

Bringing it all Together

When you improve performance in any of the key areas – pricing for profit, reducing costs, and making efficient use of working capital – you will see some kind of increase in your operating profit. The more individual target areas you can improve, the greater will be the increase in profits for the business. For example, one company reduced the costs of its materials by 5 percent; increased its inventory turnover by 6 percent; increased its debtor days by 4 percent; improved its gross margins by 4 percent; and, finally, reduced its creditors by 7 percent. As a result, the company saw its operating profit increase by more than 200 percent.

CHANGING THE LEVEL OF LEVERAGING
In this chart four different financing options show the effects of higher leveraging on the return on shareholders' investment. As the net profit drops from $10,000 to $4,600, the ROI rises from 16.6% to 30.7%.

SETTING YOUR OWN TARGET AREAS
After completing your review of past performance, and identifying specific areas where you feel improvements could be made, you should now prepare a profit improvement action plan (see the example opposite). Set targets for your business to achieve in each area and decide how those targets are to be achieved. Then take action. Start first with those targets where the opportunities are large and the work required to get the results is small. Take one area at a time, until you are ready to tackle the most difficult areas.

MY PROFIT IMPROVEMENT PLAN

BUSINESS AREA	ACTIONS	COMPLETION DATE (LATEST DATE BY WHICH IMPROVEMENTS WILL BE MADE)	EXPECTED IMPROVEMENT ($)
PRICES			
RAW MATERIALS			
WASTAGE AND RETURNS			
LABOR COSTS			
EQUIPMENT COSTS			
PREMISES			
CAR AND TRAVEL			
INVENTORY			
DEBTORS			
CREDITORS			
LEVERAGING			
TOTAL EXPECTED COST REDUCTION			

IMPROVING OVERALL PERFORMANCE

Set improvement targets for each of the key areas in the chart above, then incorporate the tasks needed to achieve them into your next budget review.

USEFUL information

*Y*ou will need to understand the legal aspects of your business to ensure that you operate legally. Your business will also face a range of taxes, covering income, capital, sales tax, and wages and payroll. This section provides a basic grounding in the regulations that are likely to affect you, and offers guidelines on taxation to ensure that you pay your dues and no more. The Glossary explains key business terms, while the Useful Contacts and Suggested Reading sections point you toward other sources of information.

Legal Matters

The financial aspects of business are less exact than the arithmetic purity of numbers might suggest. In fact, uncertainty and unpredictability are more common features of business financial affairs than you might at first think. After all, add two and two and you ought to get four, but if part of one of those twos is made up by a customer who will not, or cannot, pay, then things are not so clear. In areas of imprecision like this, it is the law that has to be relied on for help and guidance.

The law confers obligations as well as helping people in dispute. Such obligations include filing financial statements on time; paying legal charges to banks on assets, both business and personal; and accepting the responsibilities of directorship, which are beyond those of a sole proprietor running much the same enterprise.

To survive in a country ruled by laws, you need an appreciation of the main legal aspects surrounding the financing of your business.

Using the Small Claims Court

The civil courts in most states and localities have various procedures for getting legal disputes concerning payment from customers settled quickly and inexpensively.

Most commonly called the Small Claims Court, by whatever name the purpose is the same: to provide a speedy and inexpensive resolution of disputes that involve relatively small amounts of money. The advantage of the Small Claims Court is that if you cannot afford a lawyer, you can still bring your case to the court yourself. Even if you can afford counsel, the legal fees may be more than the amount you are claiming, and therefore an unnecessary and unwarranted expense. Needless to say, if you lose the case, or win but do not manage to get your opponent to pay your costs, then you will not be any better off.

As a rule, Small Claims Courts try cases for unpaid bills and for property damage, but not for personal injuries. The amount for which you can sue varies, but rarely exceeds $10,000, and may be much less. State and local lawmakers are increasing these amounts, called a court's "jurisdictional limit," because of inflation, and because the public and the judicial system need a forum to resolve straightforward claims for relatively minor sums quickly and fairly.

Some courts, especially in commercial centers, have special business sections, with judges and personnel who are trained and attuned to the language and usage of business transactions. The housing court may have a special commercial part for disputes between landlords and their business or commercial tenants.

You are entitled to ask for interest on the amount you are claiming, from the date the claim arose. The statutory interest rate varies from state to state, and may change from time to time.

A business person can use a Small Claims Court to collect bills, to obtain a judgment for breach of contract, or to seek money for minor property damage claims – for example, suing someone who broke a fence around your property or parking area. The Small Claims Court offers you an opportunity to collect money that would otherwise be lost because the amount is too small to justify suing in a regular court. It is not a perfect solution, but the Small Claims Court should still be part of the financial collection strategies of your business.

Before you start out on the legal route, investigate alternatives. If your case involves a written contract, check to see if the contract requires mediation or arbitration of disputes. If so, this may limit or cut off your right to go to any court, including the Small Claims Court. Second, consider other cost-effective options, such as free or low-cost publicly operated mediation programs. If you're in a dispute with a customer, or perhaps another business, and you still have hopes of preserving some aspect of the relationship, mediation – even if not provided for in a contract – is often a better alternative than going to court. Any litigation tends to sour people's feelings.

STARTING THE PROCESS

To start a case in a Small Claims Court, get a claim form from the court. Follow the instructions, paying particular attention to why you are making a claim, what the claim is for, the amount you are claiming, and whether you want interest.

In most courts, the fee includes the cost of serving the defendant by certified mail, return receipt requested. The court will set a date for a hearing and will send your claim, including instructions for answering the case, to the defendant. The signed receipt, or the unclaimed letter, will be returned to the court, not to you.

If the defendant refuses to accept the claim, or cannot be located at the address you gave, the court will advise you on how to proceed. Be forewarned, however, that it may be very expensive to serve a person who cannot be found, and you may have to drop the case, at least temporarily.

On the assigned court date, you must come to court with all of your evidence, including any witnesses you intend to call. If the defendant appears, your case will be set for trial, or, as increasingly occurs, arbitration before a private lawyer or retired judge assigned to rule on these minor cases. Some courts routinely send minor claims to one or more of such part-time arbitrators, whose

decision may be appealed by requesting a trial before a judge. Whether your case is tried by a judge or by one or more arbitrators, you should present your case logically and completely, without asking the court to assume any facts upon which your claim depends. Avoid "courtroom histrionics" you may have seen on television, and do all you can to convey the image of an honest business manager trying to collect a legitimate debt.

If the defendant does not appear, the case may be adjourned to another date, or you may be required to present your case in your opponent's absence. The court will generally send a written decision by mail.

Some courts are experimenting with innovative ways to hear cases. These methods include mediation, in which a neutral negotiator tries to get both parties to agree on a resolution, as well as telephone and video conferencing, especially in courts covering a wide area.

GETTING PAID

One of the frustrating things about any legal process is that winning the argument could, in the end, resolve nothing. If the person you are suing has no money, or decides to ignore the judgment against them, then the ball could be back in your court.

If your opponent looks as though they could pay, but won't, you have three options open to you: replevin, attachment, and garnishment.

■ **REPLEVIN** is where the dispute involved the ownership or possession of a particular item, and the court ordered the defendant to return the item to you. You may present the order to a marshal, sheriff, or other judicial or quasi-judicial officer, and have the officer obtain the item from the defendant.

■ **ATTACHMENT** is where the court authorizes an official to seize the defendant's property, especially a bank account, in the amount of the unpaid judgment and court costs, and to remit the funds to you, or arrange for the sale of the property. A variation of this remedy is available if the defendant owns real property of greater value than any existing mortgage or other encumbrance, but this is realistic only if the defendant is the sole owner. Be aware, however, that people who intentionally fail to pay their debts may have already placed obstacles in the way of anyone trying to collect them (see pp. 151–152 for further details).

◼ **GARNISHMENT** is where the court authorizes a judicial or quasi-judicial official to seize monies owed to the defendant by a third party in the form of wages, commissions, or other payments. This remedy is strictly regulated by federal and state laws, and is generally limited to just 10 percent of the defendant's wages. Your lawyer can put most of these remedies, and more, into action. The problem arises when you don't know the extent of the defendant's assets or where they are located, or even the name and address of the defendant's bank or current employer.

The first step is to require the defendant to answer written questions under oath about assets, income, and claims they have against a third party. If the defendant's answers are evasive or need to be further developed, you may require the defendant to be questioned under oath in person, preferably in court.

The defendant's refusal to appear, to produce documents, or to answer questions, can be punished as contempt of court, usually involving a fine payable to the court and perhaps an additional amount in costs - if you can collect it. In some states, the most flagrant cases of contempt can be punished by being jailed until the defendant agrees to obey the court order, but don't expect a former customer to be jailed for not paying a $2,000 supply or repair bill.

BEING SURE OF YOUR CASE

While the Small Claims Court, or indeed any court, is one way to claim money that is owed

to you, it is, as you can see, neither easy nor certain of a positive outcome.

First, you want to be relatively sure of your legal position. You must have a valid legal basis for a lawsuit. Before proceeding, ask yourself if you have a decent chance of proving in court that the defendant refused to pay a fair and just bill, or broke a contract, or negligently damaged your property. If not, any talk about going to court is just an idle threat that may hurt your credibility.

Filing the Audited Accounts

Sole proprietorships, partnerships, and most corporations do not have to file audited financial statements, and will do so only if they are required to in order to apply for a substantial loan or other financing arrangement. They may also need audited financial statements if they are selling or otherwise closing down the business (see pp. 154-158).

Public corporations must, however, file financial reports that have been reviewed in accordance with generally accepted auditing standards by independent auditors so as to conform to generally accepted accounting principles. Such audited financial statements, which can be much more costly than the work of an ordinary accountant, must be filed with the U.S. Securities and Exchange Commission before the company even goes public. State law may also require the filing of other, less onerous, reports.

The rules of disclosure are complex, and the resulting report may differ from accounting reports used by management to conduct the business's affairs.

AUDITORS, AND HOW TO MAKE THEIR JOB EASIER

Most corporations will be required to appoint an auditor and have their accounts audited. It is the job of the auditor to report to the members (shareholders) of the corporation as to whether the accounts have been properly prepared, taking notice of the appropriate accounting rules. The auditor must also report as to whether the accounts give a true and fair view of the state of the corporation's affairs during the period in question.

In order to arrive at their conclusion, the auditor will carry out an examination of the records on a test basis to ensure that the accounts are not materially incorrect. This does not mean that the auditor will check every detail, but they will look at a representative sample of transactions to get a feel for whether or not the books are being properly kept.

If your bookkeeping records are poorly kept, inaccurate, or missing, expect to pay a hefty bill to the auditor and to spend a lot of time answering questions about long-gone and often trivial financial events.

DORLING KINDERSLEY & CO.
CERTIFIED PUBLIC ACCOUNTANTS
95 MADISON AVENUE
NEW YORK, NY 10016

INDEPENDENT AUDITORS' REPORT
TO FAST FOOD CORPORATION, ITS DIRECTORS, AND STOCKHOLDERS

We have audited the Consolidated Balance Sheets of Fast Foods Corporation and its subsidiaries as of December 31, 2000 and 1999, and the related Consolidated Statements of Income, Cash Flows, and Stockholders' Equity for each of the three years in the period ended December 31, 2000. These financial statements are the responsibility of the Corporation's management. Our responsibility is to express an opinion on these financial statements based on our audits.

We conducted our audits in accordance with generally accepted auditing standards. Those standards require that we plan and perform the audit to obtain reasonable assurance about whether the financial statements are free of material misstatement.

An audit includes examining, on a test basis, evidence supporting the amounts and disclosures in the financial statements. An audit also includes assessing the accounting principles used and significant estimates made by management, as well as evaluating the overall financial statement presentation. We believe that our audits provide a reasonable basis for our opinion.

In our opinion, such financial statements present fairly, in all material respects, the financial position of Fast Foods Corporation and subsidiaries on December 31, 2000 and 1999, and the results of their operations and their cash flows for each of the three years in the period ended December 31, 2000 in conformity with generally accepted accounting principles.

Dorling Kindersley & Co.
February 5, 2001

AUDITORS' REPORT
Here is an example of an auditors' report, prepared on behalf of the shareholders of Fast Food Corporation. In this case, the auditors have found that the corporation's accounts are accurate and in good order.

If you have a computerized system, the year-end audit is made much simpler for you and your accountant. In fact, with some accounting software, you can do much of the work before your accountant even sets foot on your premises, thereby saving yourself some money.

You can, for example, produce the reports that all auditors will require, such as the trial balance. Some packages have utilities that enable the auditor to run random checks on the transactions and postings, and some have facilities for the preproduction of debtors' confirmation letters. Auditors will normally send those out to debtors to check that the transaction did take place.

In this way, the auditor's life is made much simpler and, hopefully, it will take less time to conduct the audit, your personnel will be free to continue with their work sooner, and there will be a smaller fee for you to pay. In addition, if you require it, your accountant can get on with some work that will be of more benefit to the business than preparing accounts for the auditor. For example, they could recommend how you could tighten up on credit control or taking inventory, or get better
and more timely management accounts, all of which are infinitely more valuable to the owner-manager than a set of audited accounts.

YOUR INTERNET REAL ESTATE, AND HOW TO PROTECT IT

As businesses make increasing use of the internet to promote themselves, to market their products, and even to raise capital, the problem of domain names has come to the forefront. After all, a sole proprietor named John Smith can use his own name in business: there can be 50 corporations named "John Smith Inc.," one in each state, but there can be only one "johnsmithcorp.com" in the entire world. ICANN (Internet Corporation for Assigned Names and Numbers), the worldwide group that governs internet naming rules, has brought good news to businesses that could not use their own name on their website.

First, it establishes procedures for the arbitration of domain-name disputes. If a name that should rightfully be yours, because it's your corporation name or trademark, was registered by someone with no right to the name beyond having claimed it first, you can ask that the name be turned over to you. (You may first want to find the registrant via a search engine such as betterwhois.com, to see whether a small cash payment will do the trick.) An arbitrator can decide the case on submitted documents, without the need for any witnesses or lawyers.

In addition, in November 2000, ICANN announced that it will soon ease the dot-com name crunch by adding new suffixes, several of which are of particular interest to the business community. Of the newly available options, any company can use the suffix "biz," but use of "coop" will be restricted to cooperatives, and "pro" will be limited to professionals such as physicians, lawyers, and accountants, who will have to provide evidence to ICANN of their licensed status.

Giving Bank Guarantees

When the assets of a business are small, anyone lending it money may seek the added protection of requiring the owner to guarantee the loan personally. For corporations, this is, in effect, stripping away some of the protection that the law is supposed to afford the risk-taking owner-manager.

These are eight important things to keep firmly in mind when your bank raises this issue, as at some stage it almost inevitably will if you want to borrow money.

1 Resist any suggestion that you should provide any guarantees at all. Make it absolutely clear that this is just not an option as far as you are concerned.

2 Your next line of defense should be to offer the new assets themselves as security.

Whatever assets you plan to buy with the funds should be comfort enough. If the bank will not accept those assets at the generally accepted discount, then perhaps you are not making a prudent investment. (A generally accepted discount might be 30 percent of the value of any inventory, 50 percent of debtors, and 80 percent of owned real estate.)

3 If pressed, make any guarantee given as specific as possible. For example, set a maximum value.

4 Try to secure the guarantee against specific assets only. Perhaps you could persuade the bank to limit its claims against you to say one particular property, even though what you actually want the funds for is to finance new inventory.

5 Set clear conditions for the guarantee to come to an end, for example when your overdraft or borrowings return to the level they were at before your most recent request for additional funds. If you do not do this, the bank may try to retain the extra comfort of the security of a personal guarantee as part of your permanent banking arrangements. This will leave you exposed to this threat forever. It will also take away a negotiating option for any further financing you may need. If the bank already has your personal guarantee, then you have little else to offer them.

6 Make sure that the conditions of the additional financing are clear, as are any events that could allow the bank to exercise its rights to demand repayment. For example, it is likely that any funds advanced by a bank will come with some strings attached. These could include what and how much of that money can be spent on which particular assets. So, if the funds are advanced for inventory and you use them to buy a new vehicle, however necessary for the business that may be, you will be technically in breach of your loan covenants, as these conditions are known.

7 If you believe that giving a personal guarantee materially changes the nature of the bank's risk, then it may be worth trying for a lower interest rate on the loan. Banks charge interest at a rate above the base rate. A more risky loan to a small firm may be charged out at 4 percent over the base rate of 8 percent, i.e. 12 percent in all. But if your personal assets include a second home worth $150,000 on which there is no mortgage, and the total financing you are looking to secure is, say, $50,000, then any financing with that home as security should be charged at the rate prevailing for a mortgage, which might be just 2 percent over base rate. If this were the case, your new borrowing rate would be a more comfortable 10 percent rather than the 12 percent formerly proposed.

8 Remember that everything in business finance is negotiable, and your relationship with a bank is no exception. Banks are in competition too, so if yours is being unreasonably hard, it may be time to move on to a more reasonable one (or at least to threaten to do so). Obviously, to be able to move on you need to have some advance notice of when the additional funds are needed. Rushing into a new bank and asking for extra financing next week is hardly likely to inspire the bank manager to have much confidence in your abilities as a strategic thinker. That is where your business plan will come into its own.

Distancing Personal Assets

Only by operating through a corporation, giving no personal guarantees, and never falling foul of the fraudulent or wrongful trading laws can you be confident that your personal assets are completely safe. If you are a sole proprietor, a partner, or have given personal guarantees to support a corporation, then your personal assets are at some risk.

It is possible, if you gave your assets away years before going bankrupt or even being in debt, to save them from your creditors, but this calls for extraordinary foresight, and even then things can go wrong.

First, the person you "give" the assets to could take off with them. After all, couples split up and over a third of marriages end in divorce. Second, anyone making a claim against you can ask the court to set aside any gift, however long ago it was made, if they can prove that it was your intention at the time to put those assets beyond their reach. Clearly you can take steps to protect your personal assets from your business liabilities, but it is not a simple matter.

Corporate Officers' Responsibilities

The corporate structure will protect owners and directors from personal liability for the business' debts, but it will not shield them from their own wrongdoing. In certain cases, their assets can be seized, they can be barred from being involved in a public company, and they can even be jailed for committing crimes on behalf of the corporation.

In practice, a corporate officer's general responsibilities are much the same as those for a sole proprietor or partner, and indeed the situation can be better. This is because by forming a corporation, you can separate your own personal assets from the business assets (in theory, at any rate, unless personal guarantees have been extracted). But this separation is conditional upon responsible business behavior.

A director also has to cope with some technical, more detailed requirements, for example sending in accounts to tax and regulatory agencies. More onerous than just signing them, a director is expected, and required by law, to understand the significance

of the balance sheet and profit and loss statement as well as the key performance ratios (see pp. 112–129).

Some of a director's duties, responsibilities, and potential liabilities are:

■ To act in good faith in the interests of the company. This includes carrying out duties diligently and honestly.

■ Not to carry on the business of the company with intent to defraud creditors or for any fraudulent purpose.

■ Not knowingly to allow the company to operate while insolvent ("wrongful trading"). Directors who do so may have to pay for the debts incurred by the company while it was insolvent.

■ Not to deceive shareholders.

■ To have a regard for the interests of employees in general.

■ To comply with the requirements of corporate and securities laws, providing what is needed in accounting records or filing accounts.

What Corporate Officers and Directors Should Avoid

Corporate officers and directors should be careful to avoid operating while insolvent; wrongful trading; fraud; "piercing the corporate veil"; and other pitfalls, including tax and payroll-related violations of the law.

■ **Operating While Insolvent** This occurs when your liabilities exceed your assets. At this point, the shareholders' equity in the business has effectively ceased to exist, and when shareholder equity is negative, directors are personally at risk and owe a duty of care to creditors – not shareholders. If you find yourself even approaching a state of insolvency, you need the prompt advice of a business bankruptcy lawyer. Directors who act properly will not be penalized and will live to fight another day.

■ **Wrongful Trading** This term can apply to a corporation if, after a corporation goes into bankruptcy, the trustee believes that the directors (or those acting as such) ought to have concluded earlier that the corporation had no realistic chance of survival. In these circumstances, the courts can remove the shelter of limited liabilities and so make the directors personally liable for the corporation's debts.

▓ **FRAUD** This is a rather more serious position than wrongful trading. Here the proposition is that the director(s) were knowingly party to fraud of their creditors. The full shelter of limited liability can be removed under these circumstances.

▓ **PIERCING THE CORPORATE VEIL** In certain circumstances, a court may hold managing owners personally liable for the apparent debts of the corporation. This process, called "piercing (or lifting) the corporate veil," may occur if the owners treated the corporation as an adjunct of their own lives, by using the corporation as a vehicle to conduct their personal affairs.

▓ **OTHER PITFALLS** Other laws that can hold officers personally liable, civilly or criminally, include certain tax and payroll-related violations. In addition, prosecutors have sometimes tried, often unsuccessfully, to charge managers with homicide in cases of egregious safety violations that resulted in workers' deaths.

Choosing an Accountant

Keeping your financial affairs in good order is the key to staying legal and winning any disputes. A good accountant inside or outside the firm can keep you on track and legal, while a bad accountant is in the ideal position to defraud you, at worst, or derail you through negligence or incompetence.

Bearing in mind the importance of finding a law-abiding, knowledgeable, and diligent person for this job, what attributes should you look for and how can you find the right accountant for your business? The key steps are as follows:

▓ Be sure that they are in good standing with the state licensing board.

▓ Have a clear idea of what services you require from your accountant. You need to consider how complete your bookkeeping records are likely to be and whether you will need the sales tax return done, budgets and cash-flow forecasts prepared and updated, in addition to an audit.

▓ Clarify the fee scale at the outset. It may make more sense to spend a little more on your staff and computer systems to do your bookkeeping internally rather than leaving it all to a much more expensive qualified accountant.

▓ Follow up personal recommendations from respected business colleagues. There is nothing like hearing from a fellow consumer about a product or service. Pay less attention to the recommendations of bankers, government agencies, family, and friends, without totally ignoring their advice. They may have a vested interest in the person they are recommending.

▓ Find out who else they act for. You do not want them to be so busy working for highly demanding clients that they cannot service your needs properly, nor do you want them to be working for any of your potential competitors.

▓ Find out what backup they have for both systems and people. The tax authorities will not be sympathetic, whatever the reason for lateness of statements and audits. It would be doubly annoying to be fined for someone else's tardiness.

▓ Take references from the accountant's clients, as well as from the person who recommended the accountant. It could just be good fortune that they get along, or it could be that they are related or in business together.

▓ See at least three accountants before making your choice. Check that they deal with companies your size and a little bigger: you want to be able to grow without having to change accountants too quickly.

◼ Make the appointment for a trial period only. Set a specific task to see how they get along.

◼ Give them the latest accounts of your business and ask them for their comments based on their analysis of the figures. You will quickly see if they have grasped the basics of your financial position.

Closing Down the Business

The lifetime of the average business is relatively short – much shorter, in fact, than the life of the typical business owner. The reasons for a business' demise range from the relatively benign sale of the business to the disastrous bankruptcy. The options open to the owner are to sell the business, close down, or go under. The financial process of a business is not complete until it closes down.

SELLING UP

Getting the best value for your business may involve getting expensive corporate finance advice to maximize the price in the minimum amount of time. Without an auction or controlled auction, you could be shortchanged by as much as 50 percent. Sweetheart deals – a popular strategy for people retiring from a business, where you sell out to someone you know or do business with – are almost always bad deals for the seller.

Having received your price, how can you be sure you will get your money? Warranties, missed earn-outs, and bad tax advice could take as much as 70 percent of the selling price out of your pocket.

These are the pointers to make sure you get the best result when selling a business.

1 Even if your business is not in the greatest of shape, or even if it is financially troubled, remember that selling an operating business almost always brings more money than closing it down and selling off the assets. Before you give up and conclude that no one will buy your business, consider that people do buy businesses, even ones with financial problems, for all sorts of reasons: Yours could be just what they are looking for.

◼ The buyer may have a similar business and can combine the two to operate more efficiently than you can. The buyer may be extremely anxious to take over one or more of your business assets – its location, key employees, or domain name if you are on the internet.

◼ The buyer may have better access to needed financing than you do and therefore be able to stay the course until your good business idea ultimately proves itself.

◼ The buyer may have greater expertise in your business than you do and see a way to turn a loss into a profit by changing how the business is run.

◼ The buyer may conclude that it is cheaper to buy your business and turn it around than to start a similar business from scratch.

2 Do not get into a sweetheart deal with a buyer who claims to be able to act quickly if you can just keep the corporate finance people out of the deal. Recently, a prospective purchaser offered $12 million for a business and insisted on a lockout deal, with no other purchasers being involved. When the business finally went to auction, they paid $25 million.

3 Do beauty pagents with corporate finance and lawyers. See at least three of each, preferably on the same day. Not only is time of the essence, but you will remember their good and bad points better.

4 Find advisers who are the right size for your deal. There is no point in getting the best guys in town to sell a business worth just $500,000 when they are used to dealing with corporations worth multiple millions. After they have sold you the deal, the partners will vanish and leave you with the office boys to do the work. Find a firm that specializes in your size of deal.

5 Everything to do with selling is negotiable. The corporate finance advisers will want upfront payments and high results-related rewards. You can get everything done on contingency and pay a smaller percentage the more the business is sold for.

6 Nail down everything with the corporate finance people and get your contract with them examined by your legal advisers; otherwise unfavorable clauses will slip through. For example, if there is a time clause, you could have to sell at a lower price or pay their bill in full when the six months' search time is up.

7 During the due diligence process done by the acquirer, get every skeleton out of every closet. If you do not, the warranties will come back to haunt you. You could be pursued years later to compensate for any liability not declared.

8 The corporate finance team should bring experience, credibility, and, hopefully, a couple of prospective buyers to the table. Two buyers makes for an auction, and auctions make for better prices.

9 Go through the term sheet (as the offer to buy document is called) very carefully. The price will be only the headline figure in a fairly complex document. That price may be dependent on customers and key staff remaining with the firm, or it may be dependent on certain projects under development being completed on time and at budgeted cost.

10 Whatever the logic behind the offer price, multiple of sales, price earnings, and so on, it is just a yardstick to make people feel comfortable. Price is just the figure people will pay at a given moment for a given business.

11 Your share of whatever the business sells for will be a lot less if you do not get good tax advice. Owners can end up paying between nothing and 51 percent tax on any gain. (Note that the gain will be calculated on the price of the share options, which may have been granted at very favorable prices.)

12 The price you agree to sell at will not be paid. The auction process pushes the price up, but the purchaser can win much of that back again using various techniques. For example, they can try to string negotiations out for long enough for other prospective bidders to have lost interest and gone elsewhere. To prevent this from happening you must keep the pressure on during negotiations. Alternatively, the purchaser can try to claim that what you are selling is not quite what they thought they were buying. You can limit this danger during due diligence.

13 Be scrupulously honest during due diligence. Once both sides are in general agreement over the terms of the sale, your business will be reviewed in detail. This will ensure that the buyer gets what they think they are getting.

The ownership of assets, patents, and copyrights will be examined, as will employment contracts, the customer terms and conditions, and so on. The basis of plans and projections will also be reviewed. If you think that your annual audit is an intrusive experience, due diligence is more like invasive surgery.

Just in case the prospective buyer has missed anything, you will be asked to warrant the deal. This basically means that, if any material liability is uncovered after the sale that was not either uncovered in the due diligence or included in your offer memorandum, you pick up the tab. The buyer may well expect a sum to be set aside to cover any such eventuality for a period of months – or even years.

If the due diligence uncovers problems, there are usually only four options: if the buyer is very eager to buy, they can be asked to live with it; if they are less enthusiastic, the price can be adjusted to reflect the potential problem; specific guarantees or indemnities can be offered to protect the buyer from such problems. This may include retention of some of the purchase monies; the deal is off.

If you can break the business into parts, separating off, for example, the property, you may be able to get some additional value from the sale.

14 To avoid horrors being uncovered in the due diligence, you may need to clean up the corporation beforehand. A change of auditors may be necessary, if you have been using a sleepy small local firm, especially if they have become particularly friendly. In preparing for a sale, you would be wise to select a more inquisitive and thorough firm, with a reputation that is likely to be known, and respected by, potential buyers.

Private businesses tend to run expenses through the business that might be frowned upon under different ownership. One firm, for example, had its sale delayed for three years while the chairman's yacht was removed from "work-in-progress." There can also be problems when personal assets are tucked away in the corporation, or when staff have been paid rather informally, free of tax. The liability rests with the corporation, and if the practice has continued for many years the financial picture can look quite messy.

The years before you sell can be used to good effect by improving the performance of your business relative to others in your industry. Going through the profit and loss statement and balance sheet, using ratios, will point out areas for improvement. Once the business is firmly planted on an upward trend, your future projections will look that much more plausible, and therefore encouraging, to a potential buyer.

You should certainly have a business plan and strategic projections for at least three years. This will underpin the strength of your negotiations by demonstrating your management skills in putting together the plan, and showing that you believe that the company has a healthy future.

PROS AND CONS OF SELLING

✓ You will be able to invest your money in a spread of businesses rather than just in your own business.

✓ You will have the time to pursue new business or personal interests.

✓ You will achieve financial security for yourself and your family.

✗ Once having been your own boss, it is hard to be anything else.

✗ The new owners will want to do things differently, which may be distressing to watch.

✗ You may find it more difficult than you imagine to stop working long hours.

✗ Selling a business can result in a sense of bereavement or loss.

✗ If family members work in your business, they may lose their jobs.

CLOSING DOWN

If your business is not insolvent, but consists largely of yourself and your relationships with customers and suppliers, then in truth you may have little to sell. It may be that a family member or an employee could take over from you and pay you out of a share of future profits. If that is the case, then a much-slimmed-down version of the process described above is all that needs to be gone through.

If neither of those conditions prevail, then you need to close the business down in an orderly fashion, disposing of assets and paying off liabilities. Subject only to any possible capital gains tax demands that may arise, the surplus is yours.

If you are in a partnership, you may be advised to take public leave of that relationship. That will prevent any misunderstandings with people doing business with any remaining partners, if some parts of the business are to continue to operate after you have gone. Once again, professional advice should be sought.

GOING UNDER

Many businesses do not enjoy the luxury of a dignified exit. They are forced into failure, usually with unpleasant repercussions. Something can usually be salvaged from the wreckage, but that requires you to know something of the likely events that lie ahead. Fortune favors the prepared mind.

The various ways in which small (and, for that matter, not so small) businesses go under are listed below:

▓ **BANKRUPTCY** This is a way of dealing with your financial affairs if you cannot pay your debts. While it is not a criminal offense to get into debt, becoming a bankrupt has serious implications. Bankruptcy is a legal procedure for businesses and individuals who are insolvent, that is, their liabilities exceed their assets, to find a way out of that situation. Bankruptcy cases are federal cases that are heard by special bankruptcy judges in each federal court district.

A bankruptcy petition can be voluntary, when it is filed by the individual or business debtor, or involuntary, when it is filed by one or more creditors.

A bankruptcy case can involve a business or an individual. Personal bankruptcy becomes an issue for sole proprietors, partners, general partners of limited partnerships, and in cases where corporate officers gave personal guarantees for their business debts.

Whether personal or business, there are two types of bankruptcy: liquidation, in which assets are sold, and reorganization, which involves developing a realistic plan to put the debtor's finances and business operations on firmer shoring.

Filing a bankruptcy petition puts an immediate halt to all other pending legal proceedings, include wage garnishment and property foreclosure. The bankruptcy court will appoint a trustee, usually a lawyer well versed in bankruptcy law, either to sell the debtor's assets, in a liquidation case, or to monitor the debtor's attempts at any reorganization.

Although bankruptcy is governed by federal law, state laws determine which assets can be retained by the bankrupt. State laws vary widely, and debtors can lose or keep their homes and vehicles, depending on where they live. Individuals and couples must file in their state of residence.

Because it is so specialized, with so much depending on state laws and the ability to negotiate with trustees and creditors, it is important to work with an experienced attorney who specializes in your type of case, the earlier the better.

For this reason, you should monitor your business' finances and contact your attorney at the first warning signs of trouble. In most cases, the signals appear long before bankruptcy is on the horizon. By facing the reality that your business is not making money, or is losing money at an increasingly fast pace, you may be able to work out issues with creditors more advantageously than you could on bankruptcy court.

The first thing to determine is whether in fact you owe the debts your creditors claim, or whether you have sufficient setoffs to avoid undergoing the intrusive process of bankruptcy.

If you do go bankrupt, there are certain debts you cannot discharge. They will be paid first (after court costs, legal fees, and the trustee's fee), and they will remain your obligation after the case is over. These include taxes, debts incurred by fraud, and unpaid alimony and child support.

Next to be paid are secured and preferred creditors (with judgments, liens, and mortgages), and some wages you may owe employees. The rest of your assets will be prorated to your unsecured creditors. In a business reorganization plan, the trustee will examine your proposed plan to determine whether you it is feasible for your business, and if it is, whether your business will survive reorganization. Your business will not be put on "life support" if the only realistic outcome is that it will die anyway, owing creditors even more money.

If your plan is declared effective, which requires creditors' approval, voting by their share of that type of debt, you can continue to operate the business as the "debtor in possession." This may actually improve your position, because creditors can advance you limited amounts of credit with the reasonable assurance of being paid.

Finally, the new presidential administration is expected to renew efforts to change bankruptcy laws and procedures, which failed to become law in 2000. As with everything having to do with law or business, make sure you consult your legal and business advisers before taking important steps.

■ **FORECLOSURE** This is a legal proceeding brought against property, not a business or person, when a loan secured by a mortgage secured by that property remains unpaid. The most usual scenario is where a borrower gives a mortgage on real property or equipment, to induce the lender to advance the necessary funds.

Whatever the terms of the mortgage, possession of the property cannot be regained without the issuing of a state court order foreclosing the owner's interest in the property. The court will appoint a receiver to sell the property, usually at public auction, in order to pay off the debt. In many cases, selling the property is not the lender's only recourse. The mortgage is usually accompanied by a promissory note to the lender, giving the lender the right to seek any deficiency from the borrower.

FINANCIAL MATTERS

Taxation is many people's bête noire: we do not like paying it, and we do not like working out how much we have to pay. If you are an employee, then your employer is responsible for calculating your taxes and payroll deductions, for withholding these amounts from your paycheck, and for remitting them to the appropriate government agency on a quarterly basis. If you are running a small business, however, you need to know how to deal with the various taxes that apply to business in your area, because the responsibility for their calculation and collection will almost certainly fall on you.

As a source of funds, taxation has proved irresistible to governments the world over. For over eight continuous decades, everyone in the U.S., with limited exceptions, who earns income, or the right to an income, has been required to account to the government for their income and profits. The same is true for most other countries, although both the amounts and methods of assessment vary widely. In the U.S., for example, tax revenues amount to a third of its GDP (gross domestic product), while in Sweden it amounts to about half.

Calculating Tax Due

The more successful a small business is, the greater its exposure to tax liabilities. Its exact tax position will depend on the legal nature of the business. The business income of sole proprietorships, partnerships of various types, and Subchapter S corporations will be added to their other income to be taxed at personal income tax rates. The owners of regular ("C") corporations are taxed twice, once on the income of the corporation at corporate tax rates, and again on their wages and dividends, at personal tax rates. Both personal and corporate rates are graduated, and the rates at which they are set may change from year to year.

Simply monitoring pretax ratios, which in themselves are satisfactory measures of business performance only, is not enough. The owner-manager is concerned with the net profit after tax. This, after all, is the money available to help the business to grow, or to meet unforeseen problems.

Managing the tax position is one area where timely professional advice is essential. This is made even more important because tax rules can change every year. Good advice can help to reduce the overall tax bill and so increase the value of profits to the business.

The various types of business are treated differently for tax purposes, so this section looks at each of the following in turn:
■ sole proprietors
■ partners
■ corporations

SOLE PROPRIETORS AND PARTNERSHIPS

Partnerships are treated as a collection of sole proprietors for tax purposes, and each partner's share of that collective liability has to be worked out. Sole proprietors (the self-employed) have all their income from every source brought together and taxed as one entity. The taxes that need to be calculated are:
■ income tax, on profits
■ Social Security and Medicare taxes, on profits
■ capital gains tax, on the disposal of fixed

assets at a profit, or when the business is sold
■ inheritance tax, paid on death or when certain gifts are made

Neither of the last two taxes are likely to occur on a regular basis, so they are not covered in detail here. When those taxes do come into play, the sums involved are likely to be significant, so you should seek professional advice from the outset.

■ **Income Tax** The profit and loss statement, while more than adequate for the purpose of running the business, is not sufficient for

working out the likely tax due. Some perfectly acceptable expenses that need to be accounted for in deciding how well or badly the business is running are not allowed for tax purposes, or at any rate not in the way we have treated them so far.

THE EFFECTS OF DEPRECIATION

By setting a low rate of depreciation, so that only $2,000 is claimed for this, Fast Food achieved a high profit before tax figure of $21,950. If the depreciation had been set higher, so that $15,000 were claimed, the profit would have been much lower at $8,950.

FAST FOOD'S DEPRECIATION OF PROFITABILITY						
PROFIT AND LOSS STATEMENT		YEAR 2 ($)	LOW DEPRECIATION (%)	YEAR 2 ($)	HIGH DEPRECIATION (%)
SALES		130,000	100	130,000	100
COST OF SALES	Materials	43,000	33	43,000	33
	Labor	25,000	19	25,000	19
	COST OF GOODS SOLD	68,000		68,000	
GROSS PROFIT		62,000	48	62,000	48
EXPENSES	Rent, utilities, etc.	20,000		20,000	
	Wages	13,000		13,000	
	Advertising	3,000		3,000	
	Depreciation	2,000		15,000	
TOTAL EXPENSES		38,000		51,000	
OPERATING PROFIT		24,000	18.5	11,000	11
DEDUCT INTEREST ON: BORROWINGS		2,050		2,050	
NET PROFIT BEFORE TAX		21,950	16.8	8,950	6.88

The rate of depreciation, for example, is broadly a matter for each businessperson to decide for themselves. In the management accounts, you can decide, for example, to depreciate an asset over one year or five years. The nominal effect on profits can be significant. The accounts for Fast Food have been used again to illustrate this point (see chart on p. 160). Only the second year's figures have been used, and in an abbreviated form. They show that the higher the rate of depreciation set, the lower the rate of profit. Were that the case, then the tax due would also be much lower. Unfortunately, the taxman does not see it quite like this.

In practice, certain business expenses are disallowed, partially disallowed, or allowed for but in a different way. Such are the ways of tax authorities the world over. Some are a little less obscure in their workings than others, but few are transparent.

The profit computation is a process that has to be gone through after you have produced your management accounts showing what you understand to be the income and expenditure for the period and a record of assets bought. This computation will adjust that profit figure to meet the tax authorities' needs. Unsurprisingly, this is usually a higher figure, and so a higher tax liability, than the one you had arrived at.

Fast Food's year 2 figures demonstrate how these adjustments are made to the accounting profit to arrive at the profit for taxation purposes (see right). The expense section has been expanded to include extra details needed for this example, i.e. transportation expenses have been separated from rent.

In the computation, some of the expenses are disallowed. These include depreciation, which is replaced by capital expenses. Capital expenses are an incentive allowed by governments to encourage investment in new equipment and technology. The rate is changed in the annual budget to reflect the foibles of the government of the day. In this example, the writing-down allowance, as this is known, is 25 percent. For the first year in which the assets are bought, however, as an

PROFIT ADJUSTMENT

Depreciation and 25% of transportation expenses have been disallowed as expenses on these accounts, bringing the net profit before tax up to $26,450. The deduction of capital allowances totaling $10,169 gives Fast Food an adjusted profit figure of $16,281.

ADJUSTMENT TO FAST FOOD'S ACCOUNTS TO ARRIVE AT TAXABLE PROFITS		
PROFIT AND LOSS		**($)**
GROSS PROFIT		62,000
EXPENSES	Rent, utilities, etc.	10,000
	Transportation	10,000
	Wages	13,000
	Advertising	3,000
	Depreciation	2,000
TOTAL EXPENSES		38,000
OPERATING PROFIT		24,000
DEDUCT INTEREST ON: BORROWINGS		2,050
NET PROFIT BEFORE TAX		21,950
ADD BACK	25% Transportation	2,500
	Depreciation	2,000
TOTAL		26,450
MINUS CAPITAL ALLOWANCES		10,169
ADJUSTED PROFIT		16,281

| CALCULATING FAST FOOD'S CAPITAL ALLOWANCES | | | CAPITAL ALLOWANCE FOR YEAR 2 |
FIXED ASSETS	YEAR 1 ($)	YEAR 2 ($)	*The fixed assets bought in the first year are written down to 25% of their cost.*
EXPENDITURE ON FURNITURE AND FIXTURES	12,500	17,610	*This figure is then added to the allowance for the cost of the fixed assets bought*
25 PERCENT YEAR 1 FIXED ASSETS	3,125		*during the second year, which are written down to*
40 PERCENT YEAR 2 FIXED ASSETS		7,044	*40% of their cost, to give the total capital allowance*
TOTAL CAPITAL ALLOWANCE YEAR 2		10,169	*figure for year 2 of $10,169.*

incentive to invest, the rate is 40 percent. Also, any private element of expenses charged in the accounts is added back.

While you may dispute that you use your car for any purpose other than for business because you have a second car, in practice it will be easier to succumb to the norms that require you to say a certain percentage (in this example, 25 percent) is private usage. You can see that the changes that have to be made to the management accounts to arrive at the profit for tax purposes can have a significant effect on the end result.

We have included only a few of the adjustments needed, by way of illustration. Other changes an owner-manager may have to make include:

■ Adjustment to telephone charges if business and personal telephone use overlap; mobile phone calls also come under this heading.
■ Heating, lighting, and other property charges if the business is run from home.
■ Use of inventory for personal use, for example food products if you run a grocery store, or car parts if you run a garage.

You will need to ensure that any expense that may have seemed reasonable in the management accounts meets the more stringent requirements of the tax authorities. You are generally allowed to set an expense against your income if it is:

■ Incurred wholly and exclusively for the purposes of business properly charged

against income (not, for example, purchase of a property lease, which is capital).
■ Not specifically disallowed by statute.
■ **NET TAXABLE PROFIT** Under the self-assessment tax system, the basis of a period of a year of assessment is the accounting year ending within that tax year.

You can maintain your accounts on a cash basis of income received and expenses spent, or on an accrual basis of income you have a right to, whether or not you received it, and expenses you are required to pay, whether or not you paid them. You can also choose as your tax year the calendar year ending December 31, or any other continuous 12-month period if, for example, you began your business in the middle of the year.

Wages paid to employees and the income of self-employed persons, such as sole proprietors, partners, and the owners of Subchapter S corporations, are subject to Social Security/Medicare tax. The employer and the employee must pay this tax, and self-employed persons are considered to wear both hats, and so must pay both the employer and the employee share of the tax.

The current rate of Social Security/Medicare tax is 15.3 percent (7.65 percent each) on the first $68,400 of annual income. Higher incomes are taxed at 2.9 percent (1.45 percent each) for Medicare. Personal income tax rates are graduated, and the highest rate is 39.6 percent on taxable

DEDUCTING A DIRECTOR'S PAY

The director's pay of $13,000 is added to Fast Food's other expenses and deducted from the gross profit. Once corporation tax of $2,442 has been paid, the remaining profit belongs to the shareholders: $4,000 is paid to them in dividends, leaving $9,839 to be flowed back into the business to help it grow.

income exceeding $278,540 on a joint return, that is, a husband and wife pooling their income. Your exact rate depends on your marital and filing status, and the number of dependants, such as yourself, your spouse, your minor children, and any other person for whom you provide more than half of their necessary expenses. This last category may include elderly parents, infirm relatives, and children from a previous marriage, depending on the terms of the child support order or agreement.

The same personal income tax rules apply to state and local income taxes, if any, which may also have different rates for residents and nonresidents.

CORPORATION TAXATION

Corporations have a separate legal identity from those who work in them, whether or not they are shareholders or directors. Everyone working in the business is taxed as an employee. The corporation is responsible for collecting tax and passing it on to the tax authorities.

Directors' pay is a business expense, just as any other wages are, and it is deducted from the corporation's revenues during the process of arriving at its taxable profits. The chart above shows how this works in practice. U.S. corporations pay tax in three main ways:

■ **ON THE COMPANY'S PROFITS** for the year, as calculated in the tax adjusted profits. This is called corporation tax. The rate of corporation tax depends on the amount of profits made; they are also subject to annual review. The tax corporate rate graduates from 15 percent on taxable corporate income of less than $50,000, to a maximum rate of 39 percent on taxable corporate income of

between $100,000 and $335,000. The rate is 34 percent for taxable corporate income between $335,000 and $10 million, 35 percent on the next $5 million, 38 percent on the next $3,333,333, and 35 percent for more than $18,333,333.

■ **ON THE DISTRIBUTION OF PROFIT** to the shareholders in the dividend payment. The dividends paid are not a deductible business expense for the corporation.

■ **ON CAPITAL GAINS** If an asset, say a

FAST FOOD'S CORPORATION TAXATION

YEAR 2		$
GROSS PROFIT		62,000
EXPENSES	Rent, utilities, etc.	10,000
	Transportation	7,500
	Director's pay	13,000
	Advertising	3,000
	Capital expenses	10,169
TOTAL EXPENSES		43,669
OPERATING PROFIT		18,331
DEDUCT INTEREST ON: BORROWINGS		2,050
NET PROFIT BEFORE TAX		16,281
CORPORATION TAX		2,442
PROFIT AFTER TAX		13,839
DIVIDEND		4,000
RETAINED PROFIT		9,839

business property, is sold at a profit, then the company will have made a capital gain. Tax itself is also a business expense for a company, so an allowance for tax must be included in the accounts. Before it is paid, you accrue for it by showing it as a creditor in the balance sheet. (See pp. 97–99 for details of accrual.) When it is paid, it will appear in the profit and loss statement.

WHICH STRUCTURE IS BEST?

The most important rule is never to let the tax tail wag the business dog. If you want to keep your business's finances private, then the disclosure requirements of publicly traded corporations will not be for you. On the other hand, if you feel that you want to protect your private assets from creditors in the event that things go wrong, then being a sole proprietor or partner is probably not the best route to take.

Corporate profits and losses are locked into the corporation, so if you have several lines of business using different trading entities, you cannot easily settle losses in one area against profits in another. But because sole proprietors are treated as one entity for all their sources of income, there is more scope for netting off gains and losses.

Unless you are seeking angel or venture-capital financing, or have more than 75 shareholders, you can have the limited liability of a corporation without the negative tax implications. A Subchapter S corporation avoids double taxation, as does a limited liability company. Furthermore, the gap between the health and retirement benefits available to corporate owners and to the self-employed has been substantially narrowed.

Self-employed people and workers, including officers, at businesses with fewer than 50 employees can establish medical savings accounts. They can then put pretax contributions in higher-growth investments, roll over the funds that are not needed for medical expenses until age 65, then withdraw the funds, paying taxes but no penalties. Unlike the medical expense plans available to employees of larger corporations, the contributions are not subject to "use it or lose it" requirements. And the self-employed have expanded retirement plan options providing simple, easy-to-maintain ways to invest a significant amount of untaxed funds that can grow, tax-free, into a sizable nest egg.

With proper planning and record-keeping, even many of the other perks of corporate life, such as car allowances, and travel and entertainment, do not require the structure and tax and disclosure provisions of a C or publicly traded corporation.

Minimizing the Taxes You Pay

There is no reason to arrange your financial affairs in such a way as to pay the most tax possible. While staying within the law by a safe margin, you should explore ways to avoid, as opposed to evade, tax liability. This is a complex area and one subject to frequent change. The tax authorities try most years to close loopholes in the tax system, while highly paid tax accountants and lawyers try even harder to find new ways around the rules.

This is a field in which timely professional advice can produce substantial benefits in the form of lower tax bills. The summary of legal tax-saving measures shown on p. 166 provides an indicative list of areas to explore.

Sales Taxes

The U.S. government imposes excise taxes on a variety of items, including alcohol, gasoline, and tobacco, but unlike most European countries, there is no federal tax on general consumer spending. States, counties, and cities, however, can and do impose sales taxes on many consumer goods and/or services.

These taxes apply to different goods or services, at different price ranges, and may or may not depend on the customer's residence.

In most jurisdictions with sales taxes, goods bought for resale (inventory) are not subject to sales tax, but goods bought for business use are taxable. If you reside in the area, you know whether there are sales taxes. Consult the appropriate government agency to obtain the applicable forms and publications, and read them carefully. Then consult your accountant for guidance on collecting the taxes from your customers, properly accounting for the taxes, and paying them to the government in full and on time.

Remember that the taxes you collect are not income, and you should be careful to avoid paying income tax on money you merely collect and hold for the government for a short time. In most instances, corporate officers are personally liable for remitting the taxes collected to the tax authority. Since the taxes collected do not belong to the business, this is not an area for poor record-keeping or gamesmanship.

Handling Employment Taxes

Employing people, including corporate officers, requires a business to withhold from their pay federal (and, if required, state and local) income taxes, Social Security and Medicare taxes, and unemployment and disability insurance taxes. The business must also pay unemployment insurance taxes and workers compensation and disability insurance premiums, as well as health insurance premiums and retirement plan contributions, which are often made by both employer and employee. As you can see, these withholdings and deductions involve a great deal of record-keeping and put employers and managers in the position of being unpaid tax collectors.

Employers must file a quarterly federal report, Form 941, but their obligation to remit taxes may be much more frequent, depending on the annual amount of tax holdings.

At the end of each year, employers must give employees a Form W-2 showing these withholdings, and must give contractors and independent contractors a Form 1099 showing their earnings, from which there were no withholdings or deductions.

Because of the onerous amount of record-keeping and the penalties for getting it wrong, many businesses outsource employment taxes and deductions, even if they do their own accounting in-house. Ask your accountant whether you should use an outside payroll service to handle payroll deductions and taxes.

There is a fine line between considering your staff as employees or as independent contractors, but there is a line: typically, they are employees if you exercise control over how they do the work, and if they use your tools and equipment.

If the paperwork is too onerous, consider outsourcing the project through a temporary employment agency.

Your employees may ask you to let them work "off the books," that is, without any deductions, or you may ask them to do so, to reduce your tax and paperwork burden. You should avoid this temptation at all costs, because it can lead to an extensive investigation with considerable penalties. Also, if you cannot run your business with committing a crime, or aiding and abetting the commission of a crime, you might consider whether you should be in business at all.

Surviving a Tax Investigation

With good bookkeeping and accounting systems, you should avoid any disputes over tax and other matters. Complete records are vital if you are to defend yourself successfully

AREAS TO CONSIDER WHEN ASSESSING YOUR TAX LIABILITY

1 Make sure you have included all allowable business expenses.

2 If you have made losses in any tax period, these may under certain circumstances be carried forward to offset future taxable profits or backward against past profits.

3 Capital gains tax can be deferred if another asset is to be bought with he proceeds.

4 Pension contributions will reduce your taxable profits.

AVOIDING TAX

This example illustrates the impact on taxable profits that taking some of the above measures could have on a business. By deducting sums for pension contributions, writing-down allowance, pre-start-up expenses, an employed spouse, and last year's loss, the business saved itself $1,900 on its tax bill.

5 If you intend to buy capital assets for your business, bring forward your plans so as to maximize use of the writing down allowance.

6 Identify noncash benefits that you and employees could take instead of taxable salaries, such as a stock option plan.

7 Examine the pros and cons of taking your money out of a corporation in salary or dividends. These are taxed differently and may provide a measure of tax reduction.

8 Any pre-operating expenses, such as designing a product or buying a computer, incurred at any stage before you started up can probably be treated as if they had been incurred after the business started.

9 If you bought any business assets on a rent-to-own plan, you may be able to include the full purchase price of the items in your capital allowances calculation.

TAX SAVING: TAKING LEGAL AVOIDANCE MEASURES

		WITHOUT TAKING AVOIDANCE MEASURES ($)	TAKING AVOIDANCE MEASURES ($)
ADJUSTED TAXABLE PROFITS		50,000	50,000
ADJUSTED TAXABLE PROFITS, LESS:	First year writing-down allowance on $10,000 worth of new equipment (40%)		4,000
	Pre-start-up expenses		3,000
	Offsetting last year's loss		2,500
TOTAL TAX AVOIDANCE MEASURES		0	9,500
FINAL TAXABLE PROFIT		50,000	40,500
TAX PAID AT 20%		10,000	8,100

from mistaken allegations of wrongdoing. There are some factors that will help you understand how tax inquiries get started and what might happen if one does.

WHY TAX INVESTIGATIONS HAPPEN

The Internal Revenue Service (IRS) gets its information from three sources. Their own investigations and tips from the public account for the vast majority of their information received. However, an increasingly effective measure is to ask people to inform on themselves. Crazy as that may sound, it seems to work. While this does not quite amount to an amnesty, those self-employed who have strayed across the boundary between tax avoidance and tax evasion can contact tax authorities anonymously and get confidential advice on how to sort themselves out.

Sometimes the tax authorities look closely at whole industries. Recently they have looked long and hard at the amusement arcade business, construction, betting and gaming, commodities dealing, and some doctors and dentists.

Tax inspectors may also do any of the following in their search for tax evaders:
▓ Drive around exclusive residential areas and look carefully at any expensive-looking renovation work.
▓ Use the services of restaurants, hotels, copy shops, and other cash businesses, while looking carefully at each business's cost structure.
▓ Read local newspapers and use press-clipping agencies to cross-check people's claimed lifestyle with their actual one.
▓ Access company databases and online records from the Securities & Exchange Commission.
▓ Check up on local parking permits in certain areas.
▓ Examine property records to monitor house purchases and property prices and sales and to keep an eye on boat and airplane sales.

The IRS put all the information that it gathers into its computers, where all these sources of data are cross-correlated with each other. They have a skilled project team looking specifically at the uses of IT for tax investigations, and they can usually uncover anything that does not look quite right. For example, if someone is claiming to make no profit from their business, but, rather surprisingly, owns a yacht, has a residence parking permit for inner-city parking in an area they do not appear to live in, and is having a new swimming pool installed at their home, alarm bells ring.

What is much more likely, however, is that someone tips the tax inspectors off. Informers are often aggrieved spouses or employees, competitors, jealous neighbors, or jilted lovers. Other informers are encouraged by the bounty the IRS pays from the proceeds of monies received from tax cheats.

Some of this information is secondhand and dangerously wrong, but that is how gossip works. Some people like to brag about how they load their expenses or take cash payments that are not entered in the books, so it is not exactly surprising that gossip starts. If that gossip reaches a tax inspector's ears, then an investigation may begin.

HOW YOU KNOW IT HAS STARTED

It is not too difficult to know when a tax investigation is underway. You will probably get a standard letter from the Internal Revenue Service (IRS), or your accountant will. It will state that inquiries have begun and will explain the procedure. By this stage you can be sure that a lot of information has already been gathered.

THE TAX AUTHORITIES' POWERS

Revenue agents have sweeping powers to demand documents from the taxpayer and from third parties. They are always entitled to obtain papers and documents under a notice if that notice is valid, and they can go back as much as 20 years into a person's affairs in cases of suspected fraud. That is way beyond the six years that you are required to keep your own accounting records. So, if you have stuck strictly to the six-year rule, you may be at something of a disadvantage in the event of a tax inquiry.

What they are not entitled to do is to insist upon an interview with the taxpayer or third parties. They cannot force people to speak.

The IRS is allowed to search premises and remove documents if they have a warrant. If they raid your premises, do not obstruct them, but do follow a few simple rules:

◼ Make sure your professional adviser gets to the premises as fast as possible.

◼ Read the warrant and make sure that you understand it.

◼ Remember you are under no legal obligation to talk.

◼ Make sure that your staff are also aware that they are under no legal obligation to talk.

◼ Ask what is the purpose of the search.

◼ Obtain a receipt for any materials that they take away.

◼ Get the name and office of the investigator in charge.

CONFIDENTIALITY

The IRS understands the real world and the fact that some people have complex financial, commercial, and personal lives. They go to great lengths to protect confidences and save unnecessary embarrassments.

This means, in practice, that disclosures can be made on a managed basis. Two spouses can go through one joint disclosure as appropriate, and then have separate meetings with the IRS in which they can make disclosures of which the other is unaware. Likewise, company directors can make disclosures of which fellow directors are unaware.

The IRS does, however, have a number of obligations to share information with federal prosecutors and state tax agencies.

PRIVILEGE

In theory, whatever you disclose to your lawyer is privileged, but in practice this is not always so. For example:

◼ Original documents recording a transaction are never covered.

◼ Any communication intended to facilitate a crime is excluded.

◼ Documents that get into the hands of a third party are usually no longer privileged.

What you reveal to your tax adviser is also covered by the privilege law, but less so. The law on privilege is not clear-cut, and you should always ask your adviser about which disclosures are covered and which are not. You have more privilege as to discussions with your lawyer than with an accountant, enrolled agent, or tax preparer.

MEETINGS

Meetings with the IRS can be tense and contentious affairs. The atmosphere is similar to that in a court between two opposing lawyers. Both parties' main task is to put their own position in the most believable light. In the process, the truth can get left behind.

If you have to have a meeting, then there are some issues to consider beforehand to make the meeting less onerous:

Do not overdress; if anything be casual. The more natural you look and behave, the better you come across.

Do not hold meetings in the IRS's own offices; opt for your advisor's office. There are even occasions when holding meetings in your own home can be advantageous. The agents are going to have a good look at the home anyway. But if they do come, make sure that the rest of the family is out for the day.

The better prepared you are, the better the outcome. People who just go straight into meetings with a tax inspector generally come unstuck. They tend to make guesses when under pressure, out of an urge to answer the questions. If these impromptu answers prove wrong later, their credibility evaporates. The best approach is to think carefully about the questions likely to be asked, and to rehearse both questions and answers with your adviser.

INCOME TAX PENALTIES AND INTEREST

The IRS exacts a high price for late payment of taxes due. For taxes due on or after April 1, 1999, the interest rate on underpayment and overpayment of taxes and the penalty for underpayment of estimated tax is 8 percent. The interest is compounded daily, except on late or underpaid estimated taxes for individuals or corporations. For large (C) corporations with underpayments over $100,000, the IRS charges the underpayment interest rate plus 2 percent. In all cases, interest is charged until the amount is paid in full.

The penalty for late filing is 5 percent of the tax due on a return filed late for each month or part of a month you filed late, up to 25 percent of the tax due. If the tax return is not filed within 60 days of the due date, the penalty is $100 or 100 percent of the tax due on your return, whichever is less. The penalty for late payment is $1/2$ percent of the tax due for each month or part of a month the payment is late, up to 25 percent of the tax due. The penalty increases to 1 percent per month if the IRS sends a notice of intent to levy, and you don't pay the tax due within 10 days from the date of the notice. The combined late filing and the late payment penalties are limited to 5 percent of the unpaid tax for that month. The deposit penalty for employment, excise, or railroad retirement tax varies from 2 to 15 percent, depending on how late the deposit is.

No one knows exactly what triggers a tax audit, but tax investigators probably know more about your business than you do, even before they contact you.

The IRS Market Segment Specialization Program publishes audit technique guides on many industries containing examination techniques, common and unique industry issues, business practices, industry terminology, and other ways to help examiners perform their job. These guides are quite thorough and quite revealing.

For example, auditors examining a laundromat know how to analyze water consumption to reconstruct the volume of business. This will help them determine whether the owner fully reported the income from operating the business. This method is to be used, the IRS says, only when there is a reasonable indication of unreported income, but coin-operated laundries and other all-cash businesses are known to frequently underreport their income.

The program addresses other cash businesses, such as taxicabs, barbers and beauty parlors, car washes, and daycare providers, but no business with opportunities for unreported income is overlooked. The IRS even has guidelines for examining a minister's tax return.

A business that engages in activities set forth in these guides is clearly susceptible to being caught if it is audited, but these guidelines, published at www.irs.treas.gov/prod/bus_info/mssp/index.html, are only the tip of the iceberg. Auditors have other ways to estimate and find hidden income, and the IRS is not required to divulge their tactics.

BARGAINING

Bargaining is inevitable in most cases. The IRS's main goal is to ensure that taxpayers pay the right amount of tax. They are also concerned with hitting their own "sales targets" in an efficient manner. They have goals as to how much unpaid tax they have to collect each year and deadlines to meet along the way. Anyone with a goal and a deadline is someone with whom you can negotiate.

At the end of the day, agents are influenced by the total conduct of the case – by the quality of the taxpayer's disclosure and by the cooperation that they receive during their investigation. Good conduct of a case reflect's in the taxpayer's favor.

Negotiation starts at the very beginning of the process. The adviser contacts the IRS – on a no-names basis if the approach by the taxpayer is a voluntary one – to discuss the terms and scope of the inquiry and the legal aspects under which it is to be handled.

TIME

The duration of an investigation varies according to the complexity of the case and the availability of information. With a technically based case, it can take years, if, for example, both sides need to seek tax counsel's advice. When parts have to be taken on appeal, a case can stretch on and on.

What is as worrying to the owner-manager as the length of time is the distraction the procedure makes. This can eat into time that could have been spent getting more customers, improving products, or introducing new equipment.

Another problem is the cost. Apart from any fine, you will have to bear the cost of your own advisers answering the tax inspector's questions. This can run into a substantial four-figure sum, even for a relatively trivial case, and even if you win you will not get those costs back. You can, however, insure against a tax investigation, which will ensure that you get good, timely advice.

GLOSSARY OF ACCOUNTING TERMS

Cross-references at the end of entries are shown in bold type.

Account
Page in the ledger recording the common aspects of different transactions; for example, cash books, and sales and purchase budgets.

Account payable
Money owed by a business, for example to a supplier.

Account receivable
Money owed to a business, for example by a customer.

Accounting
Art of preparing reports from bookkeeping records, based on accounting concepts and measurement conventions.

Accounting concepts
Practical rules that enable bookkeeping records of transactions to be converted into accounting reports.

Accounting language
Special accounting meaning of various words and phrases, rather than the usually accepted layman's meaning.

Accounting period
Period of time from one balance sheet to the next, usually a month, quarter, or year. Period of the profit and loss statement.

Accounting reports
Balance sheet, profit and loss statement, and cash-flow forecasts.

Accrual
A provision made for an event that has occurred but for which no written evidence is available yet. For example, an estimate of tax liability would be accrued for the period to which it applies, because you know the bill will come in at some point in the future.

Accumulated depreciation
Extent to which the fixed asset cost has been allocated to depreciation expense since the asset was originally acquired. This is deducted from the fixed assets.

Accumulated profit
Balance of profit retained in the business over its entire life rather than being paid out to shareholders. Also known as retained earnings.

Administrative expense
Cost of directing and controlling a business, which includes directors' fees, office salaries, office rent, lighting, heating, legal fees, auditors' fees, accounting services, etc. It does not include research and development costs, manufacturing, sales, or distribution expenses.

Amortization
Reducing a loan by making periodic payments of principal and interest on the balance.

Appropriation account
Statement of accumulated profit.

Asset
Something owned by the business that has a measurable cost.

Authorized capital
Share capital of the business authorized by law. May be only partly issued for cash.

Bad debt
Debtor who fails to pay. The amount may be written off to expenses.

Balance
Difference between the debits and credits in a ledger account.

Balance sheet
Accounting report. A statement of the assets owned by a business and the way they are financed from liabilities and the owner's equity. Does not indicate the market value of the business.

Bonds
Long-term loans, often secured on the assets. Also known as debentures.

Bookkeeping
Recording of financial transactions. Posting of transactions from journals to ledgers to provide data for accounting reports.

Book value
The value of the assets owned by a business after depreciation has been deducted from the total.

Buildings
Fixed assets unless acquired for resale, they are depreciated to expense over their working life.

Capital allowance
An allowance given against taxable profit by the IRS instead of depreciation.

Capital reserve
This is created, for example, when a fixed asset is revalued. So, while the business is clearly better off with the higher valuation, no more cash is available, unless that asset is sold.

Cash
The money asset of a business, which includes both cash in hand and cash held at the bank.

Cash discount
Discount allowed to a debtor for early payment of the debt. Terms may be "two percent for payment within 10 days or net (no discount) for payment within one month."

Cash flow
The pattern and extent of cash payments and receipts by a business over a particular period. Also used to describe the differences between total cash inflow and toal cash outflow for a specific project.

Cash transactions
Receipts or payments of cash.

Claims
The owners' or creditors' claims against the assets of a business. Owners' claims are called owners' equity. Creditors' claims are called liabilities.

Closing stock
Stock at the end of the accounting period. Part of the computation of cost of goods sold.

Collateral see security.

Conservatism
If there is a choice as to the amount of certain figures when preparing accounts, it is conservative to opt to use the lower figure for assets and the higher for liabilities.

Consistency
Accounting methods are not changed frequently. If they are changed, it is only for good stated reasons.

Contingent liability
A liability not yet recorded on the balance sheet. It may or may not become an actual liability.

Cooperative
A legal business structure, where the members who own the business must also work in the business. Each member of a coop has one vote.

Corporation
Company whose shareholders have limited their liability to the amounts they subscribe to the shares they hold.

Cost
Any expense of a business.

Cost accounting
Recording of cost data and preparation of cost statements.

Cost concept
Assets are to be valued at cost, not market value. Current assets, such as stock, are normally valued at the lower cost or the market value.

Cost of goods sold
Cost of goods actually sold during the accounting period. Excludes cost of goods left unsold. Also excludes all overhead except manufacturing overhead.

Creditor
Someone to whom a business owes money.

Credit transaction
A transaction that incurs (accrues) liability. No cash is paid or received until later.

Cumulative preference shares
Preference shares whose unpaid dividends accumulate until they are eventually paid by the company. Some preference shares are specifically noncumulative.

Current asset
Something owned by a business that is either cash, can be turned into a known amount of cash quickly, or is owned with the intention of selling it for cash within one year of buying.

Current liability
Liability due for payment within one operating period, normally within one year.

Current tax liability
Income tax due within one year.

Debenture
A document that shows that the debenture owner has lent money to the business for a specific period of time, at an annual rate of interest. In some cases the capital sum is secured against certain of the business's assets.

Debt capital
Money loaned to a business for more than a year.

Debtor
Money due to a business, usually from a customer.

Deferred income
Income received in advance of being earned and recognized. It is normally left as a theoretical current liability in the balance sheet until the sale is made and the income recognized.

Deferred shares
Shares of a corporation ranking for dividend after preference and ordinary shares. Also known as deferred stock.

Depreciation
Allocation of the cost of a fixed asset (such as a building, car, or equipment, such as a photocopier) to each accounting period over its working life.

Depreciation expense
Depreciation (at cost) during the accounting period; not the same as accumulated depreciation, except in the first year of the fixed asset.

Diminishing balance depreciation
Depreciation method charging off the cost of a

fixed asset by a level percentage of the reducing balance over its working life. The percentage remains the same but the depreciation charge decreases over time.

Director
An officer of a corporation. A member of the board of directors. Not a partner.

Dual aspect
The two aspects of each transaction – debit and credit – that form the basis of double-entry bookkeeping.

Earnings
Another way of describing profit.

Entity
A business has an entity that is legally separate from the owners or managers. It is to this entity that the accounting reports are addressed.

Equipment
This is regarded as a fixed asset if it is acquired for long-term use and not for resale. It is recorded in the balance sheet at cost less depreciation, not at market value.

Equity
The capital of a business that comes from the issue of shares.

Expenditure
Money paid for cost, expenses, assets, or other purposes.

Expense
Any payments properly chargeable to the profit and loss statement, for example, manufacturing, selling, or administrative expenses. Expenses are "matched" against revenues during the accounting period to compute the figure of profit.

Face value
Normal value of shares, not the book value or market value.

Fixed assets
Assets, such as land, plant, and equipment acquired for long-term use in the business and not for resale. These are charged to overhead expenses periodically as depreciation. They are recorded in the balance sheet at cost less depreciation, not at market value. See also **expense**.

Fixtures
Fixed assets if acquired for use and not for resale.

Furniture and fixtures
Fixed assets if acquired for use and not for resale.

Future tax liability
Reserve for future income tax computed on the current year's profit and not due for payment until a future date. It normally becomes the current tax liability in the following year.

Gearing
The relationship between a firm's debt capital and its equity. The higher the proportion of debt, the more highly geared is the business.

General expense
Expense of the business that is not part of manufacturing, selling, and administrative expense. It includes audit fees, legal expenses, etc., and is sometimes grouped with administrative expense in the income statement.

General reserve
Part of the accumulated profit set aside in the owner's equity section of the balance sheet, so that it is not distributed to the shareholders as dividends. It is neither an asset nor cash, merely part of the owner's equity, which is shown separately on the claims side of the balance sheet.

Going concern
All accounting reports and values assume that a business is a "going concern"; that is, that the business will continue to do business and is not

about to liquidate (end). Market values are based upon those expected in the normal course of business.

Goodwill
The value of the name, reputation, or intangible assets of a business. In accounting it is recorded (at cost) only when it is purchased. It is not depreciated and often written off to nil. It is never valued at market price. It is generally a hidden asset of the business.

Gross profit
The difference between sales and cost of goods sold. The profit computed before selling and administrative expenses etc. are charged.

Income
The profit of a business.

Income tax liability
See **current tax liability** or **future tax liability**.

Incomplete transaction
A transaction that is incomplete at the end of the accounting period and consequently a cause of uncertainty in accounting. The concept of profit recognition must be employed to determine in which accounting period the profit is earned or the loss sustained.

Inflation accounting
Accounts are based on historical values, assuming the purchasing power of money to be stable from one year to the next. However, because of inflation this is untrue, and various methods of accounting attempt to reconcile this with useful accounting information.

Intangible asset
Asset that cannot actually be touched, for example goodwill.

Inventory see **stock**.

Investment
Amount invested in stocks, shares, bonds, debentures, or any asset. See also **trade investment**.

Issue price of a share
Price at which a share is first sold by a company. It is normally the nominal value plus share premium or less share discount.

Issued capital
Share capital actually issued by a company. See also **authorized capital**.

Land
Property owned by a business. It is normally a fixed asset and is not depreciated.

Leverage see **gearing**.

Limitations of accounting
Accounting reports show a limited picture of a business because: (a) some important facts cannot be stated in money terms; (b) accounting periods at fixed intervals involve uncertainty due to incomplete transactions; (c) accounting reports depend on concepts; and (d) accounting is not scientific but depends upon judgment.

Liquidity
Availability of cash or assets easily turned into cash.

Loan capital
See **debt capital**.

Long-term liability
Liability not due for payment within one year, such as bonds, debentures, or loans. Holders of these are creditors and receive interest; they are not shareholders.

Loss
Opposite of profit or income. The excess of costs and expenses over sales. Reduces the owner's equity.

Loss on disposal of fixed assets
Loss due to the sale or disposal of fixed assets, treated as "other income and expense" in the income statement. Significant losses or profits are sometimes charged to capital reserve.

Machinery
Fixed asset if acquired for use and not for resale. Valued at cost less depreciation. Machinery manufactured or acquired for resale is stock. See **depreciation**.

Maintenance cost
The expense of maintaining or repairing the fixed assets of the business. Such costs are charged as expense in the income statement.

Manufacturing expenses
Overhead for manufacturing. Part of the cost of goods sold. It does not include sales or administrative expense.

Matching
Costs and revenues in the accounting period should be "matched" in order that the computed profit may be certain to be true and fair. Matching means "appropriate to" not "equal to."

Mortgage
Long-term loan normally secured on a fixed asset. It is a long-term liability rather than a current one.

Net
(a) Figure after deduction; for example, gross sales less sales returns equals net sales.
(b) Payment of the full amount with no allowance for cash discount.

Net current assets
Another term used to describe working capital.

Net profit
Profit for the accounting period after income tax.

Net worth
Balance sheet value of owner's stake in the business. It consists of both the money put in at the start, and any profits made since and left in the business.

Nominal value
Face value of shares rather than the book or market value. Authorized and issued share capital in the balance sheet shows the nominal value of the shares separately from any premium or discount.

Nonoperating expense
Expense not directly related to normal operations; for example, loss on sales of fixed assets, interest paid, etc.

Nonoperating income
Income not arising from normal operations; for example, profit on sale of fixed assets, dividends received, etc.

Notes to financial statements
Notes attached to the balance sheet and income statement that explain (a) significant accounting adjustments or (b) information required by law, if not disclosed in the financial statements.

Opening stock
Inventory at the beginning of the accounting period.

Operating expenses
All overhead of the business. The term is sometimes restricted to mean only selling, administrative, and general expenses.

Operating profit
Gross profit less operating expense in the income statement.

Order
Purchase order to a supplier for delivery of goods and services.

Ordinary shares
Normal shares in the business used to apportion ownership. See also **deferred shares**.

Other assets
Assets that are not fixed or current assets; for example goodwill, research cost carried forward, trade investments, etc. These are valued at cost not market value, unless losses are exceptional.

Other creditors
Creditors or accruals for services, not trade creditors for purchase of material and supplies.

Overhead
As in overhead expense: indirect cost that cannot be conveniently associated with a unit of production.

Owner's equity
Amount due to owners of the business, increased by profits, reduced by losses and dividends. N.B. Assets less liabilities equal owner's equity.

Package of accounting reports
Set of financial statements prepared for a business. This will include a balance sheet for the start and end of the period in question, plus the intervening profit and loss statement.

Partnership
When two or more people agree to carry on a business together, intending to share the profits they make.

Patent
The legal right to exploit an invention. This is recorded at cost less depreciation under the heading "Other assets" on the balance sheet.

Plant
Equipment and machinery. This is regarded as a fixed asset if acquired for use and not for resale.

Preference share
Share that entitles the holder to fixed dividends (only) in preference to the dividends for ordinary shares. On liquidation, the holder is normally entitled only to the nominal value and has no right to share in any excess profits.

Prepaid expense
Expense paid in advance for more than one accounting period.

Profit
The excess of sales over costs and expenses during an accounting period. Does not necessarily increase cash – it may be reflected in increased assets or decreased liabilities. See also **net profit**.

Profit and loss appropriation account
Statement of accumulated profit or retained earnings. Balance of profit and loss statement.

Profit and loss statement
Statement showing sales, costs, expenses, and profit for an accounting period.

Profit before tax
Operating profit less nonoperating expenses plus nonoperating income, as shown in the income statement.

Provision
Setting a sum aside to meet a future liability.

R & D
Research and development cost of the business. This is normally regarded as an expense but is sometimes treated as an "other asset."

Redeemable preference shares
Preference shares that may be repurchased by the company from the shareholders. Part of the owner's equity, not ordinary shares.

Research cost
Cost of research listed either as a separate

overhead or as part of manufacturing overhead. It is sometimes carried forward as an "other asset" if it is of specific future benefit for a future limited period.

Reserve
Strictly means accumulated profit. See **revenue reserve**, **capital reserve**, **provision**.

Retained earnings
The profits that have been earned and kept in the business to help finance growth.

Revaluation
Sometimes fixed assets are revalued from cost to current values. The difference between the two is credited to capital reserve.

Revenue
Earnings. Sometimes also used to mean sales.

Revenue reserve
The profit made from business, which has not been distributed. Distinct from a capital reserve, which usually arises from the sale of a fixed asset at a price higher than its cost.

Sales
Total of amounts sold, recognized normally when goods are shipped to a customer, or the service is executed, and the invoice has been raised.

Sales allowance
Special allowance to a customer against the amount due for goods sold. This is often allowed for damaged goods or shortages.

Sales discount
Trade or cash discount on sales.

Sales expense
The cost of promoting sales and retaining business. This is an indirect cost and an overhead expense, not a manufacturing, administrative, or general expense. Sales expense includes advertising, sales literature, sales salaries, cars, traveling expenses, depreciation of sales, etc.

Security
Assets claimable by some creditors in priority to others.

Share
Document certifying ownership of stock in a company.

Share capital
Money put into a business by the owners of the business in return for a stake in the venture.

Share premium
The excess of the original sales price of a share over its face or nominal value.

Shareholder
Owner of part of the share capital and owner's equity. Also known as a stockholder.

Silent partner
One who puts capital into a partnership but who does not intend to take an active part in running the business.

Sole proprietor
The simplest type of business: there are no shareholders – just the owner's money and borrowings.

Stock
Goods on hand for resale or held in raw materials or as work in progress.

Straight line depreciation
Depreciation method that involves charging off the cost of a fixed asset equally over all the years of its working life. See also **diminishing balance depreciation**.

Tangible asset
Asset that can be physically identified or touched. It sometimes refers only to those assets

that have a definite value; that is, it excludes intangible assets such as goodwill, as well as research and development expenditures carried forward.

Trade creditor
Money owed for credit purchases.

Trade discount
Deduction from the selling price of an invoice because the buyer is in the same business as the seller. It is not a cash discount.

Trade investment
Investment in shares or debentures of another company in the same trade or industry. It is a long-term investment and not a marketable security. Valued at cost unless there is a substantial loss.

Transaction
May be sale, purchase, cash receipt, cash payment, or accounting adjustment. Translated into debits and credits in the bookkeeping records.

True and fair
The balance sheet and income statement show a "true and fair" view of the business, in accordance with generally accepted accounting principles.

Uncertainty
A limitation of accounting. Uncertainty at the end of each accounting period makes it difficult to determine the "true and fair" position. Uncertainty arises from: (a) incomplete

transactions; (b) the market value of stock; (c) the working life of fixed assets for depreciation calculations; (d) the realizable values of current assets; (e) contingent liabilities not yet known or calculable.

Unpaid dividends
Dividends declared as due to shareholders but not yet paid in cash. They are shown as a current liability in the balance sheet and are deducted from accumulated profit in the owner's equity.

Value
This is one of those difficult accounting words that sounds very normal but rarely means what you would think. For example, look at the definition of book value. There is nothing in the name to suggest that the book value of an asset is the amount of money you might actually get for it.

Work-in-progress
Items for sale that are only partially ready for sale. For example, a carpenter's half-finished table would have consumed some raw materials and some labor. These would be accounted for in arriving at the value assigned to work-in-progress. Valued at the lower of manufacturing cost or market value. Real value is not known in accounting.

Working capital
Has a special meaning of current assets less current liabilities. It is not the same as "capital."

USEFUL CONTACTS

In addition to these national sites, check the internet and your telephone directory for organizations and government agencies geared to your industry and your locality.

BUSINESS ADVOCACY ORGANIZATIONS

Many trade and development groups advance their causes before national and state lawmakers and regulators. National groups, with local affiliates, are:

Internet Corporation for Assigned Names and Numbers (ICANN)

Regulates internet domain names, registrars, and domain-dispute arbitration organizations.
4676 Admiralty Way, Suite 330
Marina del Rey, CA 90292
Tel: 310-823-9358
Fax: 310-823-8649
http://ww.icann.org

National Association of Manufacturers

1331 Pennsylvania Avenue, N.W.
Washington, D.C. 20004-1790
Tel: 202-637-3000
Fax: 202-637-3182
http://www.nam.org

National Black Chamber of Commerce

2000 L Street Northwest
Washington, D.C. 20036
Tel: 202-416-1622

National Cooperative Business Association

Information on forming and promoting a cooperative, and for marketing its products or services.
1401 New York Avenue, N.W.,
Suite 1100
Washington, D.C. 20005
Tel: 202-638-6222
Fax: 202-638-1374
http://www.cooperative.org

U.S. Chamber of Commerce

1615 H Street
Washington, D.C. 20062-2000
Tel: 202-659-6000
http://www.uschamber.com

BUSINESS INFORMATION

American Business Information

1717 Pennsylvania Avenue Northwest
Washington, D.C. 20006
Tel: 202-887-8001

Business Management and Consulting Group Corporation

1201 Pennsylvania Avenue Northwest
Washington, D.C. 20004
Tel: 202-661-4625

CORPORATE INFORMATION

Corporations must generally register with the secretary of state of the state, and partnerships with the clerk of the county, in which they are registered. For information on publicly traded corporations, contact:

U.S. Securities and Exchange Commission

450 Fifth Street, N.W.
Washington, D.C. 20549-0304
Tel: 202-942-2950
http://www.sec.gov

EMPLOYMENT LAW

U.S. Equal Employment Opportunity Commission
1801 L Street, N.W.
Washington, D.C. 20507
Tel: 202-663-490

EXPORTING

American Management Association
1601 Broadway
New York, NY 10019
Tel: 212-586-6100
Fax: 212-903-8168
http://www.amanet.org

Export Administration Bureau of the Department of Commerce
Washington, D.C. 20001
Tel: 202-482-4811

U.S. Small Business Administration
409 Third Street
Washington, D.C. 20416
Tel: 800-827-5722 (800-U-ASK-SBA)
http://www.sba.gov

FINANCE

Angel and venture financing are available to businesses needing between $250,000 and $5 million, and more than $5 million, respectively. The angel site puts businesses in touch with sophisticated investors looking to become a part of their growth. Business owners seeking venture capital would do well to edit their "elevator pitch" so they can hit the high points of their business plan, and how it will make millions, within less than five minutes.

Angel Capital Electronic Network (ACE-Net)
Businesses seeking financing, and·
investors seeking opportunities, can join this network for $450 per year. Its securities registration formats are authorized by the SEC and more than 40 states.
877-ACE-NET3 (877-223-6383)
http://www.ace-net.sr.unh.edu

National Association of Securities Dealers
Information on listing requirements, investor protection, etc.
33 Whitehall Street
New York, NY 10004
Tel: 212-858-4000
http://www.nasdaq.com

National Credit Union Administration
Information on credit unions, an alternative banking and finance resource.
1755 Duke Street,
Alexandria, VA 22314-3428
Tel: 703-518-6300
http://www.ncua.gov

National Venture Capital Association
1655 North Fort Myer Drive
Arlington, VA 22209
Tel: 703-524-2549
Fax: 703-524-3940
http://www.nvca.com (also .org)

New York Stock Exchange
Information on the largest stock exchange, with the highest listing requirements.
11 Wall Street
New York, NY 10005
Tel: 212-656-3000
http://www.nyse.com

Membership in the following organizations is not mandatory, but these sites offer consumer information and referrals.

American Bar Association
541 N. Fairbanks
Chicago, IL 60611
Tel: 312-988-5522
http://www.abanet.org

American Institute of Certified Public Accountants
1211 Avenue of the Americas
New York, NY 10036
Tel: 212-596-6200
http://www.aicpa.org

National Association of Enrolled Agents
2000 Orchard Ridge Drive
Suite 302
Gaithersburg, MD 20878
Tel: 301-212-9608
Fax: 301-990-1611
http://www.naea.org

Franchising
American Association of Franchisees and Dealers
P.O. Box 81887
San Diego, CA 92138-1887
Tel: 800-733-9858
Fax: 619-209-3777

American Franchisee Association
53 W. Jackson Blvd.
Suite 205
Chicago, IL 60604
Tel: 312-431-0545
Fax: 312-431-1469
E-mail: afa@infonews.com
www.infonews.com/afa

Federal Trade Commission
Pennsylvania Avenue and Sixth Street, N.W.
Washington, D.C. 20580
Tel: 202-326-2222
http://www.ftc.gov

Government Business Development Agencies
Department of Commerce
14th Street and Constitution Avenue, N.W.
Washington, D.C. 20230
Tel: 202-482-1850

http://www.doc.gov
As part of its mandate to promote the sale of U.S.-made goods abroad, the DOC publishes *ExportAmerica*, a monthly magazine with practical tips on every step of the process, from getting started through getting paid. For details and subscription information, call 202-512-1800, or see http://exportamerica.doc.gov.

Government Offices
Board of Trade
1129 20th Street Northwest
Washington, D.C. 20036
Tel: 202-857-5900

Copyright Royalty Tribunal
1111 20th Street Northwest
Washington, D.C. 20526
Tel: 202-653-5175

Federation of Tax Administrators
444 N. Capitol Street, N.W.
Suite 348
Washington, D.C. 20001
Tel: 202-624-5890
http://www.taxadmin.org
This site provides links to state tax agencies, for information, tax rates, forms, etc.

Financial Management Service
401 14th Street Northwest
Washington, D.C. 20227
Tel: 202-874-7050

Internal Revenue Service
1111 Constitution Avenue, N.W.
Washington, D.C. 20224
Tel: 202-927-5170
http://www.irs.ustreas.gov

Occupational Health and Safety Administration (DOL)
Tel: 202-693-1999
http://www.osha-slc.gov
Although not specifically a finance-oriented agency, running afoul of safety

regulations can be costly, and proactively working with OSHA can make your business a safer place, and possibly reduce your insurance premiums.

Social Security System
820 First Street, N.W.
Washington, D.C. 20254
Tel: 800-772-6270
http://www.ssa.gov

U. S. Business and Industrial Council
220 National Press Building
Washington, D.C. 20090
Tel: 202-662-8744

U.S. Copyright Office
(Library of Congress)
101 Independence Avenue, S.E.
Washington, D.C. 20559-6000
Tel: 202-707-3000
http://www.loc.gov/copyright

U.S. Department of Labor
200 Constitution Avenue, N.W.
Washington, D.C. 20210
Tel: 202-219-6001
http://dol.gov/elaws
The department monitors federal wage and hour laws, employee pension and insurance plans, labor relations, and other areas involving employees and employers.

U.S. General Printing Office
Publishes and distributes federal government documents, booklets, etc.
Tel: 202-512-1800
Fax: 202-512-2250
http://www.gpo.gov

U.S. Patent & Trademark Office
Crystal Plaza 3, Room 2C02
Washington, D.C. 20231

Tel: 800-786-9199
http://www.uspto.gov

LABOR ORGANIZATIONS
AFL-CIO
815 16th Street, NW
Washington, D.C. 20006
Tel: 202-637-5000
Fax: 202-637-5058

SMALL BUSINESS ORGANIZATIONS
Association of Small Business Development Centers
3108 Columbia Pike
Suite 300
Arlington, VA 22204
Tel: 703-271-8700
Fax: 703-271-8701

YOUNG ENTREPRENEURS
Many trade and development groups promote initiatives by young people. In addition to local groups and universities, you may contact the following clearinghouses of such information.

Edward Lowe Foundation
P.O. Box 8
Cassapolis, MI 49031
Tel: 800-232-5693
http://www.lowe.org

The Entrepreneurship Institute
http://www.tei.net

Initiative for a Competitive Inner City
727 Atlantic Avenue, Suite 600
Boston, MA 02111
Tel: 617-292-2363
Fax: 617-292-2380
http://www.icic.org

Other Useful Websites

Business Advisor
(federal government information)
http://www.business.gov

BusinessLINC
(matches small businesses with large business mentors)
http://www.businesslinc.sba.gov

Commerce Business Daily
(federal government contracts)
http://cbdnet.access.gpo.gov

Consumer Information Center
http:///www.pueblo.gov

Hoover's
(competitive business information)
http://www.hoovers.com

Minority Business Development Agency
http://www.mbda.gov

National Foundation for Women Business Owners
http://www.nfwbo.org

PRO-Net
(procurement and marketing opportunities)
http://pro-net.sba.gov

**Service Corps of Retired Executives
(SCORE)** (free business advisory services)
800-634-0245
http://www.score.org

State Government and Legal Resource
http://www.alllaw.com

State Tax Forms
http://taxweb.com/forms

Streamlined Sales Tax System for the 21st Century
http://www.geocities.com/streamlined2000

TECHNet
(technology resources)
http://tech-net.sba.gov

Thomas Register
http://www.thomasregister.com

**University of North Carolina, Charlotte
J. Murrey Atkins Library**
http://libweb.uncc.edu/ref-bus/buselec.htm

Women's Business Center
(also young entrepreneurs)
http://onlinewbc.org

SUGGESTED READING

101 Best Home-Based Businesses for Women
Priscilla Y. Huff (Prima Communications, Inc., 1998)
For every woman who wants to work at home, maintain a flexible schedule, and be her own boss. This book provides readers with everything they need to know about different businesses, from startup costs and financing sources to the potential income the business

can generate. Actual businesswomen share their stories of success and financial reward and give advice on what works and what does not.

199 Great Home Businesses You Can Start (and Succeed in) for Under $1,000
Tyler Gregory Hicks (Prima Communications, Inc., 1999)
Home-based business guru Tyler Hicks shows

you how to achieve your work-at-home dream. Contains information on how to choose the home-based business that's right for you, getting started with minimal cost, running a business from home while keeping your day job, and using the internet to advertise and promote your home-based business.

1101 Businesses You Can Start from Home
Daryl Allen Hall (Wiley, John & Sons, Inc., 1994)
This book contains expert information on startup enterprises. The majority of businesses discussed have low startup costs and are suited for communities of any size. It includes a cost rating system for beginning a business along with a chapter discussing why people startup and run their own home-based businesses.

The Adams Businesses You Can Start Almanac
Katina Jones (Adams Media Corporation,1996)
Features hundreds of interviews and success stories from people who have started their own businesses. Each one of the business ideas presented is a realistic, professional enterprise.

Cash in on Cash Flow: 50 tough-as-nails ideas for revitalizing your business
A. David Silver (AMACOM, 1993)

The Complete Idiot's Guide to Starting Your Own Business
Ed Paulson, Marcia Layton (Macmillan General Reference, 1998)
This book offers valuable advice about financing, business planning, legal issues, technology, and more. It contains the latest information about financing, business planning, legal issues, and technology.

Entrepreneur Magazine's Start Your Own Business
(Entrepreneur Media, 1998)
A step-by-step guide that includes expert advice regarding market research, business structure, creating a winning business plan, financing, bookkeeping, and taxes.

Free Help from Uncle Sam to Start Your Own Business: Or Expand the One You Have
Gus Berle (Puma Publishing Company, 1997)
The author tells the inside story on how to generate a business plan that commands attention. The book provides advice on how to avoid wasting your time and energy on complicated business plan preparation schemes, and how to optimize your efforts to drive profits up.

High Tech Start Up: The Complete Handbook for Creating Successful New High Tech Companies
John L. Nesheim (The Free Press, 2000)
This Silicon Valley bestseller incorporates 23 case studies of successful startups, including tables of wealth showing how much money founders and investors realized from each venture. It is filled with hard-to-find information and guidance covering every key phase of a startup.

If You're Clueless about Starting Your Own Business and Want to Know More
Seth Godin (Dearborn Financial Publishing, Inc., 1997)
This addition to the popular "Clueless" series is aimed at people who want to know what it takes to get a small business up and running. Well known entrepreneur Seth Godin provides readers with everything they need to know to jump-start a new enterprise.

The Legal Guide for Starting and Running a Small Business
Fred S. Steingold, Mary Randolph, Ralph E. Warner (Nolo, 1999)
This "nuts-and-bolts" guide to starting and running a small business provides clear explanations of the laws that affect businesses. It includes the latest tax law changes that affect home-based business, as well as advice on how to

select a business name in the age of the internet.

Managing Budgets
Stephen Brookson (Dorling Kindersley, 2000)

Managing by the Numbers: Monitoring your firm's profitability
David W. Cottle (AICPA, 1993)

Mancuso's Small Business Basics
Jospeh R. Mancuso (Sourcebooks, Inc., 1997)
In this book, Joseph Mancuso draws on his more than 20 years' experience helping entrepreneurs build business enterprises. It assists readers in how to start an enterprise, how to buy an existing enterprise and how to open a franchise.

Mother's Work: How a Young Mother Started a Business on a Shoestring and Built It into a Multimillion-Dollar Company
Rebecca Matthias (Doubleday & Company, Inc., 1999)
With a new baby, little money, but lots of determination and drive, Rebecca Matthias started a business from scratch out of her home. Today her company, Mothers Work – which includes the retail outlets Mimi Maternity, Motherhood, and A Pea in the Pod – has grown to become a multimillion-dollar maternity clothing empire. This book describes how Matthias got her company off the ground, offering specific lessons for other entrepreneurs and would-be entrepreneurs on the nuts and bolts of building and growing a business.

Small Business Formation Handbook
Robert E. Cooke (Wiley, Johns & Sons, 1999)
A complete guide to formations for the new business owner. This comprehensive book describes the different types of business formations. The book offers examples of tax consequences as well as liability scenarios. Also included are sample legal forms, such

as articles of incorporation and stockholder's agreements, and relevant IRS forms.

The Small Business Handbook: A Comprehensive Guide to Starting and Running Your Own Business
Irving Burstiner (Simon & Schuster, 1997)
This instructional handbook offers practical advice on finding the right business for you, targeting customers, getting financing, choosing a location, hiring and managing employees, marketing your products and services, pricing for profit, distribution, managing the company's finances, planning for growth and expansion, and much more.

Small Business Legal Smarts
Deborah L. Jacobs (Bloomberg, 1998)

The Small Business Legal Guide
Lynne Ann Frasier (Sourcebooks, 1998)

Start up: An Entrepreneur's Guide to Launching and Managing a New Business
William J. Stolze (Career Press, Inc., 1999)
Provides advice to those who want to embark on a new venture, have started a new business in the past few years, or who are seasoned pros. It addresses key problems that are crucial to the success of any new business, including information on how to write a successful business plan, what is most important to your business's success, how to pick a mentor, and the benefits of small companies.

Starting and Building Your Own Accounting Business
Jack Fox (Wiley, John & Sons, 1999)
This book details the advantages and disadvantages of setting up and running your own accounting operation. It explains how to establish and develop a business plan, how to prospect for new clients, the types of advertising and sales promotion techniques that are successful, the fee to charge and how to

collect, how to plan for growth, and how to buy a business or sell your own business.

Success for Less: 100 Low-Cost Businesses You Can Start Today
Rob Adams, Terry Adams (Entrepreneur Media, 1999)
This easy-to-use guide is packed with the latest, up-to-date expert information on current small-business trends and opportunities. It reveals 100 low-cost, in-demand businesses you can start with little or no money down. Profiles of successful entrepreneurs who started businesses give an insider's look at the world of entrepreneurship and offer practical advice you can use to get your own business off the ground.

The Unofficial Guide to Starting a Business Online
Jason R. Rich (IDG Books Worldwide, 1999)
A guide for the cyber-entrepreneur concerning every aspect of conducting business over the World Wide Web. Information includes advice on setting up websites, advertising, and marketing. Also includes addresses for hundreds of websites that can be used as startup references.

Winning Strategies for Capital Formation: Secrets of Funding Start-Ups and Emerging Growth Firms without Losing Control of Your Idea, Project or Company
Linda Chandler (McGraw-Hill Companies, 1996)
This book focuses on the thought processes involved in planning financing and obtaining capital. It considers the determining factors in which businesses form and which sources of financing are appropriate, as well as preparing an appropriate business plan and financial statements, and a representation for investors that focuses on their needs. Included among its topics are: mental strengthening and preparation for "the money hunt"; building credibility with investors; structuring your business to meet your needs as well as your partners'; understanding the options; and attacking myths that block your path to success.

The Young Entrepreneur's Guide to Starting and Running a Business
Steve Mariotti, Tony Towle, Debra Desalvo (Crown Publishing Group, 1999)
This book contains real, inspirational stories of young people finding success in the business world. It includes the stories of Microsoft's Bill Gates, Motown Records' founder Berry Gordy, and young people who are just starting out. It provides a practical, step-by-step pathway, including everything you need to know to start your own business, from creating financial statements to developing marketing techniques.

Your Business Plan: A workbook for owners of small businesses
Pearson, 2000

INDEX

ACKNOWLEDGMENTS

AUTHOR'S ACKNOWLEDGMENTS

This book owes its existence to the insight and enthusiasm of Stephanie Jackson and to Adèle Hayward, who courageously took it over halfway through. I owe much to Alison Bolus, who continuously pushed for greater clarity, and to Jane Laing and all the editorial and design staff who worked on the book. I ar also indebted to my colleagues at Cranfield and elsewhere, on whose wisdom and information I have drawn, and to the students, on whom much of the material used in the book has been tested.

The following sources are thanked for their permission to reproduce bar charts: European Observatory for SME Research (p. 47), European Franchise Federation, Arthur Andersen, and World Franchising Council (p. 49), and Cranfield Working Papers (p. 46 and p. 119).

PUBLISHER'S ACKNOWLEDGMENTS

Grant Laing Partnership thank the following for their help and participation in producing this book:
Design: Graham Curd
Proofreading: Nikky Twyman
Index: Kay Ollerenshaw

Dorling Kindersley thank the following for their help and participation in producing this book:
Editorial: Mary Lindsay, Daphne Richardson, Mark Wallace
Design: Sarah Cowley
DTP: Jason Little, Amanda Peers

PICTURE CREDITS

2: Telegraph Colour Library 5 top: Telegraph Colour Library 5 centre: Powerstock Zefa 5 centre below: Powerstock Zefa 5 below: gettyone stone 8-9: Telegraph Colour Library 10: Robert Harding Picture Library 14: Robert Harding Picture Library 20: gettyone stone 23: Canon Colour Copier CLC 1130, courtesy of Canon 25: The Stock Market 26: The Image Bank 27: gettyone stone 28: Robert Harding Picture Library 29: Rex Features 32: Robert Harding Picture Library 36: Pictor 40: The Image Bank 42: gettyone stone 43: Pictor 44: The Stock Market 46: Richard T Nowitz/Corbis 48: Rex Features 53 above: Gail Mooney/Corbis 55: TheImage Bank 58: The Image Bank 60: The Stock Market 62: Robert Harding Picture Library 64: Robert Harding Picture Library 68: Robert Harding Picture Library 71: gettyone stone 72-73: Powerstock Zefa 74: Robert Harding Picture Library 80: Robert Harding Picture Library 98: Telegraph Colour Library 101: Robert Harding Picture Library 102-103: Powerstock Zefa 107: Robert Harding Picture Library 121: Sally and Richard Greenhill 144: gettyone stone

AUTHOR'S BIOGRAPHY

Colin Barrow is Head of the Enterprise Group at Cranfield School of Management, London, and Director of the Business Growth and Development Program. He was educated at Sandhurst, England, and earned his MBA at Cranfield. Colin has taught on business school MBA programs and on management development programs in countries throughout the world. In addition to his work at Cranfield, he is a strategic consultant and a nonexecutive director of a number of companies.